Exploiting Fandom

EXPLOITING FANDOM

How the Media Industry Seeks to Manipulate Fans

MEL STANFILL

University of Iowa Press, Iowa City

University of Iowa Press, Iowa City 52242
Copyright © 2019 by the University of Iowa Press
www.uipress.uiowa.edu
Printed in the United States of America
Design by Ashley Muehlbauer

The University of Iowa Press is a member of Green Press
Initiative and is committed to preserving natural resources.
Printed on acid-free paper

Library of Congress Cataloging-in-Publication Data

Names: Stanfill, Mel, 1983– author.
Title: Exploiting fandom : how the media industry seeks to
manipulate fans / Mel Stanfill.
Description: Iowa City : University of Iowa Press, 2018. |
Includes bibliographical references and index. |
Identifiers: LCCN 2018024853 (print) | LCCN 2018028739
(ebook) | ISBN 978-1-60938-624-5 | ISBN 978-1-60938-623-8
(pbk. : alk. paper)
Subjects: LCSH: Subculture. | Fans (Persons) | Mass media—
Audiences. | Mass media—Economic aspects.
Classification: LCC HM646 (ebook) | LCC HM646 .S73 2018
(print) | DDC 306/.1—dc23
LC record available at https://lccn.loc.gov/2018024853

CONTENTS

There are a great many people without whom this project would have been much poorer, and I begin these acknowledgments with the admission that they will inevitably be incomplete. Mentorship large and small from Kristina Busse, Anita Say Chan, CL Cole, Ray Fouché, Jonathan Gray, Mary L. Gray, Matt Hills, Bruce Janz, Derek Johnson, Cameron McCarthy, Rudy McDaniel, Jason Mittell, Sharif Mowlabocus, Kent Ono, Blake Scott, Siobhan Somerville, Angharad Valdivia, and Kristen J. Warner has been profoundly influential throughout the life cycle of this project. My year as a postdoctoral research associate in the American Studies department at Purdue University was a tremendous opportunity for sustained intellectual work in a rich intellectual community, for which the book is immeasurably better. Stephanie Brown, Megan Condis, Aimee Rickman, Michelle Rivera, Andrea Ruehlicke, and Brittany Smith, my writing group at the University of Illinois, helped sharpen my thinking and argumentation with their excellent feedback on the project that became this book. Jaime Hough, Alicia Kozma, Robert Mejia, and Laurel Westbrook have had my back for a long, long time, but new interlocutors have also made their mark: Joseph Fanfarelli, Anastasia Salter, and Anne Sullivan at the University of Central Florida have been the best colleagues anyone could ask for (Lunch Club forever). My fan studies scholarly community has been indispensable as inspiration and generous with its members' individual and collective intelligence: in particular, Alexis Lothian, J. S. A. Lowe, Katie Morrissey, Julie Levin Russo, Suzanne Scott, and Mark Stewart have all been great for a chat or a cup of coffee or a conference lunch buddy. My mom helped me move house three years running and was remarkably understanding that school breaks aren't time off for academics. Audiences at the University of Kentucky, University of Utah, Old Dominion University, Pennsylvania State University, York, and the American Bar Foundation Legal History Seminar provided valuable feedback.

Portions of this work have been previously published. Earlier versions of arguments made here appear as follows: "Doing Fandom, (Mis)doing Whiteness: Heteronormativity, Racialization, and the Discursive Construction of Fandom," *Transformative Works and Cultures*, no. 8 (2011), https://doi.org/10.3983/twc.2011.0256; "Fandom, Public, Commons," *Transformative Works and Cultures*, no. 14 (2013), https://doi.org/10.3983/twc.2013.0530; and, with Megan Condis, "Fandom and/ as Labor" [editorial], in "Fandom and/as Labor," edited by Mel Stanfill and Megan Condis, special issue, *Transformative Works and Cultures*, no. 15 (2014), https://doi.org/10.3983/twc.2014.0593. These are used with the permission of *Transformative Works and Cultures* under a Creative Commons Attribution-Noncommercial 3.0 Unported License. Parts of "'The Interface as Discourse': The Production of Norms through Web Design," *New Media and Society* 17, no. 7 (2014), 1059–74, https://doi.org/10.1177/1461444814520873, are reused under the SAGE policy that one may use the published article in a book any time after publication in the journal with the inclusion of a link to the appropriate DOI for the published version.

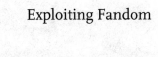

Exploiting Fandom

On March 3, 2016, CW's *The 100* aired an episode that made a common television choice: it killed off a character whose actor had taken other work to provide not only drama but finality in the story line. In response, fans launched a large-scale campaign, including "12 consecutive days of worldwide Twitter trends" (Bridges 2016). This intense reaction was because the character, Lexa, was a lesbian. "During the episode following Lexa's death, fans tweeted with the trending topic LGBT Fans Deserve Better, which has since become an international fan-led initiative. As the show returned Thursday after a two-week hiatus, fans tweeted with Bury Tropes Not Us, sending the topic trending nationally" (Butler 2016). The trend referenced the Bury Your Gays trope, or the disproportionate likelihood that an LBGTQ+ character will be killed off compared to heterosexual, cisgender counterparts ("Bury Your Gays," TVTropes.org). Additionally, showrunner Jason Rothenberg "lost thousands of Twitter followers [. . .], and the March 10 episode got the series' worst-ever ratings [. . .], demonstrating that [fans] can use their collective might to very different uses than a network might like" (Ryan 2016a).[1] One key sign of that "collective might" was fan donations to the Trevor Project, an organization providing crisis intervention and suicide prevention services to LGBTQIA youth. Fans gave $40,000 within ten days, and over $170,000 by the end of 2017 ("Fundraiser," n.d.). In the end, Elizabeth Bridges (2016) notes, "I've never seen a more widespread or more coordinated fandom response to any event, and I've been a fan and observer of the media since the 1990s."

As massive and well organized as the blowback was, what came after was even more unusual. After three weeks of outrage, Rothenberg issued a public apology, explaining that his privilege as a straight white man rendered him insensitive to the implications of killing off a lesbian character and noting that his fan management had been poor: "I realize that if somebody had that kind of a reaction and then were to look back at the way I behaved on Twitter leading up to it, which was celebrating this [lesbian] relationship that then crushed them, I can understand why they would find that reprehensible" (Ryan 2016b). Moreover, the show was chided not once but twice in *Variety*—"required reading by everyone in the entertainment industry" (Bridges 2016). Maureen Ryan (2016a) notes,

> If you wanted to come up with a playbook for how to handle TV promotion and publicity in the age of social media, a few of the major rules might look like this: Don't mislead fans or raise their hopes unrealistically. Don't promote your show as an ideal proponent of a certain kind of storytelling, and then drop the ball in a major way with that very element of your show. When things go south, don't pretend nothing happened. Understand that in this day and age, promotion is a two-way street: The fans that flock to your show and help raise its profile can just as easily walk away if they are disappointed or feel they've been manipulated. It all sounds like common sense, right? Except that *The 100* managed to break all those rules and more in the last ten days or so.

In a subsequent column, Ryan (2016c) adds, "Nobody should listen only to fans: Perish the thought. But taking their pulse to see what matters to them about your show is only smart, especially in a brave new nonlinear world in which word of mouth and fan-based marketing and promotion are more important than ever." There was a huge fan response to this incident, but there was also recognition from media industry insiders that fans needed to be reckoned with, or at least managed.

Fan management is actually the linchpin of the entire incident. The outrage was "exacerbated by the fact that the show's production team had repeatedly assured everyone that the character would not be killed off" (Busse 2017; see also Roth 2016). Specifically, the show reached out to fans using fan terms—for example, concepts like shipping: "Jason Rothenberg would repeatedly say that while he is 'ship neutral' (aka, he doesn't play favorites with regard to which characters should be in relationships together) he sees Clarke and Lexa as 'seaworthy'" (Roth 2016).[2] Moreover, not only was there standard social- and traditional-media information and impression management, but there was also active manipulation of fans. Staff writer Shawna Benson, calling herself "Your Friendly Neighborhood Lurker" and identifying herself as someone who worked on the show, went into a fan forum for rumor control and specifically denied that Lexa was going to die. Fans were particularly upset by the fact that Benson also "identified as straight, despite the forum being a safe space for lesbian individuals to engage with one another" (WeDeservedBetter .com, n.d.). This involved active lying, as the intervention took place after the decision had been made and the script likely written (Roth 2016). That a niche fan message board was thought worthwhile to infiltrate to try to keep fans watching is partially a product of the CW's overall small viewership, but it also speaks to a larger contemporary reality, one that this book explores: fans are more important to media industries than ever, and they are increasingly seen as a resource to be managed whenever possible.

Exploiting Fandom explains the underlying beliefs about fans and appropriate fan–industry relationships that made the Lexa incident possible by examining the structures that developed between 1994 and 2009 to tell the history of the present. This book is not about fans as people, fandom as a culture, or even fandom as a series of practices. Rather, it is about the fan as a concept proliferating in the internet era. A wide variety of cultures, practices, and people are all called "fan"—sports and speculative media; people who buy stuff, people who make stuff, and people who buy stuff other people make; masculine and feminine; emotional and rational; treated in a positive light and a negative light; the exotic practices of strange people and red-blooded all-American fun.[3] The term operates at various levels (and as a variety of parts of speech) sequentially or simultaneously. In recent years, "fan" as noun, verb, and adjective has been increasingly used by public figures as a positive self-identification, and to dismiss investments people have in texts, and by entertainment companies speaking to and about their consumers—and that is where things get interesting.

As the internet became broadly accessible in the United States starting in the mid-1990s, ever larger audiences engaged deeply rather than just consuming media. Engagement has been both recruited by media companies and treated as somewhere between the neutrally inevitable outcome of technological change and a triumph of democracy. Intensive and extensive engagement with media is becoming normative—falling into compliance with social norms according to industry, scholars, and the general public alike.[4] Often the belief is that expanded choices of what and how to consume and being able to talk back to industry and increasingly get at least a social media reply mean audiences now control their own media experience and media has been democratized—an interpretation promoted not only by industry, but also by some journalists and scholars.[5] This narrative says that because audiences can increasingly do things for themselves on the web, rather than only responding to what mass media does, they are increasingly powerful (Jenkins 2006a; Gray, Sandvoss, and Harrington 2007). This assumes media become freer when controlled bottom up by the people, in analogy with how we presume voting functions for governance.[6] Accordingly, the argument goes, media companies must become more responsive to retain audience loyalty or risk being cut out of (potentially lucrative) practices altogether (Murray 2004; Jenkins 2006a; Ross 2009).

This shift toward media interactivity has been interpreted as advancement for fans in particular. Being a fan has traditionally been understood as having a specialized interest or engaging in a practice rooted in intensive and extensive engagement with the object of fandom (Jenkins 1992; Hills 2002). However, this is really the only commonality among people and practices gathered under the term "fan." Certainly, it is the initial similarity between this book's two areas of inquiry, speculative media and sports fans. More specifically, to draw on Michael Warner's (2002) model, sports fans have been a subpublic. That is, although not acting as the majority Public in their participation in the subgroup, sports fans are not seen as distinct from or antithetical to the larger Public either. This leads us to seeing white men flipping and burning cars when their sports team wins (or loses) as an unfortunate but understandable moment of excessive exuberance, because boys will be boys. Speculative media fans, in contrast, have formed a counterpublic, a dominated group separated from and subordinate to the dominant group of the general or unmarked Public. This counterpublic status produces perennial news stories pathologizing men's supposedly Star Trek–induced basement-dwelling virginity and women's allegedly excessive emotional attachments to famous strangers and fictional characters. Because fans have historically been understood to have an especially participatory relationship to their object of fandom, the contemporary regularization and even celebration of media interactivity alongside the spread of "fan" as a label for people and behaviors seems to suggest that all consumers now act like fans (Jenkins 2006a; Sandvoss 2005). Fan subpublics and counterpublics are becoming indistinguishable from the Public.

Although sports and media fans have not often been considered alongside one another either academically or popularly because of this subpublic/counterpublic split, I consider them together here because both subcultures pursue intensive consumption and engagement.[7] As these behaviors become expected from the larger public, the differences between these separate fan cultures lose salience from industry's perspective in favor of "fan" as a catchall term for interactive consumers. This is one place where "fan" as a flexible concept describing certain intensive audience practices (and not others) begins to emerge. Specifically, in industry use, "fan" refers to interactive audiencing, where "audiencing" means the act of membership in an audience. This neologism both makes being an audience a verb, which highlights action, and emphasizes the audience's structurally unequal position vis-à-vis industry, which speaking of "participation" or other alternatives obscures. *Exploiting Fandom,* in a broad sense, uses fans to assess larger emerging beliefs about media use in the internet era.

From 1994 to 2009, the word "fan" and practices traditionally associated with fans were increasingly integrated into media industry logics. This expanded beyond limited consideration as audiences or eyeballs (as in Nielsen ratings) or the long-standing but industry-controlled institution of the fan club. Some media companies began to include fans as they discovered them for the first time; others began to take seriously an emotional attachment to the object of fandom they had formerly dismissed. In either case, it was a seismic shift, and fans went from marginal (as was often true of speculative media fans) or taken for granted (as was often true of sports fans) to a constituency that media companies both recognize and actively seek to incorporate, encourage, monetize, and manage. Commentators have tended to assume the contemporary cultivation of fans as a prized audience was a positive development, with talk of fans ceasing to be marginal and instead becoming central or mainstream, even powerful (Jenkins 2006a; Gray, Sandvoss, and Harrington 2007; Sandvoss 2005).

However, including fans isn't the whole story. After all, critical theory of many kinds argues that inclusion in inequitable systems does not necessarily challenge inequality, and the media system is notoriously unequal. This requires attention to power. Following Michel Foucault (1990, 2003, 2008), I argue that power does not only repress; it also produces. This means that making something more possible, more normative, or more common sense is also a form of constraint—one that encourages that outcome. This approach appreciates that "yes" indicates power relations as much as "no"; it understands that providing something is as enmeshed in power as preventing it; and it asks what power incites, encourages, or produces. Rather than assuming the incitement and recruitment of fan practices and the proliferation of the term "fan" means fans have become powerful, I take seriously the notion that this inclusion is not inherently good. It is illogical to assume that fan–industry inequalities went away rather than transformed; the playing field remains tilted in industry's favor even as the rules of the game have changed. Conversely, drawing on queer theory, I take fan desire and pleasure seriously as not only valid but vital sites of inquiry, such that inclusion, in providing enjoyment, is not inherently bad either.

Ultimately, because the concept "fan" is becoming increasingly prominent, it is important to know what it means. Posing the issue this way is quite different from how fans have traditionally been thought of as individuals or cultures. I examine the concept of "fan" as a social construct: What are the processes by which we come to understand that there is such a thing as a fan? What have we come to understand that thing to be as a result of the formative period this book examines? What do this construction process and its results mean for how we understand media audiencing? Who benefits from these processes, and who doesn't? This is not to say fans aren't people or fandom isn't a culture, because clearly they are.[8] Instead, my argument is that understanding how "fan" is constructed and deployed as an increasingly central concept in the contemporary media system gives insight into that system.

BRINGING FOUCAULT TO FANDOM: DISCOURSE, NORMATIVITY, AND BIOPOLITICS

To approach "fan" this way is to recognize it as a manifestation of social logic and to treat it as a discourse. Discourse is the set of socially possible ways of thinking about a concept, practice, or population. It delimits the framework of common sense—in this case, about what audiences do (and should do). Ruth Frankenberg's (1993, 78) description of a "discursive environment" provides a useful way to think about discourse. Like the material environment we inhabit, its shape is rooted and difficult to change, and it channels our actions in some directions more than others, even as, as Michele White (2006) rightly criticizes, it often goes uninterrogated because it is perceived as just how things are. The construction of "fan" as a concept through discourse matters because discourse creates reality. It is performative, such that when an idea carries that social authorization, the act of saying something makes it true, much like the classic example that when a judge says, "I sentence you," the saying is the sentencing.[9] Discourses are ideas with impact because assumptions about what is true or correct structure thought and action (Foucault 1972). Conceptualizing "the fan" as a discourse thus reorients the question from how fans are to how cultural common sense imagines them, and what that renders (un)intelligible or (il)legible.

As sports and speculative fiction companies came to pay more attention to their fans in the period that this book examines and invited them to participate, they represented, designed for, and had in mind certain practices and people and not others. Henry Jenkins (2006a, 3) argues that "in the world of media convergence," where content and audiences migrate across distribution platforms rather than being tied to one, "every important story gets told, every brand gets sold, and every consumer gets courted across multiple media platforms." However, it is not every consumer, so we need to ask which ones are "courted." We should recognize that it is not just the "important story" that has been supported, but the important brand and consumer too. Not everything "fan" was newly celebrated after the advent of the internet because not all fans or fan practices were included in the increasingly fanlike norm. What exactly is the idea of fans that was mainstreamed?

Instead of paying attention only to whether the media industry noticed fans, we should ask much more specific questions. What ideals, assumptions, and norms animated media industry engagement with fans as they turned toward them with the rise of the internet? When industry workers took fans into account, what did they want fans to do? Which practices comprised being a fan as represented in film, television, and news, and how were they valued? Which practices constituted being a fan as it was designed into official websites? Who were fans understood to be across industry statements, representation, and design? How much does the current construction of fans continue preinternet understandings, and how much does it differ? What do the media industry beliefs, representations, and web design practices in the period this book examines mean for how contemporary culture understands the media system? Rather than accepting the inclusion of fans in media industry practices as an improvement, I ask about inclusion for whom and on what terms, and I ask who or what is excluded.

Moments when media industry logics incorporate fans are both caused by and reinforce the broader cultural understanding about how we should interact with media. That is, discourse around fans reflects and reproduces a norm, a structuring ideal that identifies particular people and modes of behavior as correct, expected, desired—that is, normal. Importantly, while the media industry's relationship to fans through policies, web design, and representation structures norms, it is not omnipotent. I do not claim that every living, breathing fan will or must respond in a certain way to industry action. Rather, I examine which responses are invited, encouraged, and considered correct. Because what is normative is socially valued—as can be seen from the connotations attached to "normal"—there are powerful social incentives to complying with normativity, or at least trying to (Butler 1993; Ferguson 2003; Foucault 1990). The norm exerts pressure on behavior because we desire recognition and inclusion. However, the fact that fan normalization may not work seamlessly, and that the cultural common sense of what audience members should want to do may not be matched by actual, embodied fans, is not an impediment to my model. It is entirely possible that actual fans might encounter media industry strategies for fan incorporation and find themselves unwelcome. While they may then go play somewhere else, adapt, or contest media industry policies, the social power of the norm means it must be reckoned with somehow. Norms matter because they point us in particular directions (Ahmed 2006). It is therefore critical to determine where they point and what that orientation makes possible (or not). In this book, the relevant lines point to what we are normatively supposed to do when interacting with media: which people and which behaviors are recruited.

The norm is both what makes some actions socially possible or desirable and what makes others impossible or undesirable. Drawing on a framework that emphasizes the limitations of normativity, my approach highlights that second aspect: norms are inherently exclusionary. Importantly, I am interested in implications of norms and practices rather than intentions. What media industry workers try to do matters, of course. Nevertheless, this project asks about the norms actually produced by their beliefs about fans or acts of representation or web design in relation to fans, because in many cases inclusive intentions have exclusionary results. When some subcultural practices get moved into the norm and not others, the very expansiveness marks what is left behind as too strange to include. Being selective produces and reinforces one idea about who fans are and what they do as the norm for the category, and this norm benefits industry. Although increased access to media production and use is framed as democratizing, Thomas Frank's (2000) account of the "democratization of the stock market" narrative from the 1990s provides a useful counterpoint. With the rise of internet-enabled stock trading, the rhetoric was that people could now control their own economic destinies by being included in finance, but, as Frank shows, most benefits of expanded trading accrued to top-tier investors. Benefits accumulate to the top—in this case to industry—in much the same way with fan "democratization."

Audience desire to participate has gone from seen as something atypical (sometimes aberrant) that periodically happened to media to something interpreted as endemic and therefore something to manage and make productive. Although advertising and marketing have always sought to produce desire, managing desire has become newly possible as media organizations have better information about their consumers and as the norm of media use becomes increasingly interactive. As industry invites fans to participate, it attempts to recruit them into a system of management—a selective and specific system passing itself off as neutral and universal. Accordingly, I examine how two media industries—speculative media and sports—act to manage fans. I consider sports franchises to be media companies in part because a far larger number of people experience professional sports through media than in stadiums, and media revenues constitute a greater share of these companies' incomes than any other source (Buraimo and Simmons 2009). However, the second reason is that they use the same techniques of audience incitement.

Beyond productive power in general, Foucault's (1990, 2003, 2008) concept of biopolitics usefully explains fan management. In biopolitics, power operates on the population, not the individual, to manage and optimize its functioning. Foucault describes how governments manage their populations, which is obviously different from the media industry as an economic sector. Hard though it may seem to divest from media, it is considerably easier than refusing to be governed. Still, the notion of biopolitics provides insight. Broad tendencies or patterns in industry's interactions with fans function, as Foucault (2003, 246) describes the workings of this form of power, "not to modify any given phenomenon as such, or to modify a given individual insofar as he is an individual, but, essentially, to intervene at the level at which these general phenomena are determined, to intervene at the level of their generality." In this case, fans are acted on as a population through producing, disseminating, and reinforcing a norm of media use. After all, media-producing organizations do not (and cannot) generally act on individual fans.[10] Instead, metrics like Nielsen ratings, page hits, and advertising impressions permit industry to operate in terms of aggregates. This is why these processes cannot be understood by studying fans as individuals or cultures; industry does not engage them that way.

Under biopower, Foucault explains, actions and objects formerly not regulated and normalized by institutions—sexuality and the population itself in his examples—came to be so. Accordingly, if fan activities that used to happen unofficially or illicitly are now noticed and incited, this shift acts to move fans "into the order of things that are counted" (1990, 4) and to allow those practices to become known, regulated, and normalized. In this orientation toward management, media organizations—like the governments Foucault (1990, 138) describes—"foster" certain practices and "disallow" others. The fan has become, as Foucault (1990, 24) says of sexuality, "a thing to be not simply condemned or tolerated but managed, inserted into systems of utility, regulated for the greater good of all, made to function according to an optimum." In this book I demonstrate how media companies construct, orient, and manage toward optimization, a process still underway.

The organizing metaphor of this book is the domestication of fans.[11] Just as livestock are bred to be bigger and more docile, industry's invitations to fans seek to make them both more useful and more controllable, thus making fans a resource to exploit. However, exploitation is not the whole story. Livestock also lead safer, easier lives than their wild counterparts, protected from external threats. Correspondingly, fans may want to take the offer of the provision of mountains of additional content that they do not have to make themselves as well as the offer of being free from the threat of lawsuits. Indeed, fans do choose to participate, and they do benefit, although under conditions that they do not control or even always fully understand. Moreover, if domestication suggests fans are meat and milk, it also points to domesticity. Private and affective attachments underpin the extraction of surplus by capital, just as feminists argue domestic labor does (Hochschild 1989; Federici 2011). In this way, the layered meaning of "domestication" usefully demonstrates the position of fans in media industry logics. I trace a shift that worked toward bringing fan behaviors onto the media industry ranch, to incite fans' participation and production of value (emotional and monetary), but only in particular, circumscribed ways. The media industry has made a play to lock down fandom. How fans respond will determine the future course of fandom. One key purpose of this book is to give a full accounting of what the offer is so that fans can decide whether to take it.

METHODS, OR BRINGING CLOSE READING TO A BIG DATA FIGHT AND VICE VERSA

To investigate how management of fans happens, I use a method I call big reading. Big reading is close reading on a large scale. It shares the drive to comprehensiveness of big data, drawing on thousands of examples from multiple types of source across a long time period (1994–2009).

However, big reading proceeds qualitatively, asking not only whether or with what frequency fans or specific fan practices appear in the archive, but also how they appear. My first source is what media industry workers say about fans. Transmedia marketing agency Campfire was my first site. I interviewed everyone who makes decisions about producing content for fans—a total of three workers, as Campfire is a small firm. At the time of my interviews, Campfire described itself on its website as "a marketing agency that launches products and changes perceptions through storytelling. We ignite the influencers, fan cultures and communities that drive results for our clients." I also interviewed three current and former athletics marketing workers at a large public university in the US Midwest which, because interviewees asked for confidentiality, I'll call BMU, for Big Midwestern University. BMU has over 30,000 undergraduate students and over 20 intercollegiate athletics teams operating on a budget of $60 to 70 million, with a dozen employees in the marketing and media departments alone. I supplemented interviews with statements about fans and audiences by industry workers (writers, producers, directors, actors, etc.) in the 1,088 news stories and ninety audiovisual texts examined for representation.

What industry workers say about fans, whether revealing their beliefs or merely what they believe they should say, demonstrates industry common sense about fans. In selecting which workers' statements to consider, access was a constraint. I spoke with workers willing to talk to me, and I collected statements from people who had spoken publicly. I selected Campfire because I had the opportunity to meet an executive, Mike, at a conference, providing a point of entry. I selected a university athletics department because the academic mission of the broader university increased the chances that they would agree to help me with my research. Although power has nodes and any point of entry is not equally good, I did not have complete freedom to choose how and where I intervened when it came to industry workers. Within these constraints, I examined strategies workers used to incite fans and how they talked about fans with an eye toward understanding whom they imagined fans to be, what they imagined fans to do, and what they want fans to do or not do.

Second, I analyzed interfaces and terms of service (TOS) at ten official websites, five for speculative fiction and five for sports, for what happens at a key point of contact between industry and fans. Sites were selected using theoretical sampling: the companies behind them are known to be particularly controlling of fans or particularly generous with them, or their cultural status means they provide special insight. For speculative media, I examined the sites for Star Wars, whose creator, George Lucas, is notoriously controlling; the 2003 *Battlestar Galactica* reboot, whose executive producer, Ronald D. Moore, is known for providing fans with lots of behind-the-scenes information; *Dr. Horrible's Sing-Along Blog*, a project from fan-beloved auteur Joss Whedon;[12] the cable channel SyFy, which heavily uses social media to get fans involved (like inviting them to retweet announcements to get a prize); and Star Trek, which is indispensable as the most culturally mocked fan object.[13] For sports, I examined Purdue University, which integrated technology to improve fans' experience (Ault et al. 2008); University of California, Berkeley, a second college athletic site to compare to Purdue; the Seattle Mariners, who are reputationally fan friendly and new media savvy; ESPN, which was an early adopter of letting fans interact (Bryant and Holt 2006), and Major League Soccer, a net-native sports organization because it was founded in the 1990s (Wilson 2007). These sites also include both old objects of fandom established before the advent of interactive media (Star Trek, Seattle Mariners) and new objects of fandom originating in the internet era (the 2003 instantiation of *Battlestar Galactica,* Major League Soccer). This enriches the study's capacity to find continuities and discontinuities of industry logics.

My consideration of websites uses discursive interface analysis (Stanfill 2015). This method examines the "affordances" of websites, defined by H. Rex Hartson (2003, 316) as what a site "*offers* the user, what it *provides* or *furnishes,*" for their assumptions about the site's purpose and appropriate use. The analysis centers around Foucault's insight that power is productive and focuses on questions of normativity rather than control. I examine where and to what the interfaces say yes and not just no. In analyzing sites this way, I go beyond bare technological function, as affordances are often considered, examining what is possible on sites in a broader sense. I ask what features sites have, but also which features they emphasize, how they are explained, and how uses that may be technically possible are rendered more or less normative through being treated as correct. This analysis uses the following terms: "functional affordance" refers to what a site can actually do; "cognitive affordance" lets users know what a site can do; and "sensory affordance" "enables the user in sensing (e.g., seeing, hearing, feeling) something" (Hartson 2003, 322, emphasis removed). Finding patterns in these elements works to unravel cultural common sense about what fan users do, which, because it is built into the technology, becomes a normative claim about what they should do.

Third, I analyzed film, television, and web series representations of fans that either were about speculative fiction or sports fans, or that included speculative fiction or sports fan characters. I used ninety audiovisual texts released between 1994 and 2009: forty-eight films and forty-two seasons of television shows; eighty-one fictional representations and nine nonfictional ones; fifty-six representations of speculative media fans and thirty-four for sports.[14] I gathered the audiovisual archive from characters called "fan" in the Internet Movie Database (IMDb.com). IMDb is a mainstream clearinghouse popularly understood as comprehensive (delimiting what is socially relevant). It is also editable by industry, whose stake in making information about their products accessible contributes to actual comprehensiveness. I also snowball sampled media objects advertised as previews on DVDs of the texts from IMDb, objects mentioned by other scholars (Johnson 2007; Scott 2011), and representations that colleagues mentioned to me. While the archive is unavoidably incomplete, gathering all the well-known representations illuminates main currents in thinking about fans. Additionally, I examined newspaper coverage of the largest-scale events for these two kinds of fans: San Diego Comic-Con, one of the largest speculative media conventions and one made more official by being heavily attended and promoted by industry, and the Super Bowl, the annual US football championship. This archive comprises 1,088 Associated Press (AP) news stories from 1994 to 2009 retrieved from the LexisNexis database, 675 for the phrase "Super Bowl" and 413 for "Comic Con." The AP, a major source of news relied on by much of the US press, was selected to narrow down the unwieldy size of all coverage while still getting at major trends. Wire services like the AP tend to anchor discussion of news topics. Representation both acts on fans' self-understanding (Stanfill 2013; Booth and Kelly 2013; Busse 2016) and works to produce a sense of being a fan apart from actual fans—either in nonfans or when we are not seeking to learn about fans but encounter them anyway. Representations of fans therefore help produce the broad social meaning of "fan."

I began by reading closely the entire corpus of interview transcripts; web interface screenshots; TOS documentation; news articles; and television and film (and their DVD special features) transcripts. There were a total of ninety documents, which varied in scope from an eleven-page transcript of a single interview to a forty-three-page aggregated file of transcribed fictional representations of speculative media fans from sources that fell alphabetically between *Heroes*, season 2, and *O.C., The*, season 2. This close reading identified 8,589 relevant quotations for 156 codes, which were recorded using qualitative data analysis software Atlas.ti. In looking for themes, I began from the three areas of inquiry I had developed from my reading of the literature: fans as subjects, consumption, and labor. At the same time, I paid attention to emergent terms of interest as I read, like law. Once the entire corpus was coded, I read the list of themes, such as "basic consumption" or "expansive definition of consumption," alongside one another to see what groupings were emergent from their juxtaposition. I then used the Code Family feature of Atlas.ti to collate themes under the broader category of, for example, "consumption." The quotations aggregated in each family were examined again alongside one another to see what trends emerged when reading was source- and fan-type agnostic. These themes formed the basis of the argument about how the concept "fan" was shaped in the period this book examines.

Big reading shares some characteristics with what Franco Moretti (2005) calls distant reading.[15] As Moretti (2005, 4) notes, discussing literature, "A field this large cannot be understood by stitching together spare bits of knowledge about individual cases, because it *isn't* a sum of individual cases: it's a collective system, that should be grasped as such, as a whole." "Grasping as a whole" is distant reading, "where distance is however not an obstacle but *a specific form of knowledge;* fewer elements, hence a sharper sense of their overall interconnection" and their "shapes, relations, structures" (1). Close reading, in contrast, looks at the language, imagery, or other characteristics of moments fans appear for what they convey about the category "fan." I do not take the presence of fan characters, the term "fan," or fan-associated practices like video remix as the entire story. Instead, I use close reading to explore on what terms inclusion occurs and what this shows about underlying beliefs about fans. Importantly, like boyd and Crawford (2012, 667), I maintain an awareness that "the design decisions that determine what will be measured also stem from interpretation." Put into Deborah Eicher-Catt's (2003) phenomenologically derived terminology, I take seriously that my *data* (what is given) is always already *capta* (what is taken).

Big reading combines these two scales of analysis, looking both at broad commonalities and the specific moments that make them up. The general understanding of the concept "fan" then becomes visible in accumulated commonalities across disparate locations, even when different people produced the different objects, and even if the sources were produced in apparent isolation from each other. Simultaneously, I pay attention to how this relates to larger technical, economic, social, and political structures like consumer capitalism or the tendency to seek the broadest possible intellectual property (IP) protection for corporations. Using Atlas.ti, I aggregated thousands of close readings at the level of the sentence or paragraph to get a big picture made up of small, specific analyses, like tiles in a mosaic. One key benefit is that the software allows a single piece of text to be classified in potentially infinite ways, permitting attention to how a given textual moment may work on multiple levels. In this way, much as Mary Gray (2012) has argued about ethnographic data, this is a form of big data not only because of its sheer pervasiveness but also because any given data point in isolation seems insignificant; only as a body do they become meaningful. This is a particularly good way to approach discourse, which exists in and as quotidian micromoments that reflect (and can be used to investigate) larger systems of which they are part.

Through the accumulation of individual data at scale, it is possible to read back the discursive formation driving them. The patterns illuminated by big reading emerge out of (and demonstrate) the underlying beliefs animating industry's turn toward fans, as demonstrated in web page layout, statements to news media, the visual construction of film and television scenes, and all the rest. By combining the various angles of vision from interviews, representations, and design, much like ethnographic triangulation (Fetterman 1998), a richer picture emerges. I argue that, while the fan has proliferated throughout the mediascape, attending to how fans are constructed shows the fundamental, intractable limitations of achieving (apparent) normativity in a structurally unequal media system.

ROAD MAP

This book moves from the most typical approaches to studying fans to the least common: fan subjects (Chapters 1 and 2), consumption (Chapter 3), law (Chapter 4), and labor (Chapters 5 and 6). Each chapter draws promiscuously from fictional and nonfictional representations of fans, policies and structures of official websites, and statements from media industry workers. By considering these different sources simultaneously, rather than organizing the book as case studies, I examine contemporary norms for fans as a single system.[16] Deliberately mixing source types lets the big picture of emerging norms for media use become visible from commonalities across different sources at the same time that the specificity of particular appearances of the concept "fan" grounds the analysis.

Chapter 1, "Fandom's Normativity: Assuming and Recruiting the Socially Dominant Fan Subject," considers which people—in terms of race, gender, and age—are assumed and constructed as ideal or default fans. It demonstrates that white bodies numerically dominate visual representations of fans during the time period this book examines. This combines with the tendency of industry, fans, and scholars alike to limit all discussion of race to concerns about racism and the marginalization of fans of color to construct fans as white. Moreover, men are the normative fans represented, and practices disproportionately performed by men are what industry encourages, with women both indirectly marginalized and sometimes directly classified as not proper fans. This constructs being a fan as "rightfully" belonging to men. Being a fan is also constructed as "normal" by being appropriate for families and is more specifically linked to the high social valuation of children. Overall, how fans appear as people shows "fan" to be associated with valued social categories, both increasing its social valuation and inevitably shifting the former marginality of the category "fan" onto less powerful people.

In contrast, the second chapter, "The Fandom Menace Straightens Up and Flies White: Failed Normativity to Redemption," examines how these white men are paradoxically also constructed as failing at masculinity and whiteness because they fail at adulthood and heterosexuality. This recapitulates stereotypes that the internet and industry's embrace of fans have supposedly made obsolete. What is new in the period this book examines is that representations of failed masculinity include redemption for white men fans through their ability to exercise constructed-as-white self-control. These redemption narratives work both to reinforce the cultural common sense of privilege as a natural property of white, heterosexual masculinity and to produce fans as white. In this way, these narratives link fans to dominance despite the seeming marginalization from which they start.

Moving from people to practices, "Consumption and the Management of Desire," Chapter 3, analyzes what kinds of audience consumption are considered normative. Consumption is both constructed as an innate fan desire and actively encouraged, demonstrating how the fan–industry relationship works through managing desire. Constructions of normative consumption fundamentally tie proper fan desire to consumptive modes. Particularly, while transmedia—projects that use multiple platforms like TV, the internet, and games—is premised on interactivity and seems different from consumption, further investigation reveals it to be Consumption 2.0. Media industry approaches undoubtedly recruit and desire fan desire, but only as reaction, attempting to domesticate fan desire into manageable and lucrative forms. This structure therefore disputes arguments that being courted by industry empowers fans. To be the ideal consumer is still to be distinguished from a contributor.

Chapter 4, "The Long Arm of (Beliefs about) the Law," examines what beliefs industry demonstrates about the law and argues that industry legal action does not follow the letter of the law but rather chronically overreaches. Overall, the tendency in industry's legalistic practices is toward private gain at the public's expense. Assertions of control, technological design, and TOS as contracts all take place without a representative of the public interest, even as the public is the supposed beneficiary of the entire copyright enterprise. Although the copyright system is meant to cultivate more "science and useful arts," industry engagement with fans shows that it instead supports extraction of monetary value.

Additionally, fans are both assumed and recruited to do what I contend is labor. "Fandom and/as Labor," Chapter 5, analyzes how fans are asked to work in the period this book examines. First, fans labor by watching the ads that support "free" media, generating direct monetary value for the media industry through ad sales as an audience commodity. Fans also produce value through data sales, where knowledge about user activity has value. The norm expects and invites fans to work to make themselves known—to do the work of being watched. Fans are even encouraged to make the object of fandom interesting for themselves, thus making their own free lunch. Moreover, fans normatively do promotional labor to increase awareness of and interest in the object of fandom. Fan work also contributes to producing media objects themselves through content labor. Finally, the norm assumes and encourages fans to do what I term "lovebor," the work of loving and demonstrating love that generates intangible value for the media industry. What these forms of normative and recruited activity have in common is that industry extracts surplus value from them.

Chapter 6, "Enclosing Fandom: Labors of Love, Exploitation, and Consent," grapples with the key challenge of the labor model: fan work does not seem like labor because fans do it out of love. Thus, it seems like fans do not require payment because they engage out of enjoyment, or perhaps because fans are anticapitalist and resistant to market exchange. Such arguments are insufficiently structural, and they are inattentive to both the unequal playing field on which fans make those choices and how being a fan on industry's terms fundamentally differs from fandom by and for fans. Fan labor can only be understood in relation to labor-cost reduction on industry's part, the rise of pleasurable labor, and the rejection of capitalist projects by many fans, which together produce perfect conditions for exploiting fan labor. Given the low awareness of the full implications of fan activity and the structural coercions involved, fans' willingness to participate is not true consent to this labor and value extraction. Ultimately, the industry embrace of fans as an enclosure of the commons of fandom turns fans into a workforce for industry; it is thus necessary to call for greater attention to how the benefits of fan work are distributed.

Finally, the Conclusion, "Two Futures of Fandom," returns to the 2016 moment that opens this Introduction to examine the two potential directions the fan–industry relationship can take from here. On the one hand, lamentations that fans have become entitled and demand too much proliferated in summer 2016, which I analyze as a "moral panic" (Cohen 1972). This moral panic works to conserve industry power and rearticulate fans as passive as a mode of backlash to slight fan gains. On the other hand, at times industry workers have prioritized fan desires over financial considerations or have expressed a sense of owing fans something for their loyalty. Particularly, the (white, boy) child as a worthy fan to whom industry has a responsibility, the rude, unsympathetic celebrity who takes fans for granted, and the fan hero mobilize the notion that fans matter. I use this profan tendency to consider what potential there may be for decentralized information technologies to increase participation in media by those formerly excluded.

CHAPTER ONE

FANDOM'S NORMATIVITY

Assuming and Recruiting the Socially Dominant Fan Subject

Fans, the triumphalist narrative goes, are the new ideal audience. Fans have, after long suffering from undeserved stigma, been mainstreamed, and everything is now wonderful. But of course all is not wonderful. In August 2014, the internet exploded with what came to be known as Gamergate. This online campaign took the premise that gaming had become too mainstream and that inclusion of women as game players and makers was the result of a vast conspiracy to take over and shove out gaming's traditional fans: young white men. A similar public conflict arose in early 2015 around science fiction's Hugo awards, when two interrelated groups who called themselves the Sad Puppies and the Rabid Puppies, feeling that the genre had become too inclusive and was harming straight white men by pushing their work and experiences aside for fiction with social justice themes, attempted to stack the awards in favor of a collection of nominees whose wins would return science fiction to its supposed rightful owners.[1]

These panics—that fandoms of various speculative genres are becoming too inclusive, and that straight white men are consequently excluded (when in fact rightfully they should be central)—seem to suggest speculative media fandom is a paradise for white women, people of color, and queer folks. The members of the latter groups who were subjected to online rape and death threats (some of which met criteria to involve police), the posting of their personal information online (known as doxing), and other large-scale, coordinated online harassment when they opposed these reactionary campaigns would probably beg to differ. In fact, violent mob action to defend being a fan from heretical outsiders made these moral-panicking fans resemble neither downtrodden, stigmatized fans nor newly empowered ideal consumers but instead something more like football hooligans, fans notorious for acting to assert white heterosexual men's authority on the Other (Müller, van Zoonen, and de Roode 2007; Nielsen 2013).

This tension drives contemporary beliefs about fans as people. In contrast to the powerful stigma cataloged by early fan studies scholars (Jenkins 1992; Jensen 1992; Lewis 1992a), many believe being a fan is now seen as something regular people do, but the mainstream fan is tightly linked to culturally powerful categories. It is certainly true that positioning fans as ideal media users differs substantially from their traditional associations with danger, violence, and pathology or just loneliness, alienation, and loserdom, as well as the greatest hits of dysfunctional and murderous fans that formerly seemed almost required any time fans came up—Mark David Chapman, John Lennon's fan and killer; John Hinckley, a fan of Jodie Foster's, who tried to kill Ronald Reagan to impress her; and Robert Bardo, the fan who killed actress Rebecca Schaeffer. Compared to these images, more recent ideas of being a fan as a reasonable or even expected pastime for a socially powerful group like white men suggests that being a fan is normative in contemporary culture.

Yet normativity relies on fans occupying socially valued positions like masculinity and whiteness, as well as on connecting fans to the high social valuation of family and children. This is the counterpart to Kristen J. Warner's (2015a, 36) point that it is strange to contend "fandom wholesale operates as Other—especially when considering the fact that many fans are part of dominant identity groups—White, cis-gendered, and heterosexual." If fans, because of their whiteness, cisness, or straightness—and, I would add, because they are popularly understood as men—are not really as marginal as is sometimes claimed, the obverse is that these characteristics are central to how, when, and why they are granted normative status. In this chapter, I examine how race, gender, and age appear across representation, web design, and industry interviews. Through combining source types, the larger beliefs animating any given instance become visible. In particular, it become clear that what makes a socially valued fan is largely the same across sports and speculative media despite the differing lived experiences involved. Ultimately, the supposed embrace or normalization of fans remains selective.

RACE: THE (WHITE) ELEPHANT IN THE ROOM

I both begin from and emphasize race in this chapter and the next. One key reason is to counterbalance the underexamination of race in fan studies so far. From time to time, race does appear in lists of characteristics fans have; scholars note that media industries segment their audiences by gender and race, or that white people and men are privileged as audiences, or that populations of fans are diverse by race, age, and class, or that populations of fans are substantially white, middle class, and women. However, analysis rarely moves beyond this mention to a serious consideration. In recent years, awareness of fan studies' gaps around race has emerged, with criticism of how generalizations about media fans often disregard race as a relevant structure (Pande 2016; Wanzo 2015; Warner 2015a). Fan studies, Rebecca Wanzo (2015) charges, has focused on people who reject the mainstream, not those rejected by it, putting disproportionate emphasis on those who have the choice. Accordingly, she argues, "one of the primary ways in which attentiveness to race can transform fan studies is by destabilizing the idea that fans choose outsider status" (Wanzo 2015, ¶ 2.1). Making a similar argument from another direction, Christine Scodari (2012) is critical of studying white women fans and then acting as if findings apply to all women fans. However, it might be more exact to say the implicit assumption is that white women are all women because, as Warner (2015a, 48) notes, there is little awareness of women of color's participation as fans, leaving gaps in our understanding because these fans "go about fan labor in ways that speak to specific cultural experiences that traditional fan studies has yet to consider." While these discussions are not yet numerous, they make important moves toward examining how race matters to being a fan.

Sports studies, in contrast, has relatively consistently analyzed race, largely because of the history of overt racism that makes sports fans "a much less likely and indeed likeable subject of study" compared to media fans, who are traditionally seen as underdogs (Gray, Sandvoss, and Harrington 2007, 5). In Wanzo's (2015, ¶ 1.4) more sharply worded summary, "One of the reasons race may be neglected is because it troubles some of the claims—and desires—at the heart of fan studies scholars and their scholarship," namely that fandom is marginalized and/or progressive. Sports studies finds that being a sports fan privileges whiteness and alienates fans of color (Crawford 2004; Newman 2007; Ruddock 2005). Against this baseline of whiteness, fans' engagement with particular practices or sports reflects their sense of racial, ethnic, and/or national belonging (Gibbons 2011; Rommel 2011; Burdsey 2006). Sports studies scholarship also shows that numerically and structurally dominant white fans are frequently either passively or actively racist (Müller, van Zoonen, and de Roode 2007; Newman 2007; Carey 2013).

Failing to consider race has the effect of whitening being a fan. Whiteness is the unmarked category (marking others), the unexamined category (subjecting others to examination), and the norm (making others abnormal), and the cumulative effect is privilege (and disadvantage for others). Ross Chambers (1997, 189) adds, "There are plenty of unmarked categories (maleness, heterosexuality, and middle classness being obvious ones), but whiteness is perhaps the primary unmarked and so unexamined—let's say 'blank'—category." Because whiteness is unmarked, "race" is often taken as a synonym for "people of color," and if people of color are who "have" race, whiteness becomes race free, or, crucially, race neutral. As Chambers (1997, 192) argues, "In contrast to those whose identity is defined by their classificatory status as members of a given group, whites are perceived as individual historical agents." This difference makes the category "white" what he calls "the unexamined." That is, whiteness is not perceived as relevant because white people are "just people," whereas others are both classified as hyphenated Americans and always imagined to represent their group.

Although whiteness is constructed as blank and nothing in particular, it clearly is something. It is the norm-defining something (Frankenberg 1993). It is the kind of person meant when something is framed as universal. Disappearing the racialized character of whiteness is therefore a distinctly white perspective (although often not explicitly or consciously). Additionally, to ignore race is to support the "racial status quo," also an implicitly white position relying on benefiting from current racial systems (Bonilla-Silva 2003, 8). Simply declaring race irrelevant, without undoing its social impacts, is consequently troublesome, making current inequalities harder to recognize, let alone disrupt (Bonilla-Silva 2003; Warner 2015b). This means racism is not simply overt "'resentment' or 'hostility' toward minorities" (Bonilla-Silva 2003, 8), as it is often defined. It is also a refusal to examine or even acknowledge existing racial inequality. Eduardo Bonilla-Silva (2003) terms this color-blind racism and notes that it supports white supremacy. Similarly, Warner (2015b, 5) calls color blindness "a means of progress that did not significantly threaten white privilege."

In light of this, following Kyle Kusz's (2001, 393) insistence that it is necessary to "read Whiteness into texts that are not explicitly about race if one is to disrupt Whiteness as the unchallenged racial norm," this chapter and the next insist on recognizing and analyzing whiteness in fan norms. As Warner (2015a, 2015c) notes, the normative, universal, or unmarked fan identity is implicitly a white one, against which fans of color must struggle for recognition or form their own fan groups. Corresponding to Wanzo's (2015) argument that fan studies would look different if African Americans were taken into account as fans, that the default notion of "fan" is racialized as white must be recognized. The whiteness of fans is not neutral or inevitable but rather the product of power relations. We must name and examine it as the result of a process reproducing racial inequality.

Attending to the absence and not just presence of discussion about race, then, the loud silences in the discourse of the fan need to be named. The whiteness of being a fan often emerges indirectly through race being unmarked. In five of my six interviews with marketing workers at Campfire and BMU (all of whom are white), race was never mentioned as a characteristic they thought about in relation to who fans are, unlike gender, age, and class. The single worker who did mention race was James of BMU, who was somewhat differently positioned from the other interviewees as both a practitioner and an academic—although as I will explain, James's consideration of race, like other exceptions to overall color blindness about fans, tends to reinforce whiteness as central.[2] Industry workers also ignore race in public statements like DVD features and news stories.

Whitening by near omission also occurs with websites. Race does not appear in interfaces at all; websites do not ask this when you register to use them. Although some might object that race is irrelevant to a website, sites collect equally irrelevant data about birthdates (the law would only require affirmation that users are over thirteen, eighteen, or twenty-one, depending on the purpose of registration) and gender. This is part of a larger tendency to downplay race online. Early narratives about the internet took the premise that without immediately visible bodies, since all could (in theory) contribute, racial (and gender) inequality would simply go away. Accordingly, the internet is often perceived to be race free, with evidence to the contrary provoking surprise or even anger (Daniels 2013; Brock 2011). Heather Hensman Kettrey and Whitney Nicole Laster's (2014, 269, 265) research shows that "online spaces are presumed to be nonracial until they are racialized by the presence of users of color," but as this equation of "people of color" with racialization suggests, they also discover that users "assumed white identities, white privilege, and white space to be the default," thus demonstrating a blurring of "nonracial" and "white." In fact, digital technologies are often racialized as white, which can be seen when they are represented using tropes of frontiers and colonial exploitation (Daniels 2013; Noble and Roberts 2016) as well as the ways Black-specific content is perceived as lesser than "an internet where Blackness is (at best) a minor presence in a universe of content supporting a White ideological frame" (Brock 2011, 1101). Indeed, André Brock (2011, 1088) directly contends that "the Western internet, as a social structure, represents and maintains White, masculine, bourgeois, heterosexual and Christian culture through its content" even while this white internet is framed as neutral.

Beyond the ways racial silences tend to be filled with whiteness, fans are most often understood as white people, particularly white men. Fans as directly depicted in media texts, especially primary characters, are overwhelmingly (although not exclusively) white. We should take seriously and examine the sheer overpowering number of white fans in audiovisual sources, particularly against the belief white people have no race. Even if these representations did reflect a fan population that is actually substantially white—which is many people's anecdotal sense, but we do not know because fan demographics have not been systematically studied and the population would be difficult to adequately sample—fandom has often been able to be unaware of its own whiteness. Indeed, even the few prominent discussions like RaceFail '09, a months-long conflict around fandom racism and the exclusion of fans of color, were directly caused by unexamined whiteness (TWC Editor 2009). Such instances demonstrate that "if we see attachments to whiteness and xenophobic or racist affect as frequently central to fan practices, then sports fandom ceases to be an outlier" (Wanzo 2015, ¶ 1.4).

In fact, even acknowledging race as a system or that fans of color exist tends to happen in ways that center whiteness. That is, race appears as (and only as) racism and people of color are marginalized as fans. Race appears on websites only in their TOS and only as a source of trouble. SyFy forbids "harassing, offensive, vulgar, abusive, hateful or bashing communications—especially those that put down others' sexual orientation, gender, race, color, religious views, national origin or disability." ESPN tells its users, "You agree that you will not Distribute any Submission that," among other things, "is bigoted, hateful, or racially or otherwise offensive." Website design and policy equating race and racism echo the belief that, the quip goes, only racists notice race. Sites assume that race will only come up as a result of racism. Consequently, platforms only notice race to prohibit racism, which is the cause of noticing race. Equating talking about race with racism blurs injunctions not to be racist and injunctions not to talk about race—or a don't ask, don't tell policy. Like the original DADT, this assumes that the presence of difference causes strife, so we should behave as if there were no difference; "even to suggest that difference might be important would transform them into instigators of racial division" (Warner 2015b, x). The unintended consequence is that, as the military was structurally straightened by DADT, being a fan is whitened by these logics.[3] White people tend to have the luxury of ignoring race; indeed, Jessie Daniels (2013) contends that white people tend to be invested in not having any awareness of race. This is visible in the intense insistence by fans like those of George R. R. Martin (Young 2014) and the Disney film Song of the South (Sperb 2010) that race does not matter in their objects of fandom. Importantly, as Frankenberg (1993, 145) notes, "The idea that noticing a person's 'color' is not a good thing to do, even an offensive thing to do, suggests that 'color,' which here means nonwhiteness, is bad in and of itself." In short, the idea that it is rude to talk about race is rooted in white supremacy.

Treating race as always already racism is common in sports TV and film, where the racialized division of labor between (substantially) Black players and (substantially) white fans foregrounds race. The opening scene of *The Express,* a biopic about African American football player Ernie Davis, depicts the 1960 Cotton Bowl, and the Dallas crowd seems to be encouraging the white players from the University of Texas to beat up the Black players from Syracuse University. Whether or not the film reflects actual events, using such a scene to address race and fans reduces race to racism in line with color-blind logic. In fact, when Davis rallies the other Black players to resist this racism for the sake of the few Black spectators in the stands, it feels like a contrived opportunity for a grand lesson about overcoming racism, because previously African American fans were shown gathered around televisions rather than in the stadium. The same belief that race matters only as racism drives a scene in football film *Friday Night Lights,* when the coach of an opposing team argues, "There'd be a problem with our fans sitting with your fans" because one team has multiracial fans and the other team's are entirely white, a tension that also appears in the *Friday Night Lights* television show. Clearly these scenes wish to mark racism as unacceptable, but the way they do it acts to center whiteness.

Having fans of color present but centering whiteness also shows in the tendency of fans of color to be represented, but rarely as main characters. (Hiro of the NBC superhero drama *Heroes* is the only exception, and he is part of a large ensemble cast.) While admittedly it is absurd (and essentialist) to count instances of nonwhite people, to some extent that is what I have to do. Frequently fans of color appear only in backgrounds of convention scenes or sporting events, and locating them tends to be a bit like finding Waldo. As Sara Ahmed (2012) notes, the presence of those who look different from the white norm—like, in her example, having students of many races in college brochures—is often taken as proof of sufficient diversity. Presence appears to be progress, Ahmed contends, but it actually undermines substantive equality because diversity appears achieved, meaning that visual diversity can shore up white dominance. Similarly, Warner (2015b, 20) notes that "by including diverse racial types as extras but not providing them with speaking parts," viewers are not required to empathize with those characters or even see them as people. This research suggests that while fans of color prevent a monochrome crowd, without personalities or plot significance they are indistinguishable from set decoration.

Additionally, fans of color tend to be unable to speak for themselves. In the first few seasons of the nerd sitcom *The Big Bang Theory*, South Asian character Raj literally does not talk in many scenes because his pathological inability to talk to women (or even to speak in their presence) silences him, which is treated as funny. More figuratively, when an East Asian fan in the Star Trek documentary *The Captains* asks regarding the camera, "Is it on?" actor William Shatner mishears her as calling him "Spock" and is offended. This silences her actual statement and demonstrates Gayatri Chakravorty Spivak's (1988) point that marginalized people structurally cannot speak because they cannot be heard within existing systems of power. Fans of color do sometimes appear and speak, but these tend not to be fleshed-out characters. Instead they show up only briefly. Overall, fans of color are generally denied relevance.

In these ways, fans of color are often framed as an exception, thus reinforcing a norm of whiteness. James from BMU, for example, takes whiteness as standard when he describes the racial composition of the university's fan base:

> Part of my job was, you know, you see these like half—these time-out promotions, where they do activities, you know, Coca-Cola whatever basketball shot. And as a marketing person they used to want me to go out and select the contestants, and at basketball in particular we would try to get a cross section of people and get different—Trying to find an African American at a bas[ketball game]—walking around, looking for—so they could participate in a time-out activity. Generally when I found somebody they were somehow connected to the team. They were somebody's uncle or they were a guest of the player and so they were ineligible.

Here African Americans appear not as true fans but as family members of players. There is no consideration that Black people might be absent from games for reasons other than not being fans. For example, the cost may have been too high, an issue that James had previously acknowledged; work schedules may not have permitted attendance; or Black fans may have felt unwelcome in the predominantly white arena space. Although James was the only industry worker I interviewed to discuss race and fans (and indeed he named race as a structure, saying, "It's a *total* race thing. Walk around a football game. I mean it's *clear*"), he does not automatically have a particularly progressive outlook, as already suggested by his checkbox model of diversity. Certainly he characterizes students from East Asia who returned home after completing their degrees solely as a "donor base" rather than as people who might really love BMU athletics, thus constructing them out of being fans in much the same way as he had with African Americans. The whiteness of fans is thus taken as a given rather than as a result of decisions that people make.

Speculative media fans are structured as white through the ways objects of fandom recruit white audiences. Taste is racialized, and consequently only certain objects fit into the popular understanding of fandom or coalesce groups with practices like fan conventions (Jenkins 2014; Wanzo 2015). Because speculative TV and film are so overwhelmingly cast with white actors, interest is facilitated for white people while being made more difficult for fans of color. While fans of color can and do engage in the work of racebending to turn white characters into characters of color, make color-blind writing into racial specificity for a character of color, or move peripheral characters of color to the center (Warner 2015a), this additional labor raises barriers to entry, thus diminishing participation. Between the numerical dominance of white people as fans, a refusal to consider race except as racism, and the marginalization of fans of color, the whiteness of the fan is overdetermined; it is simultaneously caused by multiple factors that all lead to the same outcome.

GENDERING FANS: PRACTICES, TEXTS, AND OMISSIONS

Early in the field that became known as fan studies, Jenkins (1992) identified a difference between media fans and sports fans. The former comprised mostly women and the latter mostly men. This gender breakdown is still a relatively accurate description of views taken by academic work. While analysis of race and fans is sparse, there is much scholarly writing examining gender. However, like race, the focus falls heavily on the marginalized category, as if only women have gender.

On the one hand, fan studies has been greatly (or even primarily) interested in women's fan activities (Christian 2011; Walliss 2010). On the other hand, this body of work demonstrates that media fans as a population are heavily skewed toward women (Bacon-Smith 1991; Penley 1997; Busse 2009a). In particular, commonly studied practices are understood to be dominated by women, including vidding (editing pieces from televisual texts to music to tell a new story; Coppa 2008, 2009; Scott 2011) and fan fiction (using established characters and settings to tell a new story in text format; Derecho 2006; Hellekson 2009). Some even contend that these are distinctively feminine ways of seeing (Coppa 2008, 2009; Jenkins 2006c). Scholars argue that the internet facilitates women being fans in quantity, protecting them from the appearance-based judgments they experience in embodied contexts (Hanmer 2003) or from stigma as fans (Jones 2000), although of course the problems with color blindness on the internet do not suggest gender blindness to be a good solution. Moreover, early scholarship demonstrates that women already had a strong presence in fandom before the internet was in wide use (Bacon-Smith 1991; Jenkins 1992), although, as Jenkins (2006c) notes, the Web's early dominance by men had to be overcome first.

In contrast, researchers typically understand sports fans as comprising predominantly men, while women have to struggle for recognition. Garry Crawford (2004) discusses the double bind women sports fans face. Because they are considered inauthentic by men, even the most dedicated women are not invited or allowed to engage in hard-core expressions of being a fan, which then proves that they are inauthentic because they do not do those things. Victoria K. Gosling (2007) and Katharine W. Jones (2008) describe a similar definitional exclusion, where being a traditional or authentic sports fan is defined through masculinist in-stadium heckling, where women really do not belong and where their attendance risks destroying supposedly genuine fan practices. The gendering of sports fans as masculine often rests on a sense that women do not actually like sports. Toko Tanaka (2004), Crawford (2004), and Gosling (2007) all indicate that men fans (and media outlets, and, in Gosling's case, academics) believe women attend sporting events because they want to gawk at men's bodies rather because they enjoy sports.[4] In particular, many assume women do not know enough about sports to be true fans (Pope and Williams 2010; Waysdorf 2015b; Tanaka 2004). This androcentrism occurs even though women are in fact sports fans, at times in equal (or nearly equal) numbers to men (Crawford 2004; Oates 2012), with great intensity (Pope 2013; Mintert and Pfister 2015; Waysdorf 2015b), or with long histories of participation (Pope and Williams 2010; Mintert and Pfister 2015). As with speculative media fans, women sports fans can be protected from gender-based judgment by not being visible as women on the internet (Guschwan 2011; Tanaka 2004). In the end, academic work on fans can to some extent be summarized as, "Fans: they're not just men!"

Fandom's Popular Construction as Men's Domain

The womancentric tendency of speculative media scholarship and the nuanced gender discussion of the sports work—although based in analysis of actual fan populations—differ from the industrial understanding of "fan." The default fan named and shown for both objects of fandom is a man, in particular a white one. Mike and Merrin of Campfire both mention that clients assume men or boys to be the target audience. Although they themselves have a more inclusive view, this assumption is the background for their work. Similar beliefs drive a conversation in the DVD commentary for 2004 *The Simpsons* episode "My Big Fat Geek Wedding," which is set primarily at a speculative media convention. The creative staff, including *Simpsons* creator Matt Groening, argue about the gender breakdown at San Diego Comic-Con, on which the episode was based:

> GROENING: But you know, it's easy to poke fun at these guys—and girls, but—
>
> MAN'S VOICE:[5] No, no girls, guys.
>
> GROENING: No, but that's it, here's what I've seen change over the years is that it used to be a nerdboy fest and now it's all—girls show up!

The disbelief from the other staff member that women go to Comic-Con shows men as default fans, even though all the commentators say they go to Comic-Con regularly, and Groening's interlocutor could reasonably be expected to share his experience of gender inclusion. This likely relates to the gendering of comics as masculine: Disney's purchase of Marvel Comics was specifically a strategy to balance the princess part of its portfolio with something understood as for boys (Nakashima 2009).

Likewise, journalists much more frequently interview or discuss men and boys as fans. This is certainly true of Comic-Con coverage, and the AP's pieces on "football widows" (Davis 1999) and a "men-only Superbowl party" (Associated Press State and Local Wire 2009) similarly identify men as default or assumed sports fans. These discussions assume that being a fan is something "no woman could possibly enjoy," as Suzanne Scott (2011, 118) notes in her discussion of a 2008 *Entertainment Weekly* piece about Comic-Con. In fact, men are the fans of interest even when the object of fandom is demonstrably not manly. As Anne Gilbert (2015, ¶ 2.1) points out, popular discussion of fans of *My Little Pony: Friendship Is Magic* "focuses almost exclusively on adult male participants," known as Bronies, despite the existence of adult women fans and the show's intended audience of young girls. Gilbert contends the interest in Bronies is precisely "because they are portrayed as a fandom comprising adult men—valuable audiences who already hold a great deal of cultural and industrial capital" (¶ 4.4).

Emphasis on men also shows in the term "fanboy." News coverage consistently calls Comic-Con attendees "fanboys."[6] Scott (2011, 4) identifies the fanboy as a specific, taste-based market, noting that "because journalists and the media industry are actively constructing and courting 'fanboys' as a market segment, with 'fangirls' remaining an invisible (or worse, actively excluded) part of that 'fanboy' demographic, these terms matter. How fans participate in convergence culture, and whose participation is valued, is increasingly determined by these labels." The fanboy is often seen as the core constituency for media and technology companies, from Star Wars to Apple. Ultimately, this constructs Comic-Con's "male attendees as Hollywood's most prized focus group" (60).

While infantilized as boys rather than men, and sometimes framed as overly invested in their object of fandom and overly excitable, the fanboy is not pathological by default in contemporary culture but rather is framed as a mostly reasonable connoisseur. Some exceptions to this have arisen, especially around backlash to diversity from fanboys, like Gamergate, the Puppies, and other incidents such as the anger over the all-woman reboot of *Ghostbusters,* but tellingly, when this occurs, the diagnosis is that all fans are a problem—or "fandom is broken," in one typical screed's phrasing (Faraci 2016). Although these incidents and their associated fans are constructed as caring too much about the wrong things, fanboys are nowhere near as consistently pathologized as the fangirl is constructed as a screaming, crying Twi-hard (Twilight fan) or Directioner (One Direction fan).

Much as men are framed as the default fan by being shown and named, indirect constructions assume them. Following White's (2006) attention to the way the "male" option on website forms is either the default or is seen first by being at the top or to the left, the membership forms I archived during my research construct their default users as "male" by following these rules.[7] Similarly, Major League Soccer (MLS) constructs its audience particularly as men by displaying fan contests and prizes for Father's Day and not Mother's Day. Through these defaults, both speculative media and sports fans are men like they are white—overwhelmingly, although not exclusively.

In addition to assuming fans are men, industry norms also recruit men. Purely demographically, Scott (2011, 34) argues that the contemporary embrace of the fanboy "reinforces Hollywood's ongoing allegiance to 16–34 year-old young men as their target audience." This structural valuation of media consumers surely affects sports too, given that this is the desired target of their common advertisers. Men are also engaged as fans through normalizing practices associated with or disproportionately done by them. Fan men's activities are much more often "industrially valued (that is to say, marketable or co-optable)," making them more welcomed by industry (Scott 2011, 12). Thus, as Kristina Busse (2013, 77) reminds us, "It is often the less explicitly fannish (or, one might argue, the less explicitly *female* fannish) elements that have been accepted." Gender corresponds to participation of the right kind because men more often want to join the industry and are more often interested in official materials, consuming them rather than making their own and sticking closely to official materials when they do produce their own. Industry finds these fan practices palatable and lucrative.

This approach valuing playing by the rules contributes to what Abigail De Kosnik (2009, 120–21) identifies as "interestingly gendered" distinctions in who can professionalize: "A number of *Star Wars* fan filmmakers (all men) have received development deals or employment with major studios on the basis of their fan work. Another remix genre, game modding, has also produced professional game designers from its ranks." As Busse (2013) notes, affirmational fans, who "celebrate the story the way it is" (Murray 2004) rather than tinkering with texts as transformational fans do, are welcomed by industry (see obsession_inc 2009). Busse (2013) further suggests that identification with particular fans may shape why industry is more open to this kind of fan incorporation: the trajectory may echo and celebrate the producer's own progress from consumer to industry insider.

Beyond recruiting certain practices and textual orientations directly, the normalization of fans relies on increasing production of fan-friendly media objects, but texts themselves enlist certain types of fans. Much like Jane Gaines's (1986) argument that the ability to be the default viewer has not been available to men of color or women of any race, texts encourage (but do not determine) some readers more than others, just as under Stuart Hall's ([1980] 2001) encoding/decoding model they encourage (but do not determine) some readings more than others. Although there is, of course, a long and rich history of women fans reworking masculinist texts with few women characters to make them better suit their needs (Bacon-Smith 1991; Penley 1997; Busse 2016), this, like the work done by fans of color, emphasizes that media was not for them in the first place, thus adding a barrier to entry.

In particular, as Jonathan Gray (2010, 18) argues, paratexts—additional material surrounding and supplementing, but not part of, a text, like book covers or promotional material—"can determine genre, gender, theme, style, and relevant intertexts, thereby in part creating the show as a meaningful entity for 'viewers' even before they become viewers, or even if they never become viewers." One example of how paratexts shape texts is how the suite of licensed toys gender Star Wars, such that girls who choose not to engage often do not do so because they understand the films through the paratext of the toys (especially their packaging) being for boys (Gray 2010). Derek Johnson's (2014, 896) analysis of the more recent Star Wars HerUniverse clothing line demonstrates that while it might claim "StarWars is for everyone—including little girls!" HerUniverse actually assumed it was necessary to create separate merchandise because regular Star Wars gear is actually not for girls. This, Johnson (2014, 899) argues, "may give girls a room of their own, yet such efforts simultaneously ask girls to stay in that room." I would add that it is also a marginal room.

In addition to paratexts, the genre of the text recruits certain participants and not others. Louisa Ellen Stein (2008, ¶ 5.2) identifies the tension pulling one show between sci-fi—masculinely gendered "despite the instrumental involvement of women in science fiction media fandom from its inception"—and the feminization of both romance and teen television, making it difficult to attract a large enough audience to survive. Similarly, as Busse (2013, 76–77) notes, certain practices are more acceptable with particular genres, "where melodramatic plotlines and male sexualization may be permissible in soaps but not in comics"; as Abby Waysdorf (2015a, 2015b) indicates, such sexualization is strictly forbidden in sports.[8] Genre is therefore a key way of gendering texts—and thereby their ideal audiences.

While these ways of inviting some people to be fans and not others are long-standing features of media, the recent expansion (even explosion) of narrative complexity (where there are many interlinked plots) and serialized narratives (where each episode requires having seen the previous ones) has generated new modes of selective incitement. The first decade of the twenty-first century saw an upsurge in speculative media texts that particularly recruit intensive engagement through complex mythology, layered narrative, and thorough serialization (Ross 2009; Mittell 2013). This is often particularly understood as mainstreaming fans. That is, fans are already intensively engaged and strive to string together information among episodes, and now such work is being done officially. Sharon Marie Ross (2009, 9) calls such strategies, exemplified by shows like *Battlestar Galactica, Heroes,* and *Lost,* "obscured" invitations to participate. Such an invitation "resides primarily in the *narrative structure and content* of the show itself through a certain 'messiness' that demands viewer unraveling." However, this way of inviting intense engagement is not contained to speculative media. Waysdorf (2015a) points out that the serialized nature of soccer seasons is much like narrative TV, but that more particularly the constellation of information about teams, players, and leagues across different platforms, which recruits fans to chase it down and piece it together to make sense of the sport, is a similar structure to the messiness, complexity, and layering in speculative TV.

In both areas, official materials have proliferated, such as webisodes, podcasts, and blogs, that fill in gaps in the central text with official information. The spread of gap filling in sports, Waysdorf (2015b, ¶ 3.17) argues, has come about because as sports media outlets have proliferated, there is a premium on official, insider content: "Both football clubs and football players themselves have become content producers online, and one of the things they can offer better than the established football media outlets is personality-driven content." In speculative media, this increase corresponds to the rise of what Scott (2011, 161) calls the "fanboy auteur"— figures like Joss Whedon, Ronald D. Moore, and Eric Kripke, who are understood as "simultaneously one of 'us' and one of 'them.'" On the one hand, expansive information mimics long-standing practices of seeking out details of the object of fandom and filling in gaps with speculation or creative production, and so appear fan friendly. On the other hand, having these materials arrive top down rather than bottom up, as I discuss in Chapter 3, produces a situation where the "fanboy auteur's voice is privileged and his interpretations are posed as the 'correct' reading of textual events" (Scott 2011, 168–69). As Jenkins (1992, 2006b) has persuasively argued, men tend to look for and abide by official information. Accordingly, expansion and normalization through these particular types of (para)texts act to gender the normative fan in a way that may suit fanboy auteurs as both fans and media makers. As Scott (2011, 305) notes, "Boundaries between the mainstream and the margins [. . .] are increasingly drawn along gender lines." Close examination shows that the normalization and recruitment of fan practices and approaches are tilted toward men.

Marginalizing Women

In contrast, women as fans and feminized fan practices are downplayed, ignored, or excluded. Fan fiction and vidding are deeply feminized practices, just as the fan filmmaking and modding that are sometimes a stepping-stone to an entertainment industry career are deeply masculinized. The feminine associations of fic and vids comes from both these genres' focuses on feelings and relationships and the sheer number of women producers. Perhaps unsurprisingly, fic and vid creators are not recruited to join the media industry as often. Jenkins (2006c, 44) argues that women are drawn to these particular activities because they are accustomed to having to rework texts produced by and for men. As Busse (2013, 83) puts it, because the majority of TV shows, "especially science fiction and crime drama, are geared at the 18–35 white male heterosexual demographic," that demographic does not need to rework them, but those excluded by race or gender might. Scott (2011, 81) contends, "Though not all fangirls are 'resistant' in their reading practices, they have historically been more invested in subtext rather than text, and more attached to the 'fanon' (texts produced by other fans) than the producer's construction of the canon. Moreover, the forms of fan productivity that have been historically dominated by women, such as fanfiction and vidding, actively avoid monetization and industrial detection." Between disinterest in or refusal of monetization, resistance to authorial control, and often touchy-feely subject matter, these practices and their feminized creators are not well aligned with industry's desires, and women are thus not recruited. In fact, Scott (2013) argues that the comics industry in particular has made it clear that women are at best marginal fans and potentially even actively unwanted; film and TV's focus on men as heroes and women as secondary is similar. Jenkins (2006a, 154) argues that in moments of fan–industry contact, Hollywood professionals "clearly identified more closely with the young digital filmmakers who were making 'calling card' movies to try to break into the film industry than they did with female fan writers sharing their erotic fantasies." It is important to examine what this differential identification means.

Discomfort with particular fans and their practices is both cause and effect. Busse (2013) contends that gender inequality produces low opinions of women as fans and defines marginalized practices as peculiar to women. One clear example of constructing women as inherently illegitimate is the differential acceptability of sexualizing celebrities, which is normative for heterosexual men but distressing for heterosexual women and for queers of all genders. For sports in particular, sexualizing men athletes is scandalous (Rahman 2011; Waysdorf 2015a) despite the noto-riously sexualized way women athletes tend to be photographed. Things fangirls do are not real fan things, even if fanboys also do them. Indeed, women fans themselves sometimes believe stereotypes about women fans as overly emotional and sexual, both in sports (Mintert and Pfister 2015; Pope 2014) and media (Harman and Jones 2013; Zubernis and Larsen 2012; Yodovich 2016). As this suggests, in contrast to "fanboy," "fangirl" is a marginalized category. With the exception of the embrace of the term by actor Orlando Jones (2016), a practice that is itself contested for its potential appropriation of women's culture by a man who does not experience the gendered stigma (and further complicated by this being a criticism of a Black man from mostly white women), pathologization of the fangirl is nearly total.

As this begins to suggest, women are frequently constructed as exces-sively emotional. In particular, they are shown as screaming, weeping girls—a consistent image from Beatlemania to the Twi-hard and beyond. Seeing Twilight fans as particularly inclined to screaming was established from the franchise's first appearance at Comic-Con in 2008. That year's AP story about the San Diego Comic-Con (SDCC) was entitled "*Twilight* Fans Camp Out for a Peek (and a Scream)" (Cohen 2008b), with women implicitly, but not explicitly, gendered by the screaming. By 2009, it was "*Twilight* Sequel Draws Fangirls by the Thousands" (Cohen 2009), not coincidentally specifying gender in the year there was anti-Twilight backlash. Scott (2011, 87) spends an entire chapter detailing the 2009 Twihate backlash at Comic-Con, noting, "Fanboys at SDCC were simply fans, [but] fangirls at SDCC were always already aligned with *Twilight*, even if they had no interest in the franchise or had been attending SDCC long before Teams Edward and Jacob arrived." Scott also argues, "While the Twihate protesters at SDCC were just a fraction of Twi-hards in number, the press coverage of the outrage, and how those conversations dovetailed with the prevailing construction of fangirls as 'unwelcome,'" made the protests significant in the history of Comic-Con (104–5). Twilight fans were taken as proof Comic-Con had become excessively inclusive or main-streamed (Scott 2011). Although complaints about excessive inclusivity at Comic-Con date back to at least 2000 with concern over movies and TV potentially crowding out comic books (Lin 2000), the high visibility and audibility of Twilight fangirls gave it new intensity and prompted a rallying cry to hold the line on Comic-Con (and being a fan) as a men's space, much as happened later with Gamergate and the Puppies.

Much like fans of color are used to reinforce whiteness, discussing women fans tends to reinforce men as default. Noting that women often do not attend even women's sporting events, James of BMU says he sees change:

> I think that—with Title IX, one of the big impacts of Title IX has been the fact that *girls* are exposed to things at a younger age. As a little *girl,* my wife may not have been pushed to play basketball or engage in these things, but now that they *have* been they become fans at a young age because they have access to it. And so because they have access, because they have knowledge of it, they're participating as *girls,* as they mature into *women* I think they have more—they're more active participants which I think is going to lead to more fan support.

James clearly does not want to exclude women; he even sounds excited that more women might get involved and interested. However, as with white dominance, his comment nevertheless takes women's marginalization as given. The assumption is that this is simply how things are rather than the outcome of differential inclusion.

A similar perspective drives appeals to sports as a family event, an approach common in news coverage. As Gosling (2007, 250) describes, pitching sports as for families—meaning including women and children versus the default of adult men—is precisely about increasing women's participation and diminishing the rough stadium atmosphere, which is associated with hegemonic masculinity and which is imagined to scare women off. While Thomas P. Oates (2012, 605) argues that "women spectators helped to secure football's status as legitimate entertainment during a period when the game's violence threatened its public image," this pushback, like James's, relies on sports being primarily for men. It assumes that women must be actively courted rather than attending on their own, and that women require sports to be changed rather than liking the regular version, inevitably marking them as not real fans. We might also think here of the masculinist climate of the sports stadium (Crawford 2004; Tanaka 2004), which is at times not just pro-men but actively hostile toward women (Gosling 2007; Jones 2008), as a paratext to sports that works toward excluding women. Women experiencing the different paratext of TV coverage might approach sports differently, although the practice of televising close-ups on scantily clad women in the stadium may diminish or undo that improvement.

This belief that objects of fandom must be adapted to interest women is clearest with merchandising. This is what Oates (2012, 606) calls "shrink it and pink it" for "women's jerseys." While women may on average be smaller than men, that does not imply that they want other changes, like abandoning the team colors or making jerseys form fitting. In fact, there is sometimes even backlash from women against women who dress in these sorts of normatively attractive ways at games (Jones 2008; Mintert and Pfister 2015). For their part, women fans of speculative media are often "cast as objects of nerd desire" (Busse 2016, 159). Clothing is shrink-and-pink-ed here as well. Johnson (2014, 903) describes the Star Wars HerUniverse clothing line as "based in sexual appeal, semi-provocative slogans, and objectification in relation to men," in which, for example, "several shirts featuring Rebel and Imperial logos call direct attention to the bustline." Johnson shows that women's acceptance as fans seems to rely on their heterosexual relation to men, pointing out that six-year-old Katie Goldman—who garnered widespread support after her mom posted on Facebook that she had been bullied for liking "boy" text Star Wars—was assured that being a fan was acceptable in part because someday it would make boys want to date her.

In contrast to fans of color, there are some prominent, fleshed-out women fan characters, although only for speculative media. These women's (universal) whiteness apparently outweighs being women and lets them be main characters, but that does not mean they are treated with much empathy. Busse (2016, 159) notes it is "often difficult for women to see themselves in the media with which they engage, allowing them few potential female objects of identification and even fewer that might be like them: smart and geeky." Even when a woman fan is the main character, as Liz Lemon of NBC comedy *30 Rock* or Cyd Sherman of web series *The Guild*, and even when the women who play these characters are the executive producers, as Tina Fey and Felicia Day respectively are, women are negatively portrayed as fans.[9] Scott (2011, 293) describes that "one recurring joke on 30 Rock is that Liz routinely dresses up in her Princess Leia costume and plays the part of the deluded fangirl in order to get out of jury duty." The jury duty scheme—the flip side of Barbara Adams wearing her Starfleet uniform to jury duty in the documentary Trekkies as a sign of Trek's values leading her to take civic duty seriously—relies on Lemon actually being a fan. Lemon's fandom causes her friend to reprimand her: "No, Liz. Do not talk about stuff like that on your date. Guys like that do not like Star Trek." (Liz's reply: "Wars! I'm sorry, you're right.") Similarly, across the first three seasons of The Guild, Cyd never has romantic success, never gets a job, and achieves only a modicum of competency and self-esteem.

The episodes of the CW show Supernatural featuring fan characters portray women fans even more negatively. As Scott (2011) argues, while there had been earlier, oblique engagement with fan practices in Supernatural, including fans of a diegetic novel series that paralleled the show, the show then moved to an explicit narrative representation of their own fans—one, I add, that was clear to nonfans as well. Importantly, the seeming embrace of fans, including fangirl characters who were even named after show personnel (Schmidt 2010, ¶ 2.2), is undercut by their excessive and creepy sexualization of the main characters and the clear narrative purpose of marginalizing fangirls and their textual sensibilities. As Busse (2013, 82) argues, "This mean-spirited and hateful representation of female fans seems strange, and yet it suggests the intended viewer's subject position as clearly not that of a fangirl." The intended viewer is so much not a fangirl that CW network president Mark Pedowitz actively seeks to disavow the young women that are his network's bread and butter, saying he wants to "put the final nail in the coffin (of the perception) that we're a young girls' network" (Berkshire 2015). That is a lot of antipathy for the hand that feeds them.

In these ways, men are the normative fans represented and the fans whose practices are welcome. Women are both indirectly marginalized and sometimes directly classified as improper fans. This constructs being a fan as rightfully proper to masculinity. Thus, gender is one axis along which "popular appreciation for fandom is constrained in ways that limit fans' value as cultural producers to a narrow range of normative identities" (Gilbert 2015, ¶ 1.2). In short, it is one way that fans are domesticated.

In thinking about fans and age, there initially appears to be a divergence from how race and gender function. Adulthood is the unmarked category of age, as whiteness and masculinity are unmarked, but rather than normativity for fans coming by association with the dominant category, being a fan is constructed as good and normative because it is for everyone, from newborn to octogenarian. Rather than the dominant category being taken as universal fans, "for everybody" really means that. The different functioning of age as a system of inequality also shows because it is something industry workers think about and are willing to name. Both Steve and Merrin of Campfire, for example, readily discuss age as a demographic factor usually considered to segment target markets—a response quite different from their silence around race. BMU workers were even more forthcoming, explaining specifically what ages their efforts targeted. The other notable difference between age as a system and race and gender is that, as opposed to the dominant category marginalizing others, marginal people are held up to be protected, particularly for children.

One manifestation of age-based inclusiveness is BMU workers' sense that older folks have specific needs that they were willing to meet to keep them involved. When asked about shifting advertising to social media, Lisa responds, "In this community we have a lot of older fans that are die-hards that come to *everything*, and they're the ones that read the *paper* in the morning and they're the ones that—So you *still* have to do, use that traditional media. I think that's still a *huge* outlet for us that's not going away anytime soon." Rather than centering media-savvy (young) adults, they maintain long-standing practices because not excluding older fans is important. Consideration of the needs of older fans also arises with discussion of conflict between older people who just want to watch a basketball game and rowdy BMU students. Although the donor section in the basketball arena, populated by wealthy older people, is frustrating to staff because these fans do not do the work of providing stadium atmosphere (the deadness of that section was mentioned by all three BMU workers), they still think that these fans should be accommodated because of their age (and their money) rather than brought into compliance with the norm.

Attention to youth as fans with specific needs is more intensive. Asked whom she sought in her marketing work, Lisa says, "I guess my target audience would be—is children and then families" for the primarily free-to-attend sports she manages. Kids as a major constituency is a pervasive idea. When I ask Lisa how BMU deals with geographically dispersed fans who cannot attend games in person, her first answer is: "We have a kid's club that we've offered—the first 5,000 people from [our state] are free in that. So that spans, obviously, the entire state." Lisa later adds, "We also have, like, a newborn package where people can get a signed letter of intent from one of their coaches. They get, like, a beanie hat, all these things for a newborn, so that's kind of encompassing people all around too."

Constructing being a fan as originating in childhood implies that it is wholesome and good; such an understanding relies on childhood being understood as innocence. As Jason Sperb (2010) argues about *Song of the South,* fans' attachment to the film has much to do with tracing being a fan to childhood, and nostalgia for the film requires framing it, and therefore the fan's childhood, as innocent (and not racist). This tight cultural link between children and innocence encourages adults to protect them. The figure of the child, Lee Edelman (2004) argues, is the override button in social valuation. Children must be protected at any cost, including curtailing adult freedom. Kathryn Bond Stockton (2009) adds that it is specifically the white, middle-class child who is protected and that children are especially to be protected from "premature" exposure to sexuality. This idea that children should be protected—even if it means denying adults what they want—is evident in a comment about the New York Comic-Con: "We don't want children to be exposed to an adults-only environment, with sex and violence" (Associated Press 2009). This indicates a belief that these things should be minimized even if adults desire them. This idea that children deserve protection even at the expense of adults also drives the other major sports-related moral panic (after hooliganism): the horror of the adult who elbows aside a child at a baseball game to catch a fly ball.

Website TOS insist explicitly that being a fan should normatively be safe for children. The Children's Online Privacy Protection Act of 1998

(COPPA, 15 USC § 6501–6) requires attention to children as users because no website may collect identifiable data about children under thirteen without parental consent.[10] However, sites make different choices about this legal obligation to protect children's privacy. ESPN, the Mariners, and MLS, for example, have fairly boilerplate privacy policies directed at adults. ESPN's reads: "We recognize the need to provide further privacy protections with respect to personal information we may collect from children on our sites and applications. Some of the features on our sites and applications are age-gated so that they are not available for use by children, and we do not knowingly collect personal information from children in connection with those features." SyFy and Star Trek, on the other hand, speak directly to implicitly untruthful youthful users. SyFy says, "By using the Site or Other Services you agree to respond truthfully and accurately about your age." Star Trek says, "You may not access any age-restricted Services unless you are above the required age."

However, engagement around youth can be much more intensive. Star Wars directly addresses KIDS in all caps repeatedly throughout the TOS, plus multiple warnings to PARENTS. In contrast to mentioning youth once or twice at other sites, Star Wars has pages upon pages and mentions upon mentions; dramatically more attention is paid to children as potential users. Even if this is because Lucasfilm is unusually paranoid about lawsuits, it intensively builds the notion of child as user into the site. Compliance with the legal requirements of COPPA is part of a general assumption that children should specifically be provided for. Star Wars, with its excessive, even obsessive, attention to children in its TOS, also has a whole drop-down menu for "Kids" at the top of its front page, plus a side-scrolling section with the same name near the bottom. Locating kids in prime screen real estate frames them as a major constituency. Although embedded under the "Fans" tab rather than given its own, the Seattle Mariners have a "Mariners Kids" page that, while lower profile, functions similarly to construct youth as not only part of their fan base but also worthy of special attention. These various ways children are specifically planned for demonstrate how they are valued as fans.

As Lisa's quick slide from children to families suggests, age as a system is deeply intertwined with family norms. Being a fan is often understood as part of a family tradition or transmission. Lyla in *Friday Night Lights*

(TV) became a(n American) football fan because "my parents dressed me up in cheerleader outfits and took me to Dillon Panthers games since I was five." The idea that parents, especially dads, are how people become fans is a common trope that presents being a fan as wholesome and traditional, something to be shared with the whole family—this is the other valence of selling events as family friendly. As feminist scholars (Nagel 2003; Rubin 1975) and queer scholars (Halberstam 2005; Stockton 2009; D'Emilio 1993) have noted, family does coercive social work. And as scholars of color have noted, the rejection of family is a position enabled by whiteness, because families of color serve as a respite from racism (Ferguson 2003). It therefore becomes apparent that there actually is an underlying binary hierarchy with age as there is with race and gender. Family is the norm to not-family's deviance. Children and elders are valued in the context of the norm of family, and this entails a normative trajectory of heterosexual reproduction that I will return to in the next chapter. It also relates to a narrative of child fans as pure, as worthy, and as needing protection, which I will discuss in the Conclusion, where I consider child fan characters as representing the truest and most important constituency.

MOVING THE BAR, PRODUCING EXCLUSIONS

In these various ways, fans as people are constructed as normative by being connected to highly valued categories: whiteness, masculinity, and family. Under the domestication metaphor, this selects stock for the most valuable traits. A liberal social movement–style framework would contend that although excluding white women and people of color to enable this normativity is of course troubling, we should celebrate the fact that the industry now includes fans in its norms. This view suggests that the first battle for fan recognition has been won and all that remains is a social justice issue to include less socially powerful categories. However, this is a deeply problematic tendency that I call "moving the bar" politics, where a new group is included—as with nonideal bodies to beauty (Weber 2009) or gay people to marriage (McRuer 2006)—and the norm gets to congratulate itself on its tolerance. However, alongside loudly proclaimed tolerance, some groups are still excluded, thus forcefully constructing those who remain outside as too different to include. Participating in moving the bar means saying, "The system is OK; we just want in on it." However, minor modifications or inclusions cannot salvage media's fundamentally and structurally unequal relationship to its audiences. Moreover, as I will discuss in Chapter 2, normalization is not the whole story, even for heterosexual white men.

CHAPTER TWO

THE FANDOM MENACE STRAIGHTENS UP AND FLIES WHITE

Failed Normativity to Redemption

It is almost a truism in academic research that actual fan populations are not exclusively composed of men (Bacon-Smith 1991; Tanaka 2004; Forsyth and Thompson 2007). Despite this, as Chapter 1 makes clear, the default speculative media and sports fan is a man. This was something Mike and Merrin of Campfire both noted they had to struggle against, and similar assumptions run through news coverage of and web design for fans. Most importantly for this chapter, as Scott (2011, 38) notes, the fanboy has "become the media industry's new favorite character archetype," and representations of fan men have proliferated.

In contrast to trying to correct the understanding of fans to match who fans really are, my focus on the fan as a concept means ideas that fans are men interest me not as mistaken impressions about a measurable reality but rather as demonstrations of a social belief. Using this framework, that fans are imagined to be men is not the whole story. What does it mean that fans are overwhelmingly, although certainly not exclusively, imagined to be men? To answer this, we should ask, what kind of men are fans imagined to be? If most of this book demonstrates how particular, selective visions of fans are portrayed positively or encouraged, acting as a carrot to incite those ways of being a fan, then when fans are characters whose stories are told—primarily in fictional representations but also in some documentaries—they are often losers, associated with negatively valued behaviors and traits. When "fan" is treated as their major identification, they are a particular, devalued kind of men, regardless of whether their fan object is speculative media or sports. However, this is not necessarily a stick to say "don't be like this," because these representations often include redemption narratives that demonstrate how to better comply with masculinity—and, crucially, whiteness. In this way, as I note in the previous chapter, I seek to make the often unacknowledged whiteness of fans visible, arguing that fans are popularly constructed as having a sub-standard, childish masculinity whose failings are simultaneously failings of whiteness. The features of the social category "white" shape both the specific forms fan nonnormativity takes and why and how redemption is possible for fans in popular representations. Here, through an analysis focusing primarily on the representational archive, I will first trace the basic contours of fan failed masculinity, then explain how this articulates with the interlocking systems of race, age, and sexuality. Ultimately, these representations show fans failing to live up to expectations of white men but maintain a belief in white men's essential capacity for dominance.

FAN UP! OR, FANDOM AND INSUFFICIENT MASCULINITY

Fans, when they are characters with substantive roles in fictional and nonfictional representations, overwhelmingly do not succeed at being gender-normative men. This failed masculinity is particularly interesting because sports fandom, at least, is commonly understood as integral to American masculinity. However, although they may be attached to a normatively masculine object, represented sports fans do not act manly about it. Importantly, although sports fans are associated with failed masculinity in some ways—usually through nonmuscular bodies and insufficient athleticism or failures of maturity and heterosexuality, they do not tend to demonstrate all the ways that men might be less than manly, unlike speculative media fans. While one could argue that being a sports fan affords better access to normative masculinity, I would hesitate to say so definitively simply because the archive contains many more main characters—or fleshed-out minor characters—who are speculative media fans than sports fans. This screen time provides more opportunities for a full set of masculine failures to be visible. While sports fans are ubiquitous, they are also sometimes assumed to be background in a stadium rather than full characters, as I suggest in Chapter 5; most sports TV and film foregrounds players. Given that the few complex sports fan characters show a pattern of failed masculinity, I do not think the absence of some characteristics from other sports fan depictions is especially meaningful.

First, fans fail at manly things, or even at knowing what manliness is. In one scene in the teen drama *The O.C.*, for example, fannish character Seth suggests, "Let's do what guys do," and then after a beat has to ask his more conventionally masculine adopted brother, "Ryan, what do guys do?" Fan characters are also routinely called women or compared to them. The characters of Star Wars comedy *Fanboys* are insulted as "ladies," "Spice Girls," or the perennial favorite, "pussies." Although accusations of nonmasculinity are a staple of men's insult arsenal, being open to the accusation in the first place marks the manliness of the target as vulnerable, which is reinforced by having a woman sometimes be the one to call fans something like "a little bitch" in *The O.C.* or "ladies" in *Fanboys*. Fan characters are often directly described as screaming (in fear) or crying (in sadness) in ways that sound like women or girls. The comparison is even at times unfavorable, with women outdoing fan men at masculinely gendered activities. Ditzy next-door neighbor Penny in *The Big Bang Theory* chides the fannish men, "Look, guys, for the future, I don't mind killing the big spiders, but you have to at least try with the little ones."

As this begins to suggest, fan men also frequently fail at normative masculinity through being cowardly. Jim Kontner, director of teen vampire drama *Buffy the Vampire Slayer* episode "Grave," says so directly in the episode's commentary when describing fannish characters Andrew and Jonathan: "And then we see their true colors. Cowards that they are." Writer David Fury responds, "Now Jonathan was showing a good side, what seemed to be a heroic side. But ultimately he is just a little weasel. Apologies to those people that are—those Jonathan shippers out there."[1] Perhaps the most absurd cowardly moment comes in *The Big Bang Theory*, when Sheldon flees down a hallway, squeaking, "Don't hurt us!" when the risk is not to himself but to his fighting robot. Fans' cowardice is perhaps reasonable, however, because they are constructed as unable to successfully engage in the masculine norm of violence. In *The Big Bang Theory*, Leonard attempts to convince Sheldon that they can retrieve their friend's TV from her ex-boyfriend because "there's not going to be a scene. There's two of us and one of him." Sheldon replies, "Leonard, the two of us can't even *carry* a TV." Lacking physical strength often makes fans vulnerable to being beaten up, including by (normatively weaker) women or children.

Beyond insufficient capacity for violence, lacking physical fitness is treated as a fundamental fan trait. *Invincible* is the story of Vince Papale, a fan turned professional football player discovered at a publicity-stunt open tryout for the Philadelphia Eagles. The rest of the fans are incompetent to highlight how unlikely it was to find anyone who could actually play football, and they reinforce Vince as exception. A doughy man, speaking to a reporter, declares, "I'm in the best shape of my life!" implying that he feels he is ready to be recruited onto the team. Of course, he is nowhere near ready, and neither is anyone else but Vince, as all the others are slow, easily winded, and unable to catch the ball. In *Fanboys,* a friend of the fans comments, "This is, like, the most exercise you guys have had all year," as they all run across the grounds at Star Wars creator George Lucas's production facility, Skywalker Ranch. Visually overweight fans are impressively consistent in both sports and speculative media in both fiction and documentaries, overrepresented (compared to the usual Hollywood distribution of body types) in all areas as seemingly indispensable to flocks of fans. Certainly much of the humor of the *Simpsons'* Comic Book Guy comes from how he waddles and wobbles, his constant eating, or jokes like him sweating through his jumpsuit with half a jumping jack at fat camp ("The Way We Weren't," 2004), or when wizard caps from his store get stuck on his flabby chest to give him a look reminiscent of Madonna circa 1990 ("Radioactive Man," 1995). When portly comic/actor Patton Oswalt jokes in a question-and-answer session with film viewers that he had to "get fat for the part" of Paul Aufiero in the sports drama *Big Fan,* it is clear that such a physical state is expected or necessary for a fan character. In these ways, then, fan men do not comply with several key expectations of masculinity.

As I show in the previous chapter, one way fans are (selectively) incorporated into normativity in the internet era is through articulating them to socially valued categories like masculinity, whiteness, and family. However, in the cases this chapter explores, while fans are men, white, and attracted to women, they are not positively portrayed or associated with the privilege usually accorded to masculinity, whiteness, and heterosexuality in contemporary American culture. This is a long-standing stereotype rooted in the historical stigma of the category "fan." Fans are envisioned as losers with pathetic real lives sublimated into being a fan, somewhere between laughably inept and dangerously pathological. In particular, fans have often been devalued as insufficiently manly men, infantilized as immaturely fixated on activities suitable only for childhood, and constructed as virgins, sexually deficient, and/or unable to engage in real relationships.[2] The notion that fans are not proper men is not new. It is, however, important to consider how and why it persisted at the same time that media industries began courting (particular) fans.

Significantly, the persistence of this idea of fan men as unable to become properly adult and heterosexual dovetails with another phenomenon developing in the same era, what sociologist Michael Kimmel (2008) has called Guyland. In Kimmel's book of the same name, he argues that "guy" has emerged as an intermediate stage between boy and man, a comma pausing the normative trajectory of career, marriage, and children. Kimmel identifies this stage as predominantly for privileged youth. Guyland's residents are the middle-class, white, and college-educated men who in previous eras would, and who still maybe ideologically should, be dominant and successful by the markers of normative masculinity. Indeed, I would add that it is substantially because these men in particular are not succeeding that these new models of young adulthood are so often framed as a crisis.

Kimmel's (2008) model specifically excludes geeks and nerds who share these race, class, and education characteristics, but not the machismo, and thus might not seem applicable to fans. However, delaying heteronormative adult masculinity also characterizes what David Greven (2013) calls the "beta male" character. Exemplified by the works of writer/director/producer Judd Apatow, beta males are often fans, which has not been recognized. However, a key part of "guy" as a social category of interest is that he has adult income without adult financial obligations, and therefore he is a coveted consumer and target audience (Kimmel 2008). Fannishness can thus be seen as essential to guyishness. This larger social formation is why there has been a shift compared to earlier generations of fan representation. Less hostile representations by the mid-2000s reflect fans' closer correspondence to emergent masculinities—or, perhaps, these masculinities' closer correspondence to historical stereotypes about fans. In particular, the ways fans are represented as nonnormative actually reinforces the idea that heterosexual white men should be dominant. Images of fans thus also illuminate how this contemporary crisis of masculinity is deeply racialized as white and is specific to men for whom marriage and career are normatively accessible.

THEORIZING FAN MASCULINITY BETWEEN INTERSECTIONALITY AND PERFORMATIVITY

As I've already begun to suggest, gender cannot be understood without race and sexuality. Women of color feminism has long demonstrated that systems of inequality are intersecting and impact one another.[3] Cathy Cohen (1997, 141) argues that the norm is "state-sanctioned white middle- and upper-class heterosexuality," so lacking one of those aspects—even if you have some of the others—provides less privilege. As Sara Ahmed (2006, 136) succinctly puts it, "Given that relationships of power 'intersect,' how we inhabit a given category depends on how we inhabit others." This is why we need to look at the whole system of categories that shape privilege in order to understand. Cohen (1997) gives the example of working-class heterosexual African Americans, who may be straight but who do not get automatic privilege from it as a result of their race and class. Examining such cases shows how people or practices that might seem normative relative to one system are not actually privileged when other measures of status are taken into account. In a similar way from the other direction, the notion of homonormativity from queer studies demonstrates how behavior that seems transgressive on one front—like same-sex relationships—is not particularly threatening to normativity when it is white, middle class, and gender normative (Duggan 2004). Importantly, the ebb and flow of privilege is unevenly distributed, with race in the US context tending to be the deciding factor over things like sexuality or gender. However, although whiteness is necessary for sexual or class normativity, those are also necessary for full membership in whiteness.

Although whiteness is generally understood as providing dominance, not all cultural appearances of white people equally demonstrate the expected windfall of privilege. Some argue that these constructions demonstrate, as backlash against the perceived destabilization of white men's privilege, a belief that white men are now victims of discrimination (Frankenberg 1993; Rodino-Colocino 2012; Savran 1998; Wiegman 1999). Others contend that representations of white men's nonprivilege disrupt equating whiteness with superiority and thus represent an opportunity to undo white privilege (Hill 1997; Newitz and Wray 1997a, 1997b). However, both of these views miss the insight of intersectionality. Whiteness alone does not control the meaning of these representations; rather, it depends on which other categories are at work. As a result of intersectional complexity, as Chambers (1997, 191) argues, "In the end, identity becomes a bit like a poker hand, in which the value of the ace (whiteness) can be enhanced, if one holds a couple of face cards or another ace (masculinity, heterosexuality, middle classness) or, alternatively depreciated by association with cards of lower value (ethnicity, lack of education, working classness)."

However, it is not simple possession of these cards that matters. Judith Butler's (1990) theory of gender performativity argues that we become members of gender categories by acting like it. Only through the consistent, correct enactment of certain socially determined kinds of grooming, dress, and behavior do we "know" that a person "is" (in this case) a man. Performing these socially recognized markers of manhood repeatedly, consistently, and correctly produces the social "truth" that someone "is" a man. In this way, category membership—through the anatomy or genetics socially assumed to determine gender, or through holding a social identity of "man"—is not enough. I extend this argument to say that white skin or phenotypic whiteness is necessary but not sufficient to secure whiteness. One must also behave in the way socially expected of whiteness. The idea that there is something socially understood as "acting white" can be seen from the slur "Oreo"—black on the outside but white on the inside—for an African American who supposedly acts white. The existence of behavior that performatively constitutes whiteness means that it is possible for phenotypically white people to fail at whiteness (Ahmed 2006; Dyer 1997).

Examined this way, it becomes clear that fan characters are often not simply constructed as white but are more specifically as what Richard Dyer (1997) calls "skin" white but not what he terms "symbolically" white. That is, although fans represented in mainstream cultural artifacts are most often phenotypically white, and although fans of color are indeed marginalized, images of fans frequently do not fit the positive valuation usually attached to whiteness in dominant American culture. In particular, being a fan and normative whiteness come into conflict—and being a fan becomes constructed as insufficient whiteness—around the issue of self-control. The category "white" has traditionally relied on equating whiteness with self-control (Dyer 1997; Roediger 1991; Savran 1998). As David R. Roediger (1991) has argued, the historical invention of whiteness involved defining negative traits like laziness out of whiteness by projecting them onto Blackness. Whiteness was invented as part of larger historical trends that worked to "eliminate holidays, divorce the worker from contact with nature, bridle working class sexuality, separate work from the rest of life and encourage the postponing of gratification" (Roediger 1991, 96). Contemporary whiteness functions in much the same way. In her analysis of reality show *Here Comes Honey Boo Boo,* Tasha R. Rennels (2015) demonstrates that being excessively embodied (fat, flatulent, etc.), rather than having tight bodily control, is a key marker of improper whiteness.

If we think about the question of bodily self-control, it is a failure of whiteness just as much as masculinity that fans are not strong, are not able to successfully commit violence, are soft and flabby rather than firm and muscled. The interplay between fans, poor bodily maintenance, and whiteness is particularly clear in the persistent stereotype of fans as pasty faced because they are constantly indoors consuming media. Patton Oswalt was not only "willing to bulk up for the role" as the lead in *Big Fan,* but also, as writer/director Robert Siegel joked, was willing to "stay out of the sun. He had a pretty healthy, glowing tan at the time and he promised he would go method and stay in his basement for a few months to kind of get rid of that." Oswalt was already both large and pale, but the joke demonstrates expectations about fans that this look is indispensable to the role, such that he would generate it if necessary. In fact, Siegel says Oswalt was cast because "I just thought he looked like he could be an obsessive, you know, nerdy sports fan." Paleness and tanness are phenomena of whiteness. Although historically being pale was associated with upper-class freedom from outdoor work, by the late twentieth century, being tan was a sign of health and fitness—good bodily maintenance—and became the privileged state. This reversal in valuation, however, still linked the proper condition to whiteness (Dyer 1997). Thus, the paleness of fans is an improper, insufficiently physically active whiteness. In such ways, it is clear that normativity rests on a "notion of whiteness having to do with rightness, with tightness, with self-control, self consciousness, mind over body" (Dyer 1997, 6).

Interrogating concepts of fans in relation to concepts of whiteness shows that whiteness shapes the discourse of the fan. Being a fan is one way of doing whiteness incorrectly. Much like white trash is "a naming practice that helps define stereotypes of what is or is not acceptable or normal for whites in the US" (Newitz and Wray 1997a, 4)—in which the problem is not that they are poor, but how they are poor—so too is the particular nonnormativity of fans the way they fail at white self-control. However, while fans are set up as failed men and whites through failed adulthood and heterosexuality, these representations rely on and reinforce the cultural common sense of privilege as a natural property of white, heterosexual masculinity.

"WHEN ARE YOU GONNA GROW UP?"
FANDOM VERSUS ADULTHOOD

If, as I describe in Chapter 1, framing children as appropriate fans or being a fan as originating in childhood helps fans' status by association with the high cultural valuation of children and family, then the corollary is that adult-aged fans are childish or immature. On the one hand, as Edelman (2004) argues, the figure of the child represents the ultimate social good, which must be protected even at the cost of adult freedoms, and this cannot be challenged within normative frameworks. On the other hand, as Stockton (2009) contends, there is a normative developmental trajectory, and one must hit all the right milestones in a straight line at the right time, neither too soon nor too late. Accordingly, to extrapolate from Stockton, childishness in those with calendrical or physical maturity is a perversion or diversion from that normative trajectory. Fan characters do not follow this straight line. They are often explicitly described as failing to grow up, or they are exhorted to get on with it by people in their lives with variations of "When are you gonna grow up?"

Fans are frequently compared to children. The commentator in the baseball drama *For Love of the Game* describes hostility toward an opposing team as "Yankee Stadium is like a schoolyard!" Hiro of the superhero show *Heroes* is consistently naive, enthusiastic, and committed to an oversimplified hero-villain ethic; the show identifies his attitude as childishness because Hiro shares these characteristics only with the two children in the story. Executive producer and director Greg Beeman explicitly makes this link when speaking of child character Micah, whom he identifies as "the one of all the heroes—him and Hiro—who really wants to be a superhero. He really wants to use his power."[4] That being a fan is equated to childishness is perhaps expected when calling collectibles "toys" is standard in interviews with industry workers, news coverage, and fictional sources, with one convention organizer saying that Comic-Con "is like Toys R Us on steroids" (Associated Press 2009). Thus, the sexually frustrated girlfriend of the title character in beta male comedy *The 40-Year-Old Virgin* complains, "Andy, I am throwing myself at you and all you can think about is a fucking toy!" when Andy is more concerned with an action figure that has just been damaged than her sexual advances.

Accordingly, there is a frequent narrative of fans as stuck in childhood, loving texts for children, or having the same behaviors since they were children. Boston Red Sox fan Ben in the baseball comedy *Fever Pitch* exists in a state of arrested development. A childhood trauma led to being a fan, and he likes that baseball is simple, safe, and predictable, unlike real life. When Ben's girlfriend helps him decide what to wear to meet her parents, she discovers that "this is not a man's closet." Ben's wardrobe consists almost entirely of Red Sox paraphernalia rather than more sober attire. She thus tells him, "You're a man-boy. Half man, half boy," underscoring his lack of adulthood. Being a fan is also frequently linked to immaturity. Certainly Judd Apatow, who nearly always depicts a white fanboy of some sort as his main character, links the two, noting that he has "told a lot stories of underdog, immature guys trying to figure out how to grow up" (Cohen 2007b). In one particularly colorful example of fan immaturity, Gus suggests to Clark in the nerd sports comedy *The Benchwarmers,* "Maybe this is a sign you should get a car." To this, thirty-something Clark replies, "My mother said I should hold off getting my license for one more year—you know, just to make sure my reflexes are fully developed."

In addition to childishness, however, fans in these representations have the hallmarks of Kimmel's (2008) guyishness, enjoying the freedoms of adulthood while putting off responsibilities like career and independent living. Irresponsibility is a common fannish trait. Chuck of spy sitcom *Chuck* forbids his friend Morgan access to the demonstration copy of a new video game because "the last time I lent you a game sampler it ended up all over the internet, so this one's gonna stay in my locker, and you can play it when you get some adult supervision." *Buffy the Vampire Slayer* writer and producer Jane Espenson notes of the appearance of three fannish characters as antagonists in the show's sixth season, "In a season that is about leaving childish things behind and taking on responsibility, the perfect counterpoint are villains who can't."

One key aspect of the delayed adulthood common to Guyland and fans is living with one's parents, particularly in their basement, a persistent idea since at least the 1986 *Saturday Night Live* sketch when actor William Shatner played himself at a Star Trek convention and mocked fans for precisely that (among other things). Mike of Campfire mentions the stereotype of "those boys in the basement" as something that is frustrating about clients unfamiliar with fans. Paul of *Big Fan* has this argument when his brother Jeff acts on his behalf:

JEFF: I'm acting in your best interests. You're not seeing things clearly here.

PAUL: You have no right.

JEFF: I have a right if you're my brother and you're not mentally competent to make decisions for yourself.

PAUL: I'm mentally competent!

JEFF: You're a thirty-six-year-old man who lives home with his mother, who depends on her for food, for laundry, and countless basic fucking life necessities. All right? On paper you're basically a fucking vegetable!

The character of Zaboo in the web series *The Guild* is even less independent. His mother bathes him, breast-fed him until he was eleven, "insisted on driving me to college every day for the past four years," and "used to take me into the ladies room with her. Until I was fifteen years old. Every time I try to grow up, she has a panic attack. Or an ulcer. Or some sort of breast polyp, which she makes me feel." Zaboo may be oppressed by his mother—and indeed she becomes the season's climactic villain—but he nevertheless fails at adulthood and masculinity by not standing up to her.⁵

Fans are also imagined to be insufficiently adult because they do not have successful careers, echoing Kimmel's (2008) discussion of Guyland as a time of dead-end or entry-level jobs without commitment to advancement as guys try out different options. In a basic way, the fan with a dead-end job, often in retail, has a certain cultural obviousness and is quite consistent. Chuck makes the link between career failure and failed adulthood clear when he tells off his friend Morgan: "I used to be cool? When was that, when we were thirteen? Well, I'm sorry to go changing on you, buddy, but if you hadn't noticed we are now chronologically speaking adults, so unless you want to work retail for the rest of your life, and by the way drag me down with you in the process, I would suggest that you grow up." The idea that retail jobs are only for youth is of course racialized and classed, pointing again to the specificity of this formation.

Alternatively, fans are shown as having normative white middle-class careers, but being failures at them. Playwright and Boston Red Sox fan Nicky Rogan in *Game 6* is described by the film's director as "fantasizing somehow that if, you know, the Red Sox *could* win this game—if—then somehow [. . .] this marriage will right itself, and the play will get a great review, and his genius will be recognized." Sports thriller *The Fan* establishes middle-aged white baseball fan Gil Renard as a failure in the first ten minutes, when his boss tells him he is close to being fired for poor performance. Ensuing scenes dramatically demonstrate Gil's lack of employment success as the knife salesman humiliates himself. In an effort to increase his sales and keep his job, he goes to potential customer after potential customer, demonstrating the quality of his company's knives by shaving first his arm hair and then his leg hair, eventually getting to the point where he jokes, "Any more of these demos and I'm going to have to start shaving the hairs on my ass." This frames his body as exploitable and vulnerable, emphasizing the way workers' bodies are part of customer service occupations (Nussbaum 1998). These occupations and their traits are typically associated with femininity. Additionally, the idea of Gil potentially dropping his trousers to make the sale invokes sex work, a feminized occupation that would in this case be homosexual, further contradicting mainstream understandings of normative, white masculinity. Thus, fans fail in part by violating the construction of whiteness as "enterprising" (Dyer 1997, 31), which is particularly interesting given the tight interconnection in popular culture between the geek or nerd and being a successful technological savant.

GOD HATES FANS: HETEROSEXUAL FAILURE AND FANDOM AS A SEXUAL ORIENTATION

(Hetero)sexuality is also key to normative white masculinity. The fundamental interlacing of sexuality, particularly sexual self-control, and race can be seen from how sexuality is racialized: "Sexual stereotypes commonly depict 'us' as sexually vigorous (usually our men) and pure (usually our women) and depict 'them' as sexually depraved (usually their men) and promiscuous (usually their women)" (Nagel 2003, 10). Under this construction, then, white men's sexuality, comprising vigor without depravity, is modulated and controlled. This understanding of sexuality relies on associating whiteness with civilization and rationality as opposed to (uncivilized and irrational) sexuality. The counterexamples reinforce the association. A failure of the normative expectation of not just bodily but more specifically sexual self-control undergirds the alleged failure of whiteness of white trash, a group typically constructed as having a propensity for bestiality, incest, and rape. Thus, while people are seen as deviating from whiteness for different reasons—class in the case of white trash or supposedly excessive attachment to media for fans—the stereotype often takes a sexual form. Accordingly, fans as represented in media are bad at the socially proper sexuality of normative masculinity and whiteness. They are not virile and sexually successful; rather, they are virgins or sexually desperate. Their homosocial ties impede heterosexual ones and sometimes shade into homoeroticism. They prefer the object of fandom over heterosexuality and romance. The idea of fans as virgins, sexually deficient, and/or unable to engage in real relationships has often been decried as inaccurate, but, as with constructing fans as men, what matters here is its function. If whiteness is grounded in vigorous but controlled sexuality, then fans are constructed as failures.

The Fan as Creep and Virgin

The stereotype that fans fail at normative sexuality was well established before Shatner's famous *Saturday Night Live* tirade, which includes demanding of "Trekkies" whether they'd ever "kissed a girl"—implying, of course, that they hadn't, thus foregrounding the belief that fans have no (hetero)romantic success. Related to the notion of fans as immature is the frequent conceptualization of fans as virgins. The lead character in *The 40-Year-Old Virgin* is a fan, although the *Simpsons'* Comic Book Guy outmatches him, describing himself as among "forty-five-year-old virgins who still live with their parents" ("Mayored to the Mob," 1998). Such emphasis on age shows that being virgin well into adulthood is considered late development. Even if not strictly virgins, fans are generally understood as sexually inexperienced or uninformed. When the characters in *Fanboys* are caught by the security guards at Skywalker Ranch, the head guard informs them, "Mr. Lucas is touched and mildly flattered by what you have done here" in seeking to steal the new Star Wars film so that their dying friend can see it. He explains that the breaking-and-entering charges will be dropped if they can prove their status as "fanboys" with "a simple quiz." The scene equates fans with failed heterosexuality when the quiz not only includes Star Wars trivia they are supposed to know, like "What is the name of the gunner in Luke's snow speeder?" (which they can answer without hesitation), but sexual trivia they are supposed to not know, like "Where is a woman's G-spot located?" (which causes head-scratching). Fans consistently lack knowledge and/or experience. It is not just sexuality they do not comprehend, but romantic relationships more broadly. When Leonard of *The Big Bang Theory* attempts to cajole Sheldon into helping their friend with her boyfriend problem, he says, "Come on, you know how it is with breakups," only to have Sheldon reply, "No, I don't. And neither do you."

To underscore their cluelessness and immaturity, fans are frequently shown as less romantically or sexually knowledgeable than younger people. In particular, adult fans know less about these topics than teens or tweens. Ben in *Fever Pitch* asks for relationship advice from a high school student he coaches, thus showing that he is less mature and knowledgeable than a teenager. High school senior Seth in *The O.C.* asks younger boys whose voices haven't even finished changing. Needing help from younger people dovetails with the idea of being a fan as arrested development; fans' attachment to childhood through being a fan makes them sexually incompetent. Certainly youth are normatively supposed to be sheltered from sexuality (Rubin 1993; Stockton 2009; Edelman 2004). The converse is that adults are supposed to know, and to not know is childish.

Part of fans' lack of heteroromantic success comes from being awkward with women. This is displayed by characters like Leonard and Raj in *The Big Bang Theory*, Windows in *Fanboys*, and the cosplayers in *Supernatural*.[6] At times, awkward becomes creepy through being tactlessly sexual or just eager to the point that it resembles stalking—simultaneously examples of failed whiteness as sexual self-control. A comedic version of awkward comes from *The Big Bang Theory*'s Howard Wolowitz, whom creator Chuck Lorre describes in the commentary track on the first season DVD as being like Pepe Le Pew. Likewise, actor Simon Helberg describes Wolowitz in the same special feature as "a genius, but he's an idiot with girls, because he thinks he's as brilliant with them as he is with, you know, science." Howard's creepiness is played for comic effect, as when he plots to find the house where *America's Next Top Model* is filmed:

HOWARD: Isn't it obvious? Every week, they kick out a beautiful girl, making her feel unwanted and without self-esteem, aka the future Mrs. Howard Wolowitz.

LEONARD: Are you insane? You're not going to party with them! You're not even going to get anywhere near that place!

HOWARD: That's what they said to Neil Armstrong about the moon.

SHELDON: No one said anything of the kind to Neil Armstrong; the entire nation dedicated a decade of effort and treasure to put a man on the moon.

HOWARD: Well, my fellow Americans, before this year is out we will put a Wolowitz on one of America's top models.

RAJ: And a large number of people will believe it never happened.

However, creepiness can also be sinister, as in *Buffy the Vampire Slayer*, when the fannish villains the Evil Trio use a cerebral dampener to make a woman do what they want. When the effect wears off, she tells them, "You bunch of little boys, playing at being men. Well, this is not some fantasy. It's not a game, you freaks. It's rape. You're all sick." Here, as with fans being guided by younger people, failure of heterosexuality and immaturity are shown to be tightly linked. The articulation to violent crime considerably amplifies the nonnormativity. Desperation for heterosexual contact conditions these fan men's behavior, clearly distinguishing them from the sexual self-control expected of whiteness.

Sometimes fans do not totally lack heteroromantic or heterosexual relationships, but they are not exactly successful at them either. Paul of *Big Fan* has this discussion with his mother after Paul disparages his brother's wife:

MOM: You should only meet somebody as good as Gina.

PAUL: Oh, boy, that'd be tough to top.

MOM: Yeah, for you.

PAUL: Yeah, give me about an hour.

MOM: You have to actually date someone to top it.

PAUL: I date.

MOM: Oh, sure. You're dating lots of girls.

PAUL: You don't think I date?

MOM: I know exactly who you're dating. Your hand.

Paul here insists that he does date women, despite his mother's doubts—and his sexual practice is reinforced as nonnormative by drawing on the cultural common sense, described by Gayle S. Rubin (1993), of masturbation as inferior to partnered sex. The idea that fans generally do not succeed in heterosexual relationships with women is common, with *Heroes* actor Masi Oka saying of his character, "This is actually Hiro's first time that he was able to get the girl and kiss—though it ends tragically." The tragic end is a common theme, with fans often being left by their wives. In all of these ways, then, fan men attempt heterosexuality, but fail.

Between Homosocial and Homoerotic

In keeping with being a fan as men's activity, as I suggest in Chapter 1 with the inconceivability of women sports fans and the idea that girls never attend conventions or visit comic book stores, fan friendship networks are represented as thoroughly homosocial. In keeping with fans' not quite normative gender and sexuality, fans' represented relationships with other men constantly threaten to become homosexual. Such slippage between gender and sexuality is routine. As Butler (1993, 238) notes, "Homophobia often operates through the attribution of a damaged, failed, or otherwise abject gender to homosexuals." Correspondingly, failed gender, such as that of fan men, is seen as a sign of homosexuality. While historically the distinction between homosocial and homosexual was tightly policed for men (Rich 1980), recent years have seen an increased willingness to raise the specter of homosexuality in homosocial circumstances among men, often specifically to refute and contain it (Jones and Wilson-Brown 2014; Pascoe 2007). The bromance has become a key genre of comedy, and it commonly incorporates the type of white complicit masculinity—aspiring to and supporting hegemonic masculinity, but not achieving it (Connell 2005)—and failed heterosexuality described here with fans (Greven 2013; Jones and Wilson-Brown 2014). Men's primary relationships being homosocial is a key feature of bromance, Guyland, and fan representations. Moreover, that young white men's primary relationships are with each other, impeding their "progress" toward heterosexual marriage (Greven 2013; Kimmel 2008), echoes in important ways the Freudian contention that homosexuality is arrested development, evidence of getting stuck in the Oedipal process before moving from same-sex desire to same-sex identification and opposite-sex desire (Stockton 2009). In these ways, the boundaries between failed heterosexuality and homosociality and homosexuality are porous.

Thus, fan relationships with other men are often constructed as or described as resembling romantic or sexual relationships. When Paul goes to jail for assault after shooting obnoxious Philadelphia Eagles fan Philadelphia Phil (the villain in *Big Fan*) with a paintball gun loaded with New York Giants colors, all the other prisoners have women visiting them (presumably intending to suggest wives and girlfriends). However, Paul's visitor is his football friend Sal, paralleling their relationship with the heterosexual ones surrounding them. More explicitly, Chuck and his best friend Morgan are repeatedly called "boyfriends" or "life partners" in *Chuck,* including by Morgan himself. Certainly the show plays with this dynamic, with a reunion between the two after a fight unfolding in slow motion. Their eyes meet across the room, exactly as romantic outcomes are often staged, which creator Josh Schwartz describes in a DVD special feature as "our romantic finale, because at the end of the day, you know, the relationship between Chuck and Morgan really is a huge part of the show." The romantic framing in fan homosocial pairs thus exceeds the buddy relationship to link fans to homosexuality.

Fans are also sometimes directly said to be gay. The broad-spectrum fan that is demonstrated in relation to race and age in Chapter 1 comes into play here, with a checkbox model of diversity permitting the inclusion of actual homosexual fans, but as with fans of color, this is largely incidental rather than a sustained presence. Far more often, heterosexually identified characters deploy homosexuality as an insult against men intending to be heterosexual. The idea that fans can be made fun of this way is so pervasive that in *The Benchwarmers* an antagonist who continually hangs out with another half-naked man in seemingly sexual situations can still call fan ringleader Mel a "homo." In *Big Fan*, Philadelphia Phil goes on at length about how New York Giants fans are "giant *fags*" (extremely gay) and "*Giant* fags" (gay for their team) by varying the emphasis in the statement. *Fanboys*, as with most things, has no subtlety about this: "gay" and "fag" are common insults among these characters (and not just the men). In particular, they call Star Trek fans they encounter things like

"Kirk-loving Spock-suckers." Using the accusation of homosexuality as an insult points toward a perceived need to restabilize their heterosexuality through destabilizing other men's. Fan characters exhibit a lot of paranoia about seeming gay. At times, there are even literal accusations of homosexual conduct rather than just insults intended to mark failed masculinity and heterosexuality.

Beyond name calling, fans are sometimes linked to actual same-sex eroticism. At times this is only incidental. Ben in *Fever Pitch* is so excited about his season tickets that he leaps, half-clothed, onto the delivery man; football fan Ronald Salazar is willing to go on a date with another man to get to the Super Bowl (Goldberg 2000); Philadelphia Phil graphically and repeatedly insists in *Big Fan* that, because his is the superior football team, Giants fans should perform oral sex on him and/or he will perform anal sex on them. In contrast, *The Fan* consistently and extensively marks Gil as sexually nonnormative, whether visually, when he accosts a baseball player in a steam room in a scene visually evocative of a gay bathhouse; musically, with the consistent use of the Nine Inch Nails song "Closer," with its lines "I want to fuck you like an animal/I want to feel you from the inside," whenever he obsesses over player Bobby Rayburn; or both, as when "Closer" plays with Gil standing in Rayburn's closet among his clothes. Although Gil never directly engages in same-sex action, the slippage between being a fan of and having desire for Rayburn is thorough.

Fandom as a Sexual Orientation

As already suggested by mentions of Spock sucking and ballplayer fucking, this is a construction where fan nonnormative sexuality is frequently about directing sexual attention to the object of fandom in particular. Indeed, alongside fans' nonheterosexuality, this formulation begins to suggest that being a fan itself is treated as a nonnormative sexual orientation. This framing shows first in fuzziness between loving the object of fandom and desiring it. A guy in *Fanalysis* exclaims "I love you!" to actor Bruce Campbell and tries to kiss him. The Trekkie antagonist in *Fanboys* tenderly cradles the severed head of his prized statue of the character Khan, screams "Khan!" like Captain Kirk did in *Star Trek II: The Wrath of Khan,* and then, after using his inhaler, kisses the statue full on the lips. This, like Philadelphia Phil's invective about "Giant fags," is the idea that fans are gay for the object of fandom.

Fans sometimes eroticize their object of fandom more intensively than incidental slips from love to lust, which I distinguish from either heterosexuality or homosexuality regardless of the object's gender because it is so focused on the fan object itself. This can be in sexy versions, as with so-called cheesecake comic art, which emphasizes the physical attractiveness of characters over their skills, or nude or seminude versions of characters. In the 1998 *The Simpsons* episode "Das Bus," Comic Book Guy attempts to download a racy picture of *Star Trek: Voyager* character Captain Janeway, only to be thwarted by his slow internet connection. The scene advances a plot about Homer becoming an internet service provider. Any character could have been downloading anything, but the writers choose to use the idea that fans seek out erotic versions of the object of fandom. Fans may also eroticize the object in its regular version. This leads to Patton Oswalt acting out a fellow customer's tendency to rub his nipples while looking through comic books. That the eroticism is for the object of fandom is clearest when it does not align with the fan's ostensible orientation. Paul in *Big Fan* "dates lots of girls," but he also has a dream where his gaze lingers on various body parts of player Quantrell Bishop in a way reminiscent of Laura Mulvey's (1988) argument that the male gaze in film dismembers the female body as a sexual object. In another scene, Bishop's poster is the last image seen before Paul begins to masturbate implies that it aids his process. This scene, like the way three of four fans in *Fanboys*, in a catalog of their fan practices, acknowledge that they have "named their right hand Leia" after the Star Wars princess, is reinforced as nonnormative by the social devaluation of masturbation.

Industry workers sometimes acknowledge that fans eroticize the object of fandom, but they usually condemn it. The production staff of *The Guild* were aware of and anxious about being eroticized by fans. Star Felicia Day in particular was teased by her cast mates that a scene where she turned her shirt around on camera would be eroticized by fans and played in slow motion for the chance to peek at her chest through the arm hole. As teenager Heather Lawver ponders about Harry Potter actor Daniel Radcliffe's nude performance in the stage production *Equus*, "I would love to know how many girls are going there just to see Harry Potter naked," which she described as "so funny because Warner Bros. has been fighting that kind of angle to their franchise for so long, fighting slash fiction writers, fighting all of that. 'We don't want any of that nudity or pornography associated with our franchise,' and here their star is going off and being nude in a play" (*We Are Wizards*).[7] Similarly, some episodes of *Supernatural* discuss (with clear condemnation) the "Wincest" interpretation (that the Winchester brothers are sexually involved), and *Heroes* creator Tim Kring argues in a commentary that interpreting "the patented Nathan Petrelli shoulder rub" as anything sexual is to "misconstrue. We've seen the YouTube movies. Don't think we don't watch the YouTube movies, people out there."

At other times, eroticizing the object of fandom takes the form of incorporating it into sexual or romantic practices, since fans do in fact have sex sometimes. Ben in *Fever Pitch* finds his girlfriend especially sexy when she wears a Red Sox jacket. Dressing up as a character is how Summer in *The O.C.* tries to win Seth's attention. Fans in the documentary *Trekkies* discuss their sexual role-playing of characters, much to actor and host Denise Crosby's discomfort. And exasperated Trish in *The 40-Year-Old Virgin* asks, "What do I have to do for you to have sex with me? Do you want me to dress up like Thor? I'll dress up like Thor. I'll dress up like Iron Man." This constructs being a fan as a fetish, as when, in the episode "Arctic Radar" of the political drama *The West Wing*, White House deputy chief of staff Josh Lyman asks a staff member wearing a Star Trek pin,

> Tell me if any of this sounds familiar: "Let's list our ten favorite episodes. Let's list our least favorite episodes. Let's list our favorite galaxies. Let's make a chart to see how often our favorite galaxies appear in our favorite episodes. What Romulan would you most like to see coupled with a Cardassian and why? Let's spend a weekend talking about Romulans falling in love with Cardassians and then let's do it again." That's not being a fan. That's having a fetish. And I don't have a problem with that, except you can't bring your hobbies in to work, OK?

This scene also constructs being a fan as deeply and inevitably involving sexuality, between the practices Lyman describes, directly calling fan practices a "fetish," and how Lyman's "and I don't have a problem with that" echoes the *Seinfeld* line "Not that there's anything wrong with that" about homosexuality.

We should take the concurrence of failing at normative heterosexuality and eroticizing the object of fandom seriously because the slippage between them is not coincidental but rather indicative of beliefs about fans. Joli Jensen (1992, 16) argues that representations frame "fandom as a surrogate relationship, one that inadequately imitates normal relationships," and the replacement of being a fan for romance is telling. The trope that being a fan substitutes for romantic and sexual relationships fans lack is common, with the object of fandom offered as a consolation prize when relationships fail. However, more than sublimating failure into being a fan, at times being a fan is imagined to cause failed heterosexuality. This logic drives Harry Knowles of the entertainment website Ain't It Cool News, labeled a web guru by a chyron in documentary *Fanalysis*, to say that a fan is "someone who has a nine-to-five job in the real world, and they want to have the wife, but they're still hanging on to being a child." It is why one fan in *Trekkies* says that "my obsession with all this stuff was what always ended my relationships." Fandom also impedes heterosexuality in sports, as with the discourse of football widows or being a fan as the downfall of Ben in *Fever Pitch,* a great boyfriend during the off season whose love of baseball conflicts with his relationship once games resume. These priorities lead fan characters Zach and Seth in *The O.C.* to drop their competition over a woman when a meeting with George Lucas occurs on the same night as their senior prom. They decide that one of them will meet Lucas and the other will go to the prom—although both prefer Lucas.

More intensely, this becomes the idea that fans will choose the object of fandom over romantic entanglements. One baseball fan in *Mathematically Alive* says of being a fan, "It's almost perhaps too important to me because I will blow off anything, whether it's a date or wearing this jacket on a Saturday night in Manhattan. I couldn't care less. It's Mets first." Although his phrasing is hard to follow, the upshot is that his desire for the Mets is greater than his desire for women, which would make it difficult to engage in heterosexual courtship. Paul in *Big Fan* also desires his object of fandom more than women, declining a lap dance and even leaning around the dancer because she is blocking the view of his favorite player. Actor Oswalt jokes that Paul's attitude is, "Please get your gorgeous, naked body out of my way so I can look at the giant guy who's about to pummel me into a coma" (NPR, "Patton Oswalt and Robert Siegel: Serious Funny Men," 2010).

If, following Sara Ahmed (2006, 3), we understand the "orientation" in sexual orientation spatially, then "orientations shape [. . .] 'who' or 'what' we direct our energy and attention toward." The directions we face "make certain things, and not others, available," because in facing one thing we have to turn away from other things (14). This suggests that the fan, although typically constructed as intending to be heterosexual, cannot orient toward the opposite sex because he is oriented toward the object of fandom—and cannot orient toward any real person. Being a fan is thus constructed as a nonnormative sexual orientation that, being toward something other than the so-called opposite sex, precludes facing where one ought.

The decision of the famously homophobic Westboro Baptist Church to picket Comic-Con in 2010 suggests that the far right, at least, has made the same link between being a fan and nonnormative sexual orientation. As with this mingling of antifan and homophobic backlash, sexuality has a fraught position for fans. While sports studies acknowledges that fans may eroticize athletes, sexuality is generally a site of marginalization for sports fans, as there is also a tendency to treat eroticizing athletes as being a fan incorrectly, and women fans are troublingly seen as sex objects for heterosexual men, fans and players alike (Jones 2008; Mewett and Toffoletti 2008; Tanaka 2004).[8] Fan studies has a rich literature on how women and queers of all genders have explored their sexuality through fandom, generally concluding that practices like slash empower fans to discover and articulate identities and desires (Busse and Hellekson 2006; Coppa 2008; Green, Jenkins, and Jenkins 1998; Jenkins 1992; Lackner, Lucas, and Reid 2006; Lothian, Busse, and Reid 2007). Importantly, all of these analyses have no sense that fans' pleasure itself is legitimate or political. Rather, the erotic serves as at worst a source of shame, or at best a move toward discovering oneself and joining a traditional identity category.

However, in place of either of these models, I want to make a queerer move and reorient the question of fan sexuality to interrogate the norm. Somewhat like the idea that "slash fangirls define themselves in sexual terms in relation to their object of adoration" (Lackner, Lucas, and Reid 2006, 202), fans can usefully be seen as oriented toward the object of fandom in a theoretical sense—as a mode of desire and as a way identity functions. In this willingness to link fans to sexual deviance, I go beyond articulations of fan fiction communities as queer spaces (Lackner, Lucas, and Reid 2006; Lothian, Busse, and Reid 2007) to think about the fan more broadly as a concept. I also, like that work on queer space, diverge from more than two decades of work that seeks to position fans as normal. However, the single most important lesson of queer theory for this book is that "normal" is selective and always comes at the cost of narrowing possibility, inevitably not only reinforcing the rightness of what is dominant but also excluding the most marginal as normativity expands only in narrow ways. What happens if we instead embrace fans' potential for queerness?

Fans' construction in representation appears to demand such analysis. The rhetoric around fan practices is closely tied to that around nonnormative sexuality. Ben of *Fever Pitch*, for example, broaches being a Red Sox fan by saying, "There's something you don't know about me," and "I've been avoiding this," framing his admission as a variety of coming out. Indeed, two different fans in *Trekkies 2* directly use the language of coming out or being in the closet about being fans. With less shame and more pride, one fan in *Trekkies* says, "Fans: we recruit!" gesturing toward the antigay idea that homosexuals recruit. A fan in the documentary *Trekkies 2* deploys a version of Queer Nation's chant, "We're here, we're queer, get used to it," by proudly proclaiming, "I'm here, I'm into Star Trek, get used to it!"

With this gesture toward Queer Nation, the queer potential of being a fan as a refusal, rather than failure, of normative sexuality comes into view. Although fans usually redeem themselves into heterosexuality in these representations through an exercise of white masculine self-control, there are other possibilities. Paul in *Big Fan*, for example, does not have a career or a girlfriend, and he lives with his mother, thus not complying with any of the dictates of normative white heteromasculinity. However, unlike the narratives that have fans learning their lesson, Paul has no interest in normativity. He is quite content to be exactly who he is, refusing marriage and children as the ultimate future, just as queer theorist Edelman (2004) valorizes. As actor Oswalt says of the character, "You realize it only looks like loneliness from the outside, so I didn't play Paul as this yearning, lonely guy. I played him as a guy who, in his mind, he thinks it's all settled, it's perfect. [. . .] What I tried to tap into was, in his mind, his satisfaction of the circumstances of his life" (NPR 2010). Oswalt also notes that Paul "just wants to stay working in the garage, and he's very offended by the pressure on him to take another job." He experiences a similar contentment with his living arrangements and nonpartnered status, which can be inferred from Oswalt's further comments: "Paul, for all of his faults, and he has a lot of faults—he does not desire to reach out to anyone. [. . .] If anything, his battle is to keep the world away from him." Writer Siegel adds, "If he could just be left alone I think he'd be happy."

These formulations show the importance of taking seriously that excessive or misdirected love or desire is at the heart of marginalization of fans. As Ahmed (2006, 101) points out, "The choice of one's object of desire makes a difference to other things that we do. In a way I am suggesting that the object in sexual object choice is sticky: other things 'stick' when we orientate ourselves toward objects, especially if such orientations do not follow the family or social line." Because normativity relies on enactment of a whole complex of norms, desiring the wrong thing and too much undermines normativity on multiple axes. It is no coincidence that fans are both failed men and failed heterosexuals—and also failed white people. In orienting themselves toward the object of fandom, fans do not follow the normative line, and what accordingly sticks to them in the cultural imaginary is failed whiteness, masculinity, and adulthood.

REDEEM YOURSELF NOW! (RESTRICTIONS MAY APPLY.)

If white men are normatively dominant, then fans fail by every measure. However, in representations that have a "happy" ending (generally comedies), it comes when fans are recuperated toward hegemonic masculinity, primarily through successful heterosexuality. Greven (2013) notes that beta male comedies seem to challenge marriage through a homosocial premise, but they ultimately resolve into it, which he attributes to the trajectory of comedy as a genre. Although this may be true, in relation to being trapped in Guyland at the beginning of these narrative trajectories, marriage or other forms of "get the girl" plots function as a redemption into heteronormativity. Although heterosexual romance coming to fruition commonly drives the happily ever after in film, and although some fans do simply learn heteronormativity, being a fan is often positioned as the specific impediment, which does particular cultural work that requires closer examination. If whiteness depends on sexual self-control, and if fans are constructed as white people sexually out of bounds, then they are also constructed as fully able to be salvaged by exercising the supposedly innate white capacity for self-control to end some of their bad behavior. The deviance of fans comes from correctable bad decisions by people who can and should do better, much as the crisis of Guyland is that these men should have high-powered jobs, marriage, and kids, but do not. In these ways, fans' divergence from socially valued categories does not contest dominance but rather reinforces it.

This is why the most explicit articulations of a positive outcome to being less of a fan are closely tied to heterosexual success. Some fans must get rid of their excessive fannish possessions in order to obtain a more restrained appreciation that permits them to succeed as heterosexuals. In *The Big Bang Theory*, Leonard's fannish acquisition of a large movie prop blocks the stairway in his building and ruins his neighbor Penny's day, causing her to scream at him and his fan friends: "My God, you are grown men! How could you waste your lives with these stupid toys and costumes and comic books and—and now that—that—" before trailing off in disgust. Later, although Penny has apologized, saying, "You are a great guy, and it is things you love that make you who you are," Leonard decides to sell his fannish possessions, declaring, "Still, I think it's time for me to get rid of this stuff and—you know—move on with my life." Penny replies, "Oh. Wow. Good for you," and kisses his cheek, positively reinforcing his decision with affection from his unrequited love interest. Similarly, Andy in *The 40-Year-Old Virgin* sells his extensive toy collection, makes half a million dollars, and uses it to finance the wedding that his move away from fannish virginity permits.[9]

Following similar trajectories, fan characters refocus on their relationships in place of immature fan dreams. In *Fever Pitch*, Ben loses his girlfriend and decides he needs to grow up and give up being a fan by selling his lifetime season tickets to the Red Sox. Ultimately, she does not let him make the sacrifice, saying, "If you love me enough to sell your tickets, I love you enough not to let you." However—much like Penny's approval of Leonard—his willingness to abandon his excessive attachment proves to her that he is worth it. The narrative of moving past all-consuming obsession to contained appreciation compatible with heterosexuality turns up even in documentaries. In *Trekkies,* we meet Gabriel Koerner, who is excessively nerdy and focused on being a fan, but by *Trekkies 2,* he has become a man, calmed his appreciation of Star Trek, begun a career, and found a girlfriend, thus collecting all the normativities.[10]

In all these cases, although being a fan does not have to be given up, it does have to be controlled, and alignment with the white norm, made possible by being white men, makes these fans eligible for redemption into heterosexuality. Fans of color and women fans never reform and control their attachment. Hiro and Zaboo never become less childish, and fannish women like Liz Lemon of *30 Rock,* Cyd of *The Guild,* and Becky in *Supernatural* make no appreciable progress toward normativity. The exclusion of fans other than white men from the recuperation narrative either constructs other groups of fans as incapable of being normalized or assumes everyone will identify with and want to emulate the redemption of white men fans. In either case, it reinforces the construction of self-control as characteristic of white men: the nonnormativity of fans serves to reinforce normativity. This demonstrates the importance of the distinction that queer and disability theorist Robert McRuer (2006, 30), borrowing from and extending Michael Warner (1999) and Judith Butler (1993), makes between virtually crip or queer and critically crip or queer, which I reframe as a distinction between nonnormative and queer. Simply not conforming to one or more norms is not the same as challenging normativity. Fans are not normatively white, straight, adult, or masculine. However, this being portrayed negatively and "fixed" with a redemption arc reinforce rather than challenge normativity as the goal. These characters are nonnormative, but they are not queer. To conceptualize this as a queer framework is to extend the notion of queer beyond sexuality proper, but as Ahmed (2006, 78) notes, "queer" as a form of disorientation from the norm "can contest not only heteronormative

assumptions, but also social conventions and orthodoxies in general,"
and certainly fans' orientation—or not—to orthodoxy is the key question
in these representations.

Deviant whitenesses, like being a fan, seems to disrupt the normativity
and dominance of whiteness. However, constructing fans as lacking
normativity and dominance relies on assuming that whiteness should be
normative and dominant. As Dyer (1997, 12) points out, "Going against
type and not conforming depend upon an implicit norm of whiteness
against which to go." Kusz (2001, 394) argues, "Constructions of Whiteness as unprivileged, victimized, or otherwise disadvantaged—images
that seem to contradict the ideology of Whiteness as privileged—can
work in particular contexts as a mechanism to resecure the privileged
normativity of whiteness in American culture." I argue that images of fans
constitute one such context. Like other representations of nonprivileged
whiteness, this is seen as abnormal; something has been done to these
men, or they have strayed. Guyland needs an explanation because for
these men, deviance from norms and privileges signals a crisis, whereas
having a job rather than a career or not being in a position that permits
marriage, children, and property ownership has routinely not been accessible for many on the basis of race and class.

Thus, the norm makes fan deviance intelligible as deviance, reinforced
by the narrative of recuperation. In the end, these constructions show that
privilege can be regained in the happy ending of normativity because fans'
skin whiteness—their imagined innate capacity for self-control—makes
them eligible for symbolic whiteness, thus making these narratives reinforce rather than undermine the connection of whiteness and privilege.
Ultimately, this articulation of white bodies, being a fan, and nonhet-
eronormativity in representation constructs the supposed inadequacy
of fans as caused by substandard—but standardizable—self-control. In
this sense, these representations tell a story about that most neoliberal of
buzz phrases, "personal responsibility." Constructing fans as normative
failures resulting from bad decisions makes their deviation from the
white norm of self-control correctable, domesticating the threat they

might seem to pose and making them useful for normativity. Because their phenotypic whiteness carries a cultural expectation of an essential ability for self-control, fan redemption seems to actualize that capacity, getting whiteness right. As Ahmed (2006) points out, some bodies are more interpellated than others. Simply by being white, normativity is possible for these fans, because "bodies that pass as white, even if they are queer or have other points of deviation, still have access to what follows from certain lines" (136–37). By being heterosexual white men, these fans have access to normativity, if only they can straighten up and fly white.

CHAPTER THREE

CONSUMPTION AND THE MANAGEMENT OF DESIRE

Consumption is expected or obvious for fans. A montage of merchandise or a panning shot across piled-up goods either in fans' homes or at conventions is a standard establishing shot, and verbal catalogs of collections are similarly used to identify individuals as fans. These patterns are remarkably consistent in fictional, news, and documentary representations. Consumption's centrality to contemporary beliefs about fans is also clear because every website in my archive lets fans buy things, and almost all of them use an on-site store.[1] Given that consumption is so essential to ideas about who fans are and what they want, we might assume that it would be fundamental to fan studies; after all, the most basic act of being a fan is consuming the object of fandom. Crawford (2004, 113) argues, "The activities of fans and fan cultures are principally constructed around consumer activities." More intensively, both Matt Hills (2002) and Cornel Sandvoss (2005) define being a fan specifically as consistent, emotionally invested consumption of the object of fandom. However, these authors are in the minority among sports or media studies scholars in linking fans to consumption.

This is because consumption carries negative connotations. Consumption is seen as being about waste or destruction rather than creation (Arvidsson 2005; Campbell 2000; Sandlin and Maudlin 2012), as natural rather than civilized (Baudrillard 2000; Campbell 2000), as personal or private (Baudrillard 2000; Sandlin and Maudlin 2012; Sandvoss 2005), as irrational or emotional (Campbell 2000; Hebdige 2000; Rafferty 2011), and as feminine (Hebdige 2000; Sandlin and Maudlin 2012; Veblen

[1899] 2000). All of this means that although a purely capitalist model encourages selling as much as possible, it is not correspondingly seen as in good taste to buy as much as possible. As Thorstein Veblen ([1899] 2000) notes, conspicuous consumption to display wealth must have good taste and consume only socially valued goods. Taste is both racialized and classed, as, for example, African Americans sometimes demonstrate wealth through clothing, shoes, and jewelry in a way white culture considers tacky, and poor people are chastised for not spending their limited funds in ways that the better-off think they should. More particularly, as Pierre Bourdieu (1984) argues, taste is understood as a judgment that is not based on personal pleasure in the object but rather, like Immanuel Kant's ([1790] 2001) notion of aesthetic judgment, should be rational and disinterested and therefore objective and universal. Pleasure is not supposed to matter, and if it does, the judgment is compromised.

As this suggests, the social devaluation of consumption is about pleasure. Both are seen as personal, private, irrational, and emotional—and not tasteful. Each negatively valued characteristic of consumption is in turn associated with femininity. Lynn Spigel (1992, 61) argues in general that "culture critics have often expressed their disdain for mass media in language that evokes contempt for those qualities that patriarchal societies ascribe to femininity. Thus, mass amusements are typically thought to encourage passivity, and they have frequently been represented in terms of penetration, consumption, and escape." If we reorient this constellation of devalued concepts to center consumption, it is clear how, as a form of taking culture in, consumption is associated with passivity and penetration—concepts themselves devalued as feminine. Additionally, the interrelation of these concepts overdetermines consumption as illegitimate—that is, its negative meaning is caused by so many factors it is almost inevitable.

In this chapter, through an analysis of industry worker statements, web design, and representations of fans, I examine how consumption functions as part of the domestication of fandom, identifying it as an abstracted industry logic applied regardless of whether the fan object is sports or speculative media. I first explain why consumption is an uncommon lens, and I make a case for taking it more seriously in studying fans. The chapter then constructs a typology of the forms of consumption

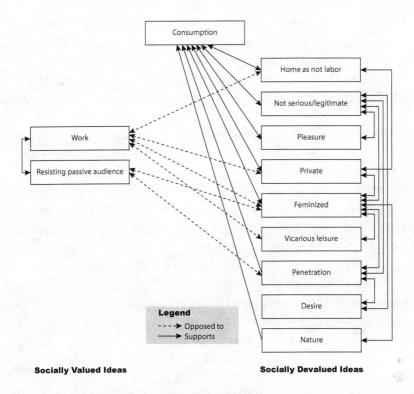

<table>
</table>

Consumption		
	Home as not labor	
	Not serious/legitimate	
Work	Pleasure	
Resisting passive audience	Private	
	Feminized	
	Vicarious leisure	
	Penetration	
	Desire	
	Nature	

Legend
---▶ Opposed to
——▶ Supports

Socially Valued Ideas   **Socially Devalued Ideas**

Consumption is overdetermined as illegitimate

that industry recruits and normalizes for fans, arguing particularly that transmedia projects seem to be interactive but actually promote consumption. After this, I argue that although fans consume extensively and intensively, that does not mean fan consumption practices are coextensive with industry's new norms. I conclude by considering the potential for leveraging consumption as power through buycotts.

RECLAIMING PLEASURE, DESIRE, AND CONSUMPTION

One common response to the negative associations of fans with consumption and of consumption itself has been trying to avoid contamination by consumption. Hills (2002) notes that there is widespread resistance to calling fans "consumers," which he links to valuing production over consumption, as when scholars like Nick Abercrombie and Brian Longhurst (1998) describe practices that move toward professionalization as higher forms of being a fan. Hills (2002, 27) points out that often, "'good' fan audiences are constructed against [. . .] the 'bad' consumer." Crawford (2004, 34) argues that at least part of the rejection of consumption is because men scholars want to celebrate their own "masculine" behaviors and reject modes of being a fan "deemed as more 'feminine' and hence less 'resistant' and 'authentic.'" The argument that consumption is feminized is not new—it was made by Veblen in 1899 and Dick Hebdige in 2000—but evidently the gendered implications of rejecting consumption are not apparent to those doing it. That consumption is feminized is complicated by the ways consumptive or curatorial fandom is associated with men, as opposed to women more often engaging in transformative productive practices. It may, however, be the specific conjunction of consumption and men that makes these scholars, and popular culture in general, uneasy about fan consumption.

There is such a strong drive to identify fan practices as productive that it would be comical if it wasn't because of rejecting femininity, pleasure, and desire. Hills (2002, 30) notes that John Fiske (1992) takes it so far that he categorizes "'semiotic' and 'enunciative' productivity, in which reading a text and talking about it become cases of 'productivity,'" because everything fans do must be productive. Sports studies has a similarly strong anticonsumerist streak. Opponents of consumerism make arguments like Richard Giulianotti's (2005) that shifting from "fans" to "customers" has destroyed traditional sports support. This is a common type of complaint from a tradition that strictly rejects commodified sports as inauthentic.

Another key reason consumption tends not to appear in discussions of fans is that when the field of cultural studies turned its attention to media reception, it was to reject the idea that audiences were passive consumers mindlessly obeying media. One unintended consequence of this active audience argument is that consumption, already associated with passivity, becomes taboo even while cultural studies examines reception, which commonsensically includes consumption. This separation of reception from consumption also shapes fan studies. Similarly, when people do discuss consumption, it is nearly always to describe how active and productive consumers are these days and to argue the producer–consumer distinction is no longer useful, so we ought to ignore consumption/consumers and speak only of production/producers. From different angles, then, these areas of scholarship have a horror of consumption.

I would argue that these responses to consumption's devaluation are accommodationist. To advocate that being a fan is valuable, they avoid association with consumption rather than challenging its negative associations (and in fact implicitly agree with them through trying not be mistaken for "those people"). However, since being a fan inevitably involves consumption, consumption's social devaluation haunts fans and could be used to remarginalize them at any time. In this chapter, instead of accepting that consumption is devalued and trying to insulate fans from it, I take consumption seriously as an integral aspect of being a fan. I ask what kinds of consumption—so necessary to capitalism—are understood as valuable fan behavior. These valuations produce norms of proper and improper consumption, which I conceptualize as an attempt to manage fan desire.

Recognizing that fans' desire to consume is both sought by industry for profit and feared as excessive and destructive, I take a similar line of inquiry with consumption as Michel Foucault's (1990) about sexuality: fan desire is not universally repressed, but rather some behavior is incited, and therefore we need to examine how this works rather than accepting the taboo and moving on. This analysis parallels the tradition of feminist and queer scholarship in fan studies that reclaims pleasure and desire as having political and intellectual value rather than shying away from them as illegitimate subjects that harm fans by association (Busse and Hellekson 2006; Busse 2013; Coppa 2008; Willis 2006; Russo 2010). This tradition has shown that being a fan is a space of specifically sexual desire, whether as fans eroticizing the object of fandom (Coppa 2008, 2009; Green, Jenkins, and Jenkins 1998) or using the object of fandom, fan community, or fan practices to better understand their desires or identity (Busse 2006; Hanmer 2003; Penley 1997, 2012; Willis 2006). Working in this vein lets me center consumption while refusing to accept stigma around pleasure and desire.

If we take this queer stance that pleasure is political—meaning both that our understanding of pleasure is the product of social power and that pleasure carries potential to disrupt social power—this shows why, as Julie Levin Russo (2010) points out, desire is essential to fans and capitalism alike. This desire is reciprocal but uneven, disjointed, and triangular (if not some other polygon). Industry desires (some) fans. Fans desire the object of fandom (the text or team), for which the industry is a (potentially obstructionist) provider. As the nonparallel terms between these sentences already suggest, fan and industry desires do not always match up. Because they are poorly aligned, and because fans desire in more directions than the straight lines industry desires them to, from industry's perspective, fans are challenging.

The idea that desire does not automatically lead to orderly consumption—that it might, if it is not managed, point in directions that are not considered normative or productive—has a long history. Not desiring properly, after all, is what Sigmund Freud ([1905] 1995, 247) classifies as sexual perversion—that is, cases of desire that are not genitally focused or that linger too long rather than getting on with "the final sexual aim." Fan desire is similarly divergent from industry's desire for fans. It lingers too long rather than consuming more and more things serially; it does not necessarily want what industry wants fans to want. If, as Kathryn Bond Stockton (2009, 25) argues, building from Freud, "perverts are 'diverts,'" then from industry's perspective, fans are perverts because they desire out of line. Industry desires fans; they desire fans' desire. Wanting fans to want them is fundamental to the speculative media or sports business model, but as the framework of desired audiences or demographics shows (Hills 2002; Jenkins, Ford, and Green 2013; Scott 2011), the recruitment of fan desire is specific and limited. In fact, Jenkins, Ford, and Green (2013, 129) raise the possibility that the "surplus," undesired audience can actually harm a media product financially if it outnumbers the preferred one. For example, because children's television shows are sharply market segmented by gender, shows targeted at boys that become popular with girls are sometimes canceled as failures despite high overall viewership (Davis 2013). Fan and industry desires as both mutual and mismatched is long-standing, but the internet era has seen new efforts to regulate, manage, and domesticate fan desire.

Contestation over proper consumption emphasizes that both "consumption" and "the consumer" are social constructs. Producing the consumer has a long history. Kyle Asquith (2015, 116) describes how marketers in the early twentieth century invented the child consumer they sought to measure. Although there is "a financial incentive to 'get it right,'" industry may end up measuring its own desires more than consumers themselves, as when marketers selected for children who would participate in mail-in offers and then "learned" that kids are outgoing and open. The historical processes by which consumption was taught and people came to be understood as—and understand themselves as—consumers provide important precedents for how industry worked to domesticate fan desire in the period this book examines. Adam Arvidsson (2005, 243), for example, describes "Fordist marketing" that tried to standardize mass consumption through managing consumer taste and/or desire just like the standardized mass production of Fordism. Sandvoss (2003, 9) similarly speaks of "Fordist leisure" as stable, cyclical, and centralized. As Hebdige (2000, 139) points out, mass producing something new is so expensive that it is only logical to prepare consumers as carefully as any other component; "corporate viability was seen to rely increasingly on the regulation of desire." New attention to fan desire and appeals to them as an emerging market therefore resemble the trajectory that Alexandra Chasin (2000) identifies as happening with groups like women, African Americans, and gays and lesbians as they became seen as legitimate citizens and markets.

Managing markets and rationalizing consumption require educating desire. Colin Campbell (2000) argues that needs for food and shelter could be satisfied by many different things, but under a consumption model, they generally attach to something specific, indicating that this desire is socially shaped. This is also why Jean Baudrillard (2000, 20) notes that "use value—indeed utility itself—is a fetishized social relation"; what we think things are useful for is a social phenomenon mystified into a property of the object. Similarly, Campbell (2000) argues that the idea that consumers are inherently insatiable is an ideology of mass production, not transhistorically true about humans but only practicable with mass production. In such ways, it is clear that "consumer culture also *produces consumers* [. . .] *in a variety of ways*" (Sassatelli 2007, 6). If consumption and consumers are products of social construction, then we should ask how they are constructed—in this case, how industry incites, recruits, and tries to domesticate fan desire. Although the management of desire of course is not unique to fans, I ask how it is instantiated in this case, and with what implications for media use.

PROMISCUOUS CONSUMPTION AND THE PARATEXTUAL ORIENTATION

Instead of insisting that everything fans do is productive and disregarding consumption and desire, I make the reverse move, thus expanding the framework of consumption. Although in some ways it is an equal and opposite step to the blanket insistence on production criticized above, it is a strategic rather than uncritical (or indeed panicked) one—a deliberate, analytic reorientation of the question to see what consumption shows about contemporary beliefs about fans. To do this, I move beyond economistic or commonsensical definitions of consumption. Jonathan Gray's (2010) theorization of the paratext is helpful here. Gray identifies paratexts as both "distinct from" and "intrinsically part of" a text, which is useful to think about how audiences consume around a primary object; "while purists may stomp their feet and insist that the game, bonus materials, or promos, for instance, 'aren't the real thing'" (2010, 6, 2), consuming these things shapes our experience of the ostensible real thing, so that they are vital to understanding how people interact with an object of fandom.

Here I construct a four-part taxonomy of the kinds of consumption normalized for fans. First is Consumption 1.0, consuming the object of fandom itself, whether watching in person or via media, whether paid or free; second is subconsumption, or consumption that is supplementary and supports the main experience rather standing alone; third is the supraconsumption of licensed goods, which can circulate independent of the object of fandom; and fourth is Consumption 2.0, or transmedia and interactive consumption. Throughout, I deemphasize a definition of consumption as buying. Much like Russell Belk's (2014) argument that collaborative consumption, like time-shares and luxury-bag borrowing services, expands markets to people who would otherwise simply not consume such things, contending that there is explanatory power if we redefine "market," there is explanatory power in redefining consumption to recognize that both paid and unpaid activities have structural commonalities as forms of consumption if we understand it broadly as taking in something related to the object of fandom.

Ninety Percent of Success is Showing Up:
Attendance, Eyeballs, and Consumption

Media industry constructions of fans consistently believe in and recruit basic consumption of the object of fandom itself, whether watching in person or via media, whether paid or free, which I call Consumption 1.0. Perhaps the most obvious way Consumption 1.0 manifests is the norm that fans show up to events. Primarily this is the expectation that sports fans attend games, which all BMU workers stressed as central to their jobs. Although sports clearly has more investment in in-person consumption, attending speculative media conventions is also constructed as fundamental to the fan experience, demonstrated by listings of upcoming events at the Star Trek and Star Wars websites and the frequency of fans attending conventions in fictional and documentary representations.

When sports industry workers discuss attendance, they often, perhaps unsurprisingly, focus on fans paying for tickets. When James at BMU was asked, "What types of things that fans do would make it easier for you?" he replied, "Coming in groups" almost before I had finished the question, suggesting this was obvious for him. He continued, "And so we—if you *focus* on group sales and group attendance, particularly at the nonrevenue events, you could really pad—you could make an impact."[2] Using quantitative measures shows what matters to BMU is their desire for fans and their need for proof of fans' desire for sports—to the exclusion of a qualitative concern for fulfilling fan desires. The combination of the norm that fans attend and the desire to incite them to attend leads sports organizations to blanket their websites with opportunities to buy tickets. The Seattle Mariners baseball team does this more than most, with general invitations to buy and self-advertisements for season tickets, tickets to specific matches, and multigame package deals. Additionally, when college sports site CalBears.com says "Buy Tickets," it rests in the grammatical space between assuming fans buy—"Here's where you can buy"—and commanding them to buy with the imperative verb. In such ways, consumption as paying to attend events is both normatively expected and actively encouraged.

However, attending events is consumption—in the sense of taking in a product—even when no money changes hands. The marketing staff at BMU cares about attendance even at games that do not charge for admission; as Lisa notes, "For football, we're obviously concerned about revenue, and just making money, whereas with the *other* sports I'm concerned about just getting butts in seats, and just getting people there." The belief that fan presence is essential leads to media representations showing sports fans attending practices, free events, or children's games. These examples suggest that like all norms, fan desire to consume through attendance is both optional and not, both claimed as something fans inevitably do and actively recruited because it is not actually automatic.

However, fans may not attend in person. Rather, they may consume the object of their fandom through media. Clearly this is the primary means of consumption for speculative media. Substantially more media consumption is unpaid than that which occurs via in-person events because both broadcast and basic cable are supported by advertising and their content is not purchased directly by consumers. The low cost of media consumption drives one memorable scene in *Big Fan*, where football fans Paul and Sal attend a tailgate party outside the New York Giants' stadium. While other fans then go inside to watch the game, Paul and Sal gather around a television hooked to their car battery. Being a fan in person at the tailgate party transitions to mediated consumption because they are unable to buy tickets. Consuming via TV can also make sports more accessible for those for whom the stadium might be hostile, such as women fans and fans of color, whose exclusion is discussed in Chapter 1. Because watching is a norm, appeals to watch are part of recruiting fan desire. This explains why SyFy devotes website space to explicit invitations to watch its shows and why ESPN uses an imperative verb exhorting website visitors to "Watch." Additionally, the sensory affordance of motion draws attention to ESPN.com's ticker labeled "Live Now" at the top of the screen that cycles through currently airing programming on their TV outlets (ESPN, ESPN2, etc.), making the website an invitation to also consume ESPN's traditional-media presence.

Beyond inciting fans to watch TV, organizations often construct watching through other distribution channels as normative. There is encouragement to consume content on the web. For example, *Dr. Horrible's Sing-Along Blog* was first released via a free web event; Star Trek and SyFy offer full episodes of their respective series; ESPN provides clips; and Purdue University has live audio streaming of its sporting events. These forms of consumption are both free to the fan and positioned as normative fan desires by being easy to find on sites. Of course, at other times, media consumption is clearly something fans are expected to purchase. They are assumed—and encouraged by the ease of it on the website—to buy *Dr. Horrible* on iTunes after the initial streaming event. Fans are also understood to buy DVDs of the object of fandom (as opposed to, say, renting them or borrowing from the library), and they are frequently hailed as buyers in special features and commentaries, as when actor Sandeep Parikh of web series *The Guild* follows up the introduction of the actors at the beginning of the second season commentary with the words, "Thanks for purchasing a DVD and for listening to our commentary track." Thus, whether it is in person or at a distance, paid or free, there is a consistent norm of basic consumption as necessary to fandom.

Subconsumption: Lesser, Supplementary, Integral

Consumption 1.0 is basic, perhaps even obvious, but it provides a baseline for a several other kinds of consumption. The first I call subconsumption because it is dependent on, always copresent with, and seen as supplementary to and supporting the main consumption rather than existing for itself. In some ways, this is like Crawford's (2004, 77, 113) contention that both buying and watching are consumption, and the "wearing of clothing that signif[ies] certain team allegiances" and "going to a bar or pub before or after games, consuming food and drinks at the game, using your car or public transport to get to games, [and/or] buying in beers and food to watch the game at home" are also "related acts of consumption." However, subconsumption is more systematic, expanding beyond physical objects and beyond purchasing.

One kind of consumption that supports basic watching or attendance is when fans consume freely provided souvenirs. As Jenkins, Ford, and Green (2013) note, the intent is that people receiving such objects use them regularly, are reminded of the company, think positively of it for giving them something, and then buy things down the road. Similarly, Lisa at BMU mentioned "T-shirt toss" two different times as something she routinely did to improve the fan experience when they are already consuming the game. In addition to increasing fans' commitment, subconsumption is clearly an expected or normative mode of fan desire. There is, for example, a storied tradition of giveaways of swag at Comic-Con, which is mentioned repeatedly in news coverage. Indeed, "fans snap up freebies such as postcards, stickers and graphic novels, hauling huge tote bags through the crowded convention floor," and fans reach peak desire for swag with entertainment writer Sandy Cohen's (2007a) parenthetical aside that "some waited in hour-long lines for the free totes."

While free objects are clearly related to the object of fandom but not the purchasing typically associated with consumption, subconsumption also includes the mirror image: buying things tangentially related to the object of fandom. Fans wearing nonbranded clothes in team colors to games, like the plain red sweat suit worn by the parent of a high school basketball player in sports film *The Winning Season* (much to his daughter's embarrassment), is subconsumption. Fans need to buy these things to have them, but they are not official merchandise. Since it is indirect, this consumption is often not considered, but it is routine for fans. Purchasing concessions at a live event, which Lisa of BMU mentioned as a place they can recoup costs at free-admission events or after offering reduced-cost admission to groups, is also subconsumption. In typical *Simpsons* fashion, the 2003 episode "Pray Anything" takes the emphasis on concessions to extremes for comedic effect, with young Lisa Simpson commenting, "Dad, it's so enlightened of you to take us to a WNBA game," only to have Homer reply, "Yeah, well, nachos are nachos."

Costs of attending events, like air and ground transportation and hotels, are also subconsumption. The Purdue University and UC Berkeley (Cal) websites helpfully provide travel information to their fans, building this form of consumption into their menu options. Discussions of travel-related subconsumption are also a staple of news coverage, with frequent mentions of increased hotel rates or availability problems when fan demand outstrips supply for events like San Diego Comic-Con and the Super Bowl. An intertitle in the documentary *Mathematically Alive* makes it clear that subconsumption is serious business: when two New York Mets fans went to spring training, "in all, they spent close to $500 on gas and tolls, another $180 on hotels, and 46 hours driving, to see 1 meaningless exhibition game." In such ways, various forms of subconsumption are (constructed as) vital to enabling or supplementing Consumption 1.0, both assumed and recruited by industry practice.

Supraconsumption: A New (Licensed) Hope

Building beyond basic consumption begins with normalizing desire for licensed or franchised extensions of an object of fandom. These expanded forms of consumption add something because they are not the thing itself or consumed while consuming the thing itself, and they can circulate independently of the thing itself, just like the team lunch box is not only used while watching sports and might be purchased by someone who has never seen a game. The first object of fandom to turn licensing and merchandising into a high art was Star Wars, which Jonathan Gray (2010, 177) describes as the "most voluminous paratextual entourage in entertainment history." Although the unprecedented proliferation of licensed merchandise for the Star Wars franchise was the result of George Lucas's shrewd decision to forgo salary on the films in exchange for retaining licensing rights (Jenkins 2006a), it has affected fans' relationship to consumption far beyond one contract. Massive merchandising is now routine, even expected. This is used for comic effect in the film *Kick-Ass,* when the protagonist's decision to become a homegrown superhero produces an immediate merchandise explosion, with his local comic book store featuring bumper stickers, hats, mugs, T-shirts, posters, a replica of the hero's wetsuit-based costume, a cappuccino special in the coffee shop, and a comic announced as "Coming Soon." There is such a surge in interest that children start having Kick-Ass-themed birthday parties, leading the henchmen of the movie's villain to assassinate an impersonator by accident—news the boss receives with disgust, exclaiming, "They got paper plates and napkins down at the store now, too?"

Of course, licensing means serious money. The magnitude of revenue involved in licensing is apparent from discussions in the business press when Disney acquired Marvel Comics:

> Through the deal, Marvel gains the ability to quickly reach more markets worldwide. Disney is by far the world's top licenser of its character brands, with $30 billion in retail sales in fiscal 2008, compared with fourth-place Marvel at $5.7 billion, according to *License! Global* magazine. "It gives Marvel the opportunity to expand internationally and leverage the Disney retail relationships as well as their licensee relationships," said Tony Lisanti, the magazine's global editorial director. (Nakashima 2009)

In fact, it is likely the 2012 Disney purchase of Lucasfilm (and thus Star Wars), bringing together two juggernauts of merchandising, resulted in a previously inconceivable deployment of the licensed good; while the corresponding figure after the merger is a combined number, by fiscal 2017, Disney's overall licensing revenue had grown to $55.14 billion (License Global 2017). Although it is easy to critique licensed merchandising as pure greed to milk properties for all they are worth, this might misunderstand the business companies are actually in: "When Disney might make several hundred dollars' worth of product sales off a single young consumer, compared to the child's paltry five dollars at the box office, we might be foolish to see the film as ipso facto the 'primary text'" (Gray 2010, 38).

The most consistent kind of licensed-good consumption constructed as normative for fans is clothing. When asked, "When I say 'fan,' what kind of person do you imagine? What pops into your head?," Lisa from BMU replied, "Here especially, I think people decked out in [BMU] gear. I think that's the biggest thing. I think it's—I mean, obviously you have fans that don't. But the majority of the fans that come to a lot of the games are the ones that are all—obviously, always wearing their [school colors] and into it and things like that." After describing the ways BMU fans vary in age, from older donors to kids with their families, she circled back to identify wearing team clothing as what they all had in common. Similarly, websites consistently emphasize T-shirts or replica jerseys as a type of merchandise they sell, reaffirming how central clothing is thought to be for fans.

Beyond clothes, normative licensed merchandise consumption has a few other standard components. Between representation, interview mentions, and web design, it is clear fans are understood to buy licensed figurines and toys. They also normatively acquire collectibles around their object of fandom, like statues and autographed merchandise. More frequent on the sports side is purchasing official support merchandise: pompons, pennants and flags, noisemakers, foam fingers—and whole foam hands and foam cowboy hats and foam paws representing animal mascots and foam sticks to wave or beat together for noise. Through these instantiations of supraconsumption, fans acquire additional objects, primarily but not exclusively by purchasing them, independently of whether or how they consume the "main" or "real" object of fandom.

Consumption 2.0: Transmedia and Interactivity as Reactivity

Transmedia is a form of media production that releases multiple inter-related objects that contribute to a larger media phenomenon across different platforms, like websites that go beyond aired TV episodes or video games that let people play stories that never happened on the football field. Transmedia spreads a story across texts or platforms, or it spreads a world or character across texts, stories, or platforms. It has cohesion or commonality across the different objects, but each piece additionally enriches the overall experience rather than duplicating others—and it is not just one story in serialized pieces. Transmedia is usually modular; audiences can consume as many or as few parts as they desire. Transmedia projects vary in whether they are centralized—that is, whether there is a core and a periphery, or whether all texts are equal. Transmedia allows immersion or filling out detail of an object of fandom. It also calls on specific audience reactions, inviting them to be involved and to chase down the pieces to consume. This is why I call it Consumption 2.0.

Transmedia has similarity across the different texts or platforms, but it does not just provide multiple ways to consume more of the same thing. Jenkins (2006a, 96) explains, "Reading across the media sustains a depth of experience that motivates more consumption. Redundancy burns up fan interest and causes franchises to fail. Offering new levels of insight and experience refreshes the franchise and sustains consumer loyalty."

It is important that he frames transmedia as fulfilling fan desire as well as consumption because it is both. Transmedia, as Consumption 2.0, differs from traditional consumption because it has a proliferation of objects rather than scarcity (Arvidsson 2005; Jenkins, Ford, and Green 2013). It also, much like Web 2.0, runs on user-generated content (Van Dijck and Nieborg 2009; Hadas 2009; Bruns 2012) and relies on consumer action to function.

Usually transmedia is thought of as storytelling, where pieces of the same narrative are distributed in different locations and/or formats. One of the most common models is having a core text—a TV show, a sports team—that is clearly the master text and that is merely enriched by other texts. This produces transmedia strategies like webisodes, which are short episodes released on the internet by shows like *BSG* and *Heroes* that fill narrative gaps in and between full aired episodes. That the center–periphery model is the norm can be seen from widespread dissatisfaction with the transmedia ecosystem of the Matrix franchise. People had an expectation that the film would be the core, but in fact the second film in the series "assumes we have almost complete mastery over its complex mythology and ever-expanding cast of secondary characters" developed in a video game and short animated films released separately (Jenkins 2006a, 94). The narrative of *The Matrix* was lateral and dispersed, so the movie alone did not provide everything one needed to know. In fact, Gray (2010) argues that *The Matrix* alienated audiences and was a failure because it made transmedia obligatory rather than optional. Part of the problem with *The Matrix* was the usual expectation that transmedia is modular and audiences can consume as much or as little as they desire, distinguishing it from the more familiar serial model (Ryan 2015). It is not a case where you need every piece, in a particular order, to understand the others. Instead, there are usually multiple objects that exist in the same world or feature the same characters that can be mixed and matched without the overall experience feeling incomplete.

Transmedia also takes the form of world building, particularly in speculative media contexts (Edmond 2015; Ryan 2015). Marie-Laure Ryan (2015, 5) argues that world building is the primary form and calling it storytelling is a "misnomer." However, I argue that world building is the same structure as transmedia where a character travels across platforms or stories, seen with texts set in the quotidian world like reality TV (Edwards 2012), the Indiana Jones franchise (Hernández-Pérez and Rodríguez 2014), and sports. Therefore, because this provides depth and breadth as well as a sense of the existence of more beyond a single object, I call it transmedia dimensionality to include both world-building and traveling-character varieties. Dimensionality can, on the one hand, happen with additional objects that are modular but finite, like the DVD staple of deleted scenes, which provide more information but generally are not considered officially part of the story, or commentary that provides background on the larger system of which a given object is part. On the other hand, dimensionality can also mean producing additional objects that flesh out the world of the story, as when Felicia Day describes that the makers of *The Guild*

> actually wanted to shoot a fake trailer for *Necrotic Fury,* this thing he's acting out [in the scene from *The Guild*]. Yes. But we did not have the budget for it. Or the time to do it. But, like, our idea was to release the viral video, a fake trailer for the worst zombie movie ever, *Necrotic Fury,* and he would star in it as the stunt guy. [. . .] He was going to play multiple roles, like even for a woman, and it was obvious that he's obviously a stunt guy.

Through these additional media objects, audiences get a peek at the "more" beyond what is usually a central text, but in precise, determined chunks. This is what Hills (2014, 38) terms "de jure" transmedia; texts are formally expanded.

The second kind of transmedia dimensionality provides breadth and depth in an open format that fans can explore in their own way. One example of this *Heroes'* production of websites for its fictional organizations Primatech and the Yamagato Fellowship, which could be traversed however fans wanted for Easter eggs, which—like their namesake—people hunt for and find. This is also the kind of transmedia used when the UK instantiation of reality show *Big Brother* had twenty-four-hour web streaming of the interior of the house, letting audiences get past the editing of the aired show into a narrative and draw their own conclusions (Jones 2003). Open models often align with Hills's (2014, 38) "de facto" transmedia, where there is depth and breadth without formalized structure.

Open transmedia dimensionality is the primary kind for sports, like the "North American Soccer Almanac" at MLS.com that details the league's history to enrich (or not) one's experience, or letting people explore the Super Bowl more fully through providing "views from six camera angles (including the blimp)" (Story 1998) or "a 360-degree video camera that allowed on-line users to personally manipulate what they could see during media day" (Goldberg 2000). A staple of the Super Bowl is the NFL Experience portable interactive theme park, which celebrated its eighteenth anniversary in 2009 (Stacy 2009) and which seeks to give fans a full, immersive sports experience, including activities like "recording a voice-over commentary of memorable NFL plays, scoring a touchdown while tethered to a bungee harness, and throwing passes at a target" (Tang 2008). This immersive sports world is well known enough for a send-up in the 1999 *Simpsons* Super Bowl episode, "Sunday Cruddy Sunday," with an event that included booths for "Rosey Grier's Porta-Chapel," "Take a Leak with NFL Greats," "Caricatures by Aikman," and "Catch a Pass from Dan Marino." Thus, free-form transmedia dimensionality lets fans enter and explore the object of fandom seemingly at will.

Variation in fans' transmedia immersion motivates Campfire's "skimmer, dipper, and diver" typology of fan engagement, worth describing at length:

> To me, skimmers are kind of like that layer of, "Oh, that's interesting," you know what I mean? Like, "I'll click that link because I'm interested," but—or "I'll read that article because I'm interested," but—"Oh, that's cool" and they move on. Your dippers are kind of like the—they're the beginning of that social layer, they're very, very social. They're like "Oh, I *love* this show, I want to go *talk* to people about it, I may recommend it to friends," you know, "If I know that you watch it, we'll talk after every," whatever day we come back after it aired. "Did you see it?" or something, you know, "I'll go online, I'll engage with whatever's happening there, look for more info." And then there's the divers, who are, in the example that I gave you [a miniseries based on a book] these are the people who saw the multiple layers of depth and saw that "Wow, this thing actually extends to the whole universe and constellation of the things that I love, here." And so they are the

ones who—They're generally the ones who will do the things like the roleplaying. They'll do the—They'll dive in deep. They'll explore every nook and cranny of what we're doing. (Mike)

Everything Campfire does relies on calibrating their materials to how much fans want to submerge themselves, and their model assumes exploration beyond a single object—and it was in fact explained to me by each of them in their respective interviews.

That this is framed as a typology of the audience, rather than of transmedia, is key. Transmedia incites particular behavior from fans, and sometimes, as with Campfire, this is framed as particular kinds of people. Benjamin W. L. Derhy Kurtz (2014, 1) describes these frameworks as undertaken "to target involved audiences" as a type of person already existing out there waiting to be courted. Similarly, Steve from Campfire noted that

> a really strong element in our kind of work are fan subcultures that embrace story worlds rather than finite stories. Fantasy is very good, because it embraces a fantasy world that lives beyond the story. And we know—all those examples, from comic books to Star Wars to fantasy worlds, science fiction, like that. It gets more—Horror, sometimes. Vampires are big, right? There's a big fan culture around vampires because it's a larger mythology. [. . .] Once fans can embrace a story world, it certainly makes it less linear. It allows fans to explore pockets of the story world without contradiction.

These are framed as fan subcultures that already exist that Campfire seeks out and engages, then attempts to get them to seek out and engage with marketing materials because they enjoy exploring story worlds. Moreover, those fans are not just imagined to exist; they are constructed as the ideal. Alternatively, transmedia audiencing is constructed as requiring specific behaviors because transmedia functions by "inviting fans to look for clues outside of the program itself" (Gray 2010, 151) or by asking fans "to move between a range of different sites and media platforms," or by generally "encouraging audiences to be more actively and intimately involved" (Edmond 2015, 1576, 1567). In these ways, transmedia systems recruit particular actions as particular kinds of people, calling the ideal audience into being.

It is vital to take seriously Scott's (2011, 157) argument that transmedia strategies demand that fans invest a lot of time "consuming and (re) constructing the metanarrative the creators are carefully spreading across various media platforms." This is a construction of normative audiencing as consumption. This is true even though Consumption 2.0 is interactive and so might not seem consumptive at all. Transmedia may even be explicitly linked to consumption, as when Steve describes his role: "As a creative director, my job is to [long pause] create a story that fulfills strategic requirements of the client and consumption requirements of my target. And when I say consumption, I was going to say entertainment requirements, but it's not always entertainment requirements." Consumption is indispensable to the transmedia marketing Campfire does, unlike the "not always" criterion of entertainment.

In some ways Consumption 2.0 resembles what David Beer and Roger Burrows (2010, 7) call "participatory consumption," and this participatory aspect is the fundamental difference from old consumption. It is participatory because (desired) fans are understood to desire participation:

> If old consumers were assumed to be passive, the new consumers are active. If old consumers were predictable and stayed where you told them to stay, then new consumers are migratory, showing declining loyalty to networks or media. If old consumers were isolated individuals, the new consumers are more socially connected. If the work of media consumers was once silent and invisible, new consumers are noisy and public. (Jenkins 2006a, 18–19)

However, if we look at what these participatory audiences are understood and encouraged to do, it is limited: explore the story world, look for clues, move across platforms, and, above all. consume. Examining the apparent invitation to interactivity for how fans are asked to behave, the norm produced by transmedia is not interactive but reactive. Fans are invited to engage the options as given by the owner of the object of fandom, maintaining them firmly in a position of response. Transmedia is inherently consumptive.

The relationship of transmedia to consumption is clear when additional materials must be purchased. Tanya Krzywinska (2009, 396) points to consumption when she argues that convergence "depends increasingly on formulating devices to create long-stay audiences/consumers who will spend money to remain in contact with their preferred world." This kind of consumption is also encouraged by the sequel and the prequel, which, as Derek Johnson (2013) points out, creatively expand the story rather than simply replicating—and, I would add, they are clearly consumption in the economic sense because they come at additional cost. In these ways, providing more to audiences seeks to keep them engaged while also making more money from them (Derhy Kurtz 2014). Unpaid transmedia is also consumption, and here too what seems to be interaction is reaction, with interactivity giving fans far less control than it seems.

For example, both websites and industry workers routinely discuss polls, quizzes, games, and fantasy sports. This seems to expect a fan who wants to do something, but it actually defines interactivity as "point and click and be entertained" and as a choice within precoded options. Fans are not always or inevitably passive, of course, but this is what intensive consumption recruits. Providing bare-minimum action, a choice between hard-coded options, is basically no action at all—and in fact, as the mention of polls and quizzes in the TOS at both the Star Wars and Cal sites shows, these features provide sites with data about their users, which I argue in Chapter 5 is actually their purpose. The structure of reactivity shows most clearly with the "Mind Reader" special feature on the *Heroes* season 1 DVD, which invites fans to "pick a double-digit number from 1 to 100. Add the two digits together. Subtract that number from the original. Now find the hero associated with your new number." The game then displays numbers attached to character faces. Then one clicks through and sees the character one has selected, because the game has "read your mind." It works because the math problem has a finite number of solutions (multiples of nine) that are all set to the same character. The game does not actually require fan input, but there is an illusion that it matters which number is chosen. Although generally it is less transparent than this example, all reactivity is predesigned with set choices; fans can do things, but only within these options. This is what Ryan (2015, 11) calls "internal interactivity," where "the user's mode of participation is narrowly scripted by the system."

Fantasy sports, where fans draft teams of real players onto an imaginary team to compete against each other as managers, found at the ESPN, Mariners, and MLS sites (among other places), is a related kind of reactivity. On the one hand, fantasy sports seems to allow fans to construct their own meaning or narrative around a sport, which Erica Rosenfeld Halverson and Richard Halverson (2008) argue makes it structurally comparable to fan fiction because it reworks the primary object to produce new stories. When scholars can chart a shift in how traditional media companies present sports statistics in response to the fantasy sports boom—they provide fantasy-specific information that is meaningless in terms of regular sports to maintain their relevance to sports consumption even as it changes (Comeau 2007; Dwyer 2009; Halverson and Halverson 2008)—it seems that industry is simply responding to fan desire for interactivity. Troy O. Comeau (2007) and Brendan Dwyer (2009) both chart a shift of loyalty away from teams and toward specific players, challenging the team as the traditional object of fandom, which similarly seems to put fans in control rather than industry.[3] However, these changes to sports do not change fans' position as reacting and consuming. As Nickolas W. Davis and Margaret Carlisle Duncan (2006) argue, fantasy sports requires a high level of knowledge, rooted in extensive sports consumption. Comeau (2007) identifies fantasy sports participants as much more involved than traditional fans, as they have to seek out information across sources to further their strategies—that is, they must consume. Most importantly, fans' only role is to choose players, because after that point, success or failure in the game comes from how the real players perform on the real field, meaning that again, interactivity is reactive.

THE OLD NORMAL, THE NEW NORMAL, AND THE FAN NORMAL

As we've seen, industry engagement with fans recruits many kinds of consumption, even intensive and expansive kinds. This new norm seems like the practices of intensive consumption and expansive desire historically associated with being a fan, which is why people argue that fannish intensive, interactive consumption has become normative for all consumers. These practices used to be clearly marginalized as passive and uncritical, so their incorporation into industry's engagement with fans appears to recuperate formerly excessive desire and consumption.

Hills (2002, 36) argues that considering fans resistant to industry is not totally unreasonable because they want to linger on their text (in an echo of Freudian perverse desire) rather than keep consuming new ones the way industry desires. However, Hills also recognizes that even then, more than fifteen years ago, "Fandom has begun to furnish a model of dedicated and loyal consumption [. . .]. Fan consumers are no longer viewed as eccentric irritants, but rather as loyal consumers to be created, where possible, or otherwise to be courted through scheduling practices." As Krzywinska (2009, 396) notes, "While shows that encouraged this type of consumption used to be considered 'cultish' and marginal to mainstream popular culture, they are now becoming central." Hills (2014) gives the example that BBC's *Sherlock* TV show made intertextual references to the Sherlock Holmes stories in order to hail Sherlockians as a detail-oriented fan base. However, although I am sympathetic to Jenkins's (2007) caution that fan scholars should not automatically assume (or celebrate) that fans are marginalized, declaring fan consumption normative is premature and inattentive to inequality. New norms absolutely include things fans do, but selectively, and when they are officially provided, top down, they differ in important ways from practices initiated and controlled by fans.

Discomfort with fannish consumption persists. Judgments that intense desires for the object of fandom are distasteful are still apparent in comments from industry workers, indicating that the new normal may not be as different from the old normal as it seems, and certainly it is not identical to traditional fan norms. People believe fans will buy anything even vaguely associated with the object of fandom, leading actor Greg Grunberg of *Heroes* to joke in a DVD commentary, "I'm going to go into the chimes business, because people are gonna buy chimes to try and call for the Haitian," a character who gives a friend wind chimes she can use to contact him for help. Indeed, some of the wackier licensed items industry produces seem to make exactly this assumption of unstoppable consumption. *Fever Pitch*'s Boston Red Sox fan Ben not only sleeps on Sox sheets, but does so while wearing a Red Sox shirt and matching boxer shorts. Ben also decorates wholly with Sox decor and keepsakes and uses Red Sox dishes and towels—and New York Yankees toilet paper. Belief in voracious consumption also manifests as visualizing fans' personal spaces as shrinelike. A room plastered on all surfaces with the object of fandom is a common trope: Gil in *The Fan* has a space wallpapered with newspaper clippings about player Bobby Rayburn, the Giants, and baseball in general; *My Name Is Bruce*'s teenage enthusiast Jeff has decorated his bedroom in much the same way with every Bruce Campbell item ever made (including drain cleaner); and Hutch's garage apartment in *Fanboys* has Star Wars curtains, action figures, lunch boxes, and what appear to be torn-out pages from comic books on the wall. From the other side, production personnel are often hesitant to mention things fans might rush out and buy, showing lingering distrust of unruly and excessive fan desire. Unease about fan consumptive excess therefore remains even in the supposedly profan era, showing that the fan norm of legitimately expansive desire has not been adopted.

Rather, engagements with fan desire seek to harness it to meet industry's desires. Industry certainly wants fans to consume. It is seen as essential, and the presence of stuff is often how you can tell someone is a fan in representations. Characters in *The Guild* or *The Big Bang Theory* are often wearing some licensed item—a hat, belt buckle, or T-shirt—referencing a media object of which they are a fan. Ben of *Fever Pitch*, of the previously elaborated Sox Central apartment, convinces his girlfriend to take an interest in the Red Sox, which is visually indicated when she starts wearing clothing with the logo. In these ways, to some extent, we are told, as are convention-goers in the science fiction spoof *Galaxy Quest*, "Don't forget to buy a *Galaxy Quest* T-shirt on your way out. Thank you."

Industry desires even more intense fan desire, like building loyalty or attachment to fan objects or characters. This relationship often takes time to build, which Mike notes can be difficult to explain to marketers unfamiliar with fans:

> "Oh the *first* thing I do gets this kind of response, but I've laid the groundwork, and if I *continue* and I'm smart about it, that will grow," like the way a TV show grows. Hopefully season two gets more and season three and season four and by season five you're a pop culture phenomenon like *True Blood*, right? That's the goal. And I think that— But brands haven't really recognized, they haven't thought about their marketing in terms of eliciting that kind of growth in, whatever, love for their brand or attention.

The slow build or the long-term relationship between fan and object is what is moving from fannish marginality to normativity. Recasting fan desire into industry's value system narrows the gap between the fan norm and contemporary mainstream norms, but Mike's comment also shows the shift is not complete.

We need to take seriously that embracing formerly fannish modes of consumption relies on them aligning with industry's desire. Hills (2014) notes that DVD commentaries assume and cater to the fan desire to know, but they also act to reinforce industry control over the text's meaning. Stephanie James (2013, 320–21) contends that the kinds of participation that are invited are specifically those that "do not threaten the intellectual property of the media conglomerate," and IP is only one part of what industry seems to protect. Scott (2011, 150–51) describes "conflict between those who claim that transmedia storytelling systems offer fans sophisticated webs of content to explore and enhance, and those that see these webs as precisely that: a mode of confining and regulating fannish analysis and textual production." That is, some see transmedia intensification of consumption as entrapment—including, elsewhere, Suzanne Scott (2007) herself, who terms these forms of transmedia gap filling "Moore-ing" after *BSG* showrunner Ronald D. Moore and critiqued it as tying fan creativity down by leaving no ambiguities to explore. The concern is that transmedia content, producing the same kinds of objects fans do, can displace fan activity, "making fan-produced texts that seek to engage with the *Battlestar Galactica* canon more difficult to produce and less likely to be consumed" (Scott 2007, 212). Whether or not industry intends to orient fans to consumption, enhancing consumption encourages it by making the path of least resistance that much more rewarding and fulfilling desires through consumption. By the domestication model, this is a bid to accustom fans to eating out of industry's hand rather than finding their own food.

Through such strategies, Simone Murray (2004, 10) notes, industry both seeks "maximum emotional investment by consumers in a given content brand" and wants "to corral such emotional attachment into purely consumptive—as opposed to creative—channels." Importantly—to think back to Chapter 1 and the idea that industry norms recruit some fans and not others—stoking the desire to consume can produce exclusions. After all, "consumer culture does not only create desire in those who can easily obtain" its products (Crawford 2004, 127). All forms of leisure are class stratified (Veblen [1899] 2000), but the intensive relationship of fans to consumption amplifies the effect and produces the normative fan as one with disposable income, which is itself shaped by race and gender stratification in income. Additionally, "customers have no means of registering their demand for products that are not offered to them" (Herman and Chomsky 1988, 339), and ongoing marginalization of people of color, white women, and queer folks from mainstream texts mean their authorized extensions will not serve those populations either.

However, the greater danger is a more subtle one. Scott (2011, 158) worries that "millennial consumers making the leap from casual viewer to fan may be adept at navigating various media flows and accustomed to the type of 'community' that Web 2.0 social networking fosters, but they are also more likely to mistake this form of 'mediated interactivity' for fan participation." She is absolutely right to be critical, but in place of the control framing that she and other skeptical authors use, arguing that industry deploys transmedia to try to shut fans up, I contend that selective and narrow engagement with fans is better viewed as normalization. Contemporary consumption norms pitch intensive engagement so fans get what they desire in ways that (conveniently enough) do not challenge industry interests, whether financial or reputational. It gives not so fans cannot or will not take, but so they do not have to bother. It makes intensive engagement easy in a way that defines proper fans as consumers. Describing the equation of "mediated interactivity" with fan participation as a "mistake" collapses the moral contention that fans should not be reduced that way (and I agree) into an empirical contention that the social meaning of fans is not flattened this way. However, this flattening is exactly what industry attempts in the period this book examines. The process I chart in this chapter is precisely about defining the true fan as affirmational rather than transformational—the one who enjoys the story as it is given rather than changing it.[4] Social beliefs about fans are changing. Those who appreciate what fandom has traditionally been may well contest the shift, but it is vital to recognize that the norm invites fans to desire in straight lines.

Ultimately, understanding the coalescing norms for fans in the period this book examines requires attention to consumption. Fans obviously consume because it fulfills their desires. However, at the same time, they have a constrained set of options to choose, and their desires are themselves social. The kinds of consumption discussed here are all both constructed as essential fan desires and actively facilitated, demonstrating the process of managing desire, and these norms construct fan desire as fundamentally consumptive. Even transmedia, seemingly interactive and user controlled, is inherently consumptive; it has not radically altered the traditional model of passive consumers who should grin and buy it. Industry approaches to fans in the period this book examines undoubtedly recruit and want fan desire, but they actually recruit reaction, which tries to manage fan desire, thus troubling ideas that fans are newly empowered by being courted as the ideal consumer. They are instead recruited to be docile and useful—that is, they are domesticated.

However, the counterpoint to industry's desire for fan desire is that fan consumption can be leveraged. The drive to normalize fans into useful consumption can be if not reversed then at least nudged to serve fan needs. This is the logic of the buycott. Although there are definite limits to using consumer power, and although it is a deeply neoliberal strategy, consumption can be a site for collective action (Vered and Humphreys 2014; Dawes 2014; Willis and Schor 2012). This is what *Chuck* fans did as they loudly and visibly bought from the show's sponsors to proclaim their financial power and support the show's renewal (Savage 2014). In such ways, the norms working to domesticate fan activity are powerful and pervasive, but not deterministic.

CHAPTER FOUR

THE LONG ARM OF (BELIEFS ABOUT) THE LAW

The law is popularly imagined (and likes to imagine itself) as neutral, disinterested, fact based, and objective. Justice is, after all, represented as blind. However, the law—and, for the purposes of this chapter, IP law in particular—is both produced and interpreted in a cultural context. For example, Japanese copyright laws are not more permissive than American ones, but Japanese corporations are more relaxed about enforcement, producing a thriving market for fan production (Koulikov 2010; Noppe 2015). Because beliefs about law shape behavior, then, what people believe about law and when and how they appeal to it are important to examine. My approach here is like the legal consciousness tradition, "developed within law and society [research] in the 1980s and 1990s to address issues of legal hegemony, particularly how the law sustains its institutional power despite a persistent gap between the law on the books and the law in action" (Silbey 2005, 323). Legal consciousness focuses in particular on the legal understanding of people who are not legal professionals, considering how beliefs about law shape how it functions as well as how law both comes out of and reproduces larger social structures (Ewick and Silbey 1991; Silbey 2005).

Through convergent scholarly evolution, several media studies authors have investigated what everyday media users think about copyright in parallel to this legal studies tradition. Some research investigates why user perspectives diverge from the law so they can be corrected (Aufderheide, Jaszi, and Brown 2007). Other scholars are interested in using everyday beliefs to shape law (Collins 2010). Most often, researchers treat lay legal interpretation as worthy of study like any other belief or practice, asking what people think is acceptable and unacceptable, how it differs from what the law says, and why that disconnect matters. These studies show that expansive corporate claims of IP control are viewed negatively (Benkler 2007; Collins 2010; Fredriksson 2014). People also tend to consider remixing popular culture acceptable, seeing it as free advertising for media industries (Aufderheide, Jaszi, and Brown 2007; Edwards et al. 2015). Even file sharing, which has been thoroughly propagandized as theft, is still socially unsettled (Mansell and Steinmueller 2013), with many users both classifying it as illegal and not particularly considering the law legitimate (Gillespie 2007).

Most directly relevant here is research examining fan beliefs about law. Scholars tell us fans believe they cannot sell their works (Coombe 1998; De Kosnik 2009), or that not selling them makes fan creative production legally safer (De Kosnik 2013).[1] Fans often perceive their creative work as illegal in a strict sense but not morally wrong (Fiesler 2007; Tushnet 2007a), or even, like other users, that it is helpful to rights holders as free advertising (Tushnet 2007a). In fact, the tradition of appending disclaimers to fan fiction can be seen as demonstrating fan legal consciousness. In a disclaimer, "the author would state that she did not own the copyright in the characters and situations, name the entity that did (or the original creator, who is usually not the copyright owner), and sometimes add a request that the copyright owner not sue her" (Tushnet 2007a, 154). This practice shows the fan cultural norm of proper attribution, with fans not taking credit for work that is not theirs and giving credit where it is due (Fiesler 2007; Tushnet 2007a). It also shows a belief that fans can avoid copyright infringement the same way as plagiarism (Tushnet 2007a). Casey Fiesler (2007) and Rebecca Tushnet (2007b) have in fact suggested that fan legal beliefs might be a better model than current law.

In the spirit of this work looking at fan and user copyright beliefs, this chapter analyzes what beliefs media industries demonstrate about law. In their relationships with fans, when and how do media organizations use legalistic language, when and how do they act in legalistic ways, and what does that tell us about how industry's legal consciousness shapes the fan–industry relationship? In some ways my inquiry departs from legal consciousness, which considers the legal understanding of laypeople, since media organizations surely include lawyers; indeed, lawyers write the TOS that are one of my key objects of analysis. However, as I will show through examining industry worker statements, representation, and especially the design and policies of websites, industry legal action does not particularly match the letter of the law but rather the fundamental fan–industry relationship, across both speculative media and sports, is an assumption of complete industry control. In this way, media industry action demonstrates Patricia Ewick and Susan S. Silbey's (1999, 1031) category of legal consciousness as acting "with the law." More legally knowledgeable or familiar people, they argue, perceive the law as a tool to leverage however they can, which is exactly what media organizations and their armies of lawyers do, even when that requires contradictory interpretations of law at different points. Accordingly, it is not only possible but productive to investigate the legal consciousness demonstrated by media workers and the websites and documents they produce.

My analysis, then, brings together thinking of law as a text—it does not have transcendent meaning but must be interpreted (Coombe 1998)—and as a technology (Gillespie 2007)—a tool designed and used by people to do particular things. Alexis Lothian (2009, 132) similarly interrogates how people make sense of law, contending, "It is worth determining who defines the use as fair, and what it might mean to place a value on unfair uses." I reframe the issue as "Which uses are considered fair, by whom, and for whom?"—but my concerns are comparable. Law is indeterminate; this explains and conditions its contingency or even capriciousness. After all, given two similar uses of IP, one can be found legally protected and the other not, without particularly clear criteria beyond which side had the lawyerly skill to convince a court. This is why sometimes law overrides technology, legally preventing uses that are technologically possible (Boyle 2008; Gillespie 2007; Petersen 2015). Other times, technology is used instead of law to control behavior (Gillespie 2007; Lessig 1999, 2006), or even to exceed the letter of the law (Favale 2014; Gillespie 2007; Tushnet 2014) through making legally permissible actions technologically impossible.

In this chapter I will first give a history of copyright, then discuss the three ways industry overreaches in its relationships with fans: with scary legalese, by coding for control, and through TOS as contracts. Ultimately, I argue, the tendency in media industry legalistic practices is toward private gain at public expense.

WHAT IS COPYRIGHT FOR? FROM MONOPOLY TO OWNERSHIP

Article I, Section 8, Clause 8 of the United States Constitution, known as the Copyright Clause, identifies the purpose of copyright protection as "To promote the Progress of Science and useful Arts," which is accomplished "by securing for limited Times to Authors and Inventors the exclusive Right to their respective Writings and Discoveries." This has two key components. First, the reason for securing that exclusive right is encouraging more science and arts—that is, it serves a public good (Boyle 2008; Hyde 2010). Second, exclusive control is time limited, after which materials become freely available in the public domain—that is, they become owned by the public (Hyde 2010; Khanna 2012; Olson 2012). This is because the framers of the Constitution, notably Thomas Jefferson, were wary of state-sanctioned monopolies and saw IP as the state granting monopolies on ideas (Hyde 2010). This legal formulation also, importantly, assumed IP did not automatically exist without action to establish it. IP requires active intervention because, unlike physical property, information is nonrivalrous—my use of it does not preclude anyone else's (Benkler 2007; Boyle 2003; Wittel 2012)—and nonexcludable—it is impossible (for now) to prevent people who have not paid from using it (Boyle 2003; Favale 2014; Gillespie 2007). The law therefore acts to "create private property rights in cultural forms" where they do not otherwise exist (Coombe 1998, 6) by producing "a bundle of [. . .] property-like rights" (Favale 2014, 125) to make information act like property through making use without payment a source of civil liability or a crime. While nonexcludability is a long-standing and fundamental challenge, it is particularly important in a digital era as physical media becomes increasingly less common and nonrivalrous use becomes even easier.

The eighteenth-century framework might seem strange today, when the dominant belief is that someone who creates something has complete control over it. However, under the model of creativity when the Constitution was written, creative production is only partially the work of the author, either arising from external intervention, like a muse or divine inspiration (Hyde 2010), or the result of the skillful redeployment of existing cultural materials within a tradition, like craftsmanship in a guild or musical improvisation on known melodies (Arewa 2013; Fredriksson 2014; Toula and Lisby 2014).[2] The Constitution operates from a belief that new work builds from previous work and that arts and sciences do not come into being from nothing. This is why the law is structured so works pass into the public domain after a period of protection. The public domain is seen as a cultural and intellectual commons, from which creators benefit, and which their works in turn enrich (Hyde 2010; Toula and Lisby 2014). Property claims are limited so creators pay forward the benefit they have gained and do not prevent others from creating as they themselves built on what came before (Gordon 1992; Toula and Lisby 2014). Both aspects are crucial here, because if access to previously created culture is closed off through copyright, subsequent creativity becomes harder (Boyle 2003; Gordon 1992; Lessig 2004). Despite what rights holders argue, sharing information multiplies it rather than taking something away from the first person, much like the analogy James Boyle (2008) uses in which Thomas Jefferson compares sharing an idea to lighting one candle from another. Thus, the ways physical objects or resources can be overextended do not apply (Boyle 2003). To get to the artificial scarcity needed for supply and demand, we not only need government legal intervention but we also have to reframe something that by default is infinite and not diminished by use as able to be used up or worn out.

The Constitution therefore balances rewarding creativity and not foreclosing future creativity. The reward is supposed to encourage more creativity (Boyle 2008) and benefit the public (Edwards et al. 2015), not solely the author. As Tarleton Gillespie (2007) reminds us, the reward is a means to an end, not an end in itself that the author "deserves." There was, then, a public interest rationale for withholding culture (built from other culture) from the public, although Tushnet (2004) points out it is not clear where the limit should be to protect further creativity, and Yochai Benkler (2007) adds that we only assume reward encourages production. However, even as flexible as they are, these logics have largely been abandoned in the contemporary era.

If historically copyright means the state agrees to use its power to enforce a monopoly over a thing that is made and is a privilege, particularly since the late twentieth century there has been a shift to a belief that authorship confers ownership and therefore property rights. Shifting IP more and more toward property can be seen in the ballooning of copyright lengths from a fixed term—initially fourteen years—to the duration of the author's life plus fifty years in 1976 (or seventy-five years after publication for corporate authorship) and seventy and ninety-five years, respectively, in 1998 with the Copyright Term Extension Act. Traces of the legal and rhetorical move to establish IP also show in how media industry workers and news coverage consistently call media objects "properties," which for example was routine from Steve and Mike at Campfire as they discussed their previous work and hypothetical scenarios I posed to them. Property ownership implies permanence and complete control over the owned object, overriding the limits built into copyright.

The ownership framework for copyright, like the monopoly framework before it, comes out of a specific understanding of authorship. Indeed, Rosemary J. Coombe (1998, ix) describes her book on IP as "about the conceits of authorship and the peculiar powers it confers." As opposed to the previous model of inspiration or creation within a tradition, with the rise of romanticism from the late eighteenth through the mid-nineteenth centuries, the author came to be seen as the singular origin of artistic production from nothing more than (usually) his genius (Arewa 2013; Fredriksson 2014; Toula and Lisby 2014). Martha Woodmansee (1984) argues that this shift was deeply rooted in economics, and authorial genius was invented specifically to justify and enable writing as a profession. That model of authorship as unique genius, along with the reverence it recruits, morally authorizes greater restrictions on what can be done with an author's works. It also disclaims any role for building on previous creativity and defines cultural objects as end points of the creative process that are not eligible to be used as building blocks for further creativity. If authorship is the product of an isolated creative mind, total ownership is logical in a way it is not under other models.

However, if the purpose of copyright is to encourage creation by rewarding the creator, what the current system tends to reward is the corporate rights holder, who is the legal "author" but not by any authorship model the source of creativity, and that makes the relationship to encouraging creativity even fuzzier. As Foucault (1980) reminds us, authorship is a technology, a way to assign texts to an entity constructed by the laws and institutions of its context. The idea that a corporation can be an author—like the idea that a corporation is a person entitled to free speech or protection of its religious beliefs—is an historical invention reflecting the position of corporations in the current social system. Thomas G. Schumacher (1995, 264n11) identifies this as "one of the fundamental contradictions in legal theory: its reliance on the myth of the original, individual author is coupled with the abandonment of the author-subject for the corporate rights–holding-subject." Certainly, as is clearest with music but also the case in other media, the actual people making copyrighted materials are enmeshed in "a system of contracts [. . .] that makes feudal indenture look benign" (Boyle 2008, 77); these people do not have the legal status of authors for works they create. In fact, as Tushnet (2007a) recounts, there may even be differences in attitude toward reuse between the author and corporate rights holder, as when Joss Whedon had no problem with fan creativity but Fox surely did, and fans in turn often have much clearer reverence for and knowledge of the author than the rights holder. Overall, an ownership-control model has largely supplanted protecting and encouraging creativity as the driving force of contemporary copyright action and belief.

Today, the belief is that rights holders have control by default over their copyrighted materials. This framework is "not premised upon what is the public good or what will promote the most productivity and innovation, but rather what the content creators 'deserve' or are 'entitled to' by virtue of their creation" (Khanna 2012, 1), so it also deletes the public interest rationale of copyright. To go along with extending copyright in time, contemporary models support intensive control, under the logic that people and organizations can and should control and maximize every use of materials to which they hold the rights. As Coombe (1998) notes, the belief is if things have market value, then the rights holder should be able to control them and reap that financial gain. This absolute right to economically exploit what you want, when you want, shows most clearly when there is conflict, as with a lawsuit from retired National Football League (NFL) players against the NFL Players Association over using their images without paying to license them, thus unfairly depriving them of their due revenue (Elias 2008). In this framework, for example, Disney's high purchase price for Marvel Comics is justified because control over its IP provides vast potential licensing revenues (Nakashima 2009). Of course, this is perfectly reasonable from an economic perspective, since, as Gray (2010) notes, there is much more money in selling a child every toy and T-shirt in existence than in selling them one movie ticket. This same belief system leads sports media organizations to purchase various rights to freeze out competitors or bundle them for sale to increase their market value (Boyle 2015). In all ways, precise and total control is the goal.

Total control also manifests in maximizing revenues through carefully orchestrated geographical or time-based distribution structures. For example, Merrin notes that Campfire might need to coordinate sharing materials with different marketing agencies "if they're distributing in one way in this country and in another way [elsewhere]—maybe there's a time lapse, and that sort of thing." Intranationally, both the Mariners as part of Major League Baseball (MLB) and MLS devote lengthy sections of their TOS to how their online streaming services are subject to geographical restriction: "Live games will be blacked out in each applicable Club's home television territory," MLB says, adding that "blackout restrictions apply regardless of whether a Club is home or away and regardless of whether or not a game is televised in a Club's home television territory." This reflects the sports value system where live attendance is preferred over television viewing, since broadcasting in the team's local market often occurs only when games sell out, and television is preferred over internet streaming because TV revenues, one of the largest revenue sources (Buraimo and Simmons 2009; Sullivan 2006), risk being undercut by streaming competition.[3] Importantly, not making content available creates market failure, preventing people from accessing things they would pay (or watch ads) for, but herding fans into the more lucrative pasture is evidently preferred even at the cost of losing some. In these ways, it is clear the contemporary belief is that copyright produces total control, and especially total right to micro- and macromonetize.

Belief in entitlement to financial benefit from the rights one holds drives assumptions that all unauthorized uses are harmful. Mark Andrejevic (2009a, 410) calls the idea that unauthorized uses are equivalent to lost sales "absurd on its face," and even the more neutral Government Accountability Office (2010, 18) indicates that a "one-to-one substitution rate is not likely to exist in most circumstances." R. Rob and J. Waldfogel (2006) find that illegal downloads corresponded to a reduction of only 10 to 20 percent in sales when they examine music in particular. However, rights holders often "argue that even if an unauthorized use is not substituting for current sales, the owner could be making *more* money if he had the right to authorize the use" (Tushnet 2007b, 514). This reflects the belief that the only measure that matters is revenue, as opposed to having concern for a more ambiguous measurement like value (Boyle 2015). Belief in total macro- and microcontrol thus leads rights holders to shut down fan activity even when it is not objectionable, as when Steve of Campfire notes that *The Hunger Games* had stopped an unauthorized alternate reality game "because if they don't shut it down first, then all the subsequent uses can claim that as a precedent. When I hear it most often, that's a danger, the danger of, if we've set—what would that precedent lead to." The fear of precedent undermining control also animates MLS's TOS insistence that "MLS's failure to enforce any provisions of these Terms of Service or respond to a breach by you or another user shall not serve to waive MLS's right [to] enforce subsequently any terms or conditions of these Terms of Service or to act with respect to similar breaches." There is great concern to never cede control.

This trajectory from monopoly to ownership, finite to seemingly infinite, as Coombe (1998, 6) describes, is a "massive expansion of the scope and duration of intellectual property rights since the mid-eighteenth century and an even greater growth and proliferation of legal protections in the twentieth century." This is particularly true after the Copyright Term Extension Act and the Digital Millennium Copyright Act (DMCA), both from 1998. In fact, Benkler (2007, 383) notes that the DMCA also established "new paracopyright powers" that far exceeded controlling copies, producing a model where "reading my e-book on your machine is either technically impossible, a crime, or a tort—or possibly all three" (Boyle 2003, 50). These legal and technological moves assume, or at least argue, that technological progress threatens creativity itself rather than just endangering particular business models (Boyle 2008), so companies enlist the law to protect their "rights" to monetary gain rather than adapting (Benkler 2007; Boyle 2008). As Benkler (2007) notes, the DMCA is fundamentally about separating IP from being a product of culture as well as making it behave like property.

The DMCA's premise, that rights holders should control all uses, is a major departure from the previous idea that authors had some control but other uses were permitted—that is, fair use (Benkler 2007). The Copyright Act of 1976 explicitly codified the idea that the monopoly privilege of the copyright owner was balanced with the public's free speech rights to fair use comprising specific, limited uses of copyrighted material. The relevant statute, 17 USC § 107, indicates the following:

> In determining whether the use made of a work in any particular case is a fair use the factors to be considered shall include—(1) the purpose and character of the use, including whether such use is of a commercial nature or is for nonprofit educational purposes; (2) the nature of the copyrighted work; (3) the amount and substantiality of the portion used in relation to the copyrighted work as a whole; and (4) the effect of the use upon the potential market for or value of the copyrighted work.

Courts are asked to assess alleged infringement on the basis of whether, by meeting these conditions, the use is fair.

Although fair use continues to explicitly exist in the law, the DMCA forbids circumvention of digital rights management (DRM) technologies, which functionally allows industry to technologically prevent all unauthorized uses of their products, whether a court might find them fair or not (Benkler 2007; Gillespie 2007; Petersen 2015). The DMCA is frequently seen as a departure from previous thinking like *Sony v. Universal* (1984), also known as the Betamax case, when the Supreme Court ruled that just because a technology can infringe copyright does not mean it can be outlawed if it also has substantial noninfringing uses (Boyle 2008). As Marcella Favale (2014) argues, given the existence of fair use as the public's right to use culture, DRM should not be imposed at all unless the technology allows fair use, much like when neighbors have trespass rights on land, a fence cannot be put up if it keeps them out. The ways the DMCA is often misused to restrict fair use were in fact judged improper by the Ninth Circuit in *Lenz v. Universal* (2015), which held that fair use must be considered before material is removed from the internet, but it is not clear how this is implemented in practice. In these ways, then, the historical notion of copyright as limited and public focused has largely been discarded in favor of a model of private control and gain.

SCARE TACTICS, TECHNOLOGY, AND CONTRACTS AS COPYRIGHT PROXIES

The Law as Bludgeon and Scary Legalese

Even the expansive powers created under the DMCA, however, differ from the chronic scare tactics and ownership overreach of media industries that supplement or even supplant the control provided by copyright. Importantly, although Foucault (1995) contends that overall, there has been a shift away from sovereign, repressive power to disciplinary, productive power, and although this book is mostly focused on the use of carrots to shape fan behavior, there are still sticks, and the law is the primary one. Corporations routinely assert excessive control that relies on generally low public legal literacy to compel broad compliance. On the one hand, this manifests as constructing the law as the ultimate, incontestable power. Thus, privacy policies often promise to safeguard personal data while noting that the law could compel the site owner to do otherwise: "In the event we are required to respond to subpoenas, court orders or other legal process your personally identifiable information may be disclosed pursuant to such subpoena, court order or legal process, which may be without notice to you" (University of California, Berkeley, Athletics). Alternatively, TOS indicate that the owner would like to exert more control, but they are stopped from doing so by law, as when ESPN notes that their terms "apply to the maximum extent permitted by applicable law" or that they will (perhaps begrudgingly) "obtain your consent" when "required by applicable law." Holding up the law as the highest authority in this way aligns industry's power ideologically with law's power, encouraging users to obey other terms that may not align with law at all.

As a result, in a seeming contradiction in fact enabled by the attitude that law is all-powerful, website terms routinely use legalistic language to exceed law. For example, sites declare a jurisdiction to which users must consent, but note that it is "without regards to [the jurisdiction's] principles of conflicts of law" (SyFy). What is common between the two approaches is that the legalistic language lends cultural legitimacy to industry's pronouncements, which is in many ways the fundamental characteristic of TOS. This is one way that, as Jenkins (2006a, 138) notes, "studios often assert much broader control than they could legally defend." A study by the Brennan Center for Justice (2005) finds that nearly half of all demands for content to be removed from the internet either make questionable claims to copyright ownership or target fair uses, but these claims in excess of the law still often result in content being removed because of low legal literacy. Industry often deploys cease-and-desist letters, particularly to suppress things they dislike (Jenkins 2006a; Koulikov 2010; Tushnet 2014). These are generally effective because fans are not able to contest industry in court (Fiesler 2007; Jenkins 2006a). For example, Will Brooker (2002) recounts Lucasfilm's crackdown on fan fiction that did not comply with what it considered to be the franchise's family values. Patricide and incest were apparently OK, but homosexuality not so much, resulting in self-censorship in this fandom—a case of successful domestication. Favale (2014) argues that industry itself breaks the law in this overreach by preventing people from exercising the rights the law reserves to them by fair use. It is generally agreed, however, that industry can functionally shut down fan activity at any time (De Kosnik 2013; Murray 2004; Ross 2009), as internet service providers and social media platforms tend to—and are more or less required by the safe harbor provisions of the DMCA to—err on the side of the corporation (Consalvo 2003; Jenkins, Ford, and Green 2013; Russo 2009).[4]

What became known as PotterWar demonstrates how these scare tactics are used. It began, routinely enough, with Warner Bros., as the Harry Potter film studio and rights holder, attempting to shut down unauthorized websites that it saw as infringing its IP. However, these were not just any unauthorized sites. As Heather Lawver, age fifteen, described it in the Harry Potter documentary *We Are Wizards*, "One day a friend of mine, she had gotten a letter from Warner Bros. telling her that if she did not shut down her website they would sic their lawyers on her, and basically she was scared out of her mind. She was this 12-year-old girl who thought that she was going to go to prison because she was running a Harry Potter fan site."[5] Warner Bros. had attacked children at sites like "The Daily Prophet, which was an online newspaper for children that focused on creative writing." To resist, fans orchestrated

> a worldwide boycott. We had people petitioning for us, and picketing in London. We had people in Poland. There was a *huge* group of people in Poland who had been threatened. [. . .] We didn't have an argument with J. K. Rowling, so we were going to keep buying the books like usual, but we weren't going to go see the movies, we weren't going to buy any of the toys, nothing, just anything that was Harry Potter was off limits.

In the end, Warner Bros. retreated from its complete-shutdown approach.

This incident is interesting on several levels. First, because threatening children is a PR disaster, Warner Bros. ultimately backed off. Lawver says, "It took quite a while before we got in contact with someone at Warner Bros. For a while they just kind of thought of us as the PotterWar problem. They refused to dignify our questions with an answer," because from their default perspective, these were just IP thieves. However, "once we had been on the cover of *USA Today* we finally got their attention." With news coverage, they became a public perception problem that meant Warner Bros.' approach had to change. Second, the story is explicitly framed in the documentary as overreach. The film lets Lawver speak for herself and thus discursively authorizes her contention that "we wanted the same rights that any fan should have. People used to have clubhouses for *Howdy Doody* or any other TV show or book, but because it is on the internet, it was threatening, and we wanted to show that we weren't threatening. We were just fans of the books—remind them that the fans are what gives them their money and gives them their power." In this way, interacting with copyrighted materials is legitimized as a "right any fan should have," and specifically not a threat to corporate power.

Third, the framing of the broader fight as "big, bad corporation versus children" situates copyright practice as fundamentally just but misapplied in this case. Lawver and her compatriots are treated as innocent children (as they are) when she notes, "I never really thought that I would be involved in some huge legal battle." She repeatedly uses the word "threaten" to describe Warner Bros.' actions. However, Lawver is also framed as having a "correct" baseline understanding of the law: "I don't know why I knew better, but I just knew that letter was full of baloney and I knew that I could do something about it," she says at the beginning of the PotterWar segment of the documentary, and near the end she indicates, "I understand that on a legal basis Warner Bros. does have to protect what they own. They own the rights to the words 'Hogwarts' and 'Hagrid' and 'Harry Potter.'" Lawver's approach to the law is authorized not only by the outcome of the incident being in her favor but also internally to the documentary, when the authority of scholar Henry Jenkins is deployed to support her: "Here's a young girl who at the age of fourteen or fifteen begins to become part of a conversation, publicly, to challenge the studio's rights to assert their control over intellectual property. She goes on national television and debates the value of fan participation, and through this process she gets Warner Bros. to rethink their position on intellectual property." In this way, while the documentary treats Warner Bros.' legal overreach as poor fan relations, it also constructs it as legitimate control.

The belief underlying actions like those of Warner Bros. is that rights holders take precedence. Although total control is not the letter of the law (much less its spirit), people without financial resources to pay lawyers, let alone a copyright judgment with many zeros, tend to give in (Jenkins 2006a). As Tushnet (2014) points out, people have to know a fair amount about the law to resist. The end result, therefore, is often the use of copyright to censor things rights holders dislike (Brennan Center for Justice 2005; Tushnet 2007a, 2014). This echoes how rights holders leverage legal status to seek technological control, including over third parties. Ramon Lobato, Julian Thomas, and Dan Hunter (2011) describe Viacom's lawsuit against YouTube as trying to control the entire platform rather than simply the specific works to which they hold the copyright. What is happening in these cases is that industry exceeds what law permits, or it deploys people's fear of law to try to make fans docile and compliant.

Coding for Control

Like legal overreach, the capacities designed into and out of technologies are not just neutrally what the technology does, nor equivalent to the capital-L Law as an authority, but rather the product of corporate legal consciousness. Lawrence Lessig (1999, 2006) famously calls on internet researchers to examine code—the technology itself—over law, and others note that technological control often exceeds law (Gillespie 2007; Tushnet 2007b, 2014). Technology matters, for example, because nondownloadable video formats like Flash produce a technological default of read only (Consalvo 2003; Russo 2010). When the website of SyFy TV show *Battlestar Galactica* (*BSG*) had a widget that let fans put videos of the show on their own sites, this seemingly departed from copyright protectivism. However, because of the way the widget was designed, fans could not really take the videos unless they cracked the Flash encoding, which is not default knowledge and which is also circumvention prohibited by the DMCA. Even when rights holders intend to allow reuse, technologies are often structured otherwise. Star Wars has an annual fan film contest, and filmmakers can even use official Star Wars music in their films, but they must mail their submission if they do, the instructions warn, or it may get caught in the automatic copyright filter when they upload it, because the technology is so restrictively designed it controls more than they actually seek to limit.[6] In these ways, technologies are built to enforce control, as opposed to the previous model where either people did not use other people's IP on pain of lawsuit or had to pay up if they lost one. In this way, industry can use technology to enforce laws that may lack popular legitimacy.

Moreover, technology can also be used to supersede law. Gillespie (2007) identifies one of the key shifts of post-DMCA approaches as how DRM encoding restricts not only copying but also access to a copyrighted work. This is possible because, technologically, a copy is made when a digital document is displayed, and the Ninth Circuit classified random-access memory "copies of this sort as 'copies' for purposes of copyright" (Benkler 2007, 440). Therefore, limiting access, which is not what copyright is for, is justified as limiting copies by the Ninth Circuit's interpretation of that technological quirk. Tushnet (2014) describes a similarly expansive assertion of control through technological means. Getty Images created an embed format for their copyrighted images that allows them to not only track sites using their images but also anyone who loads those pages, since their computer will retrieve the image directly from Getty. Such technological choices assert broader control than copyright itself imposes, and they do so in a way that is difficult to refuse or even negotiate.

In particular, websites often technologically prohibit fair use, as automated decision making turns what in law are case-by-case gray-zone judgment calls into black-and-white up/down determinations (Chun 2011; Gillespie 2007; Tushnet 2007b). The most notorious of these technological controls is YouTube's Content ID system, which is worth examining in depth because it directly affects fans. Where a court would assess whether use of sports footage in a fan compilation is copyright violation, fair use, or free speech, YouTube scans uploaded videos and disables or monetizes those matching works uploaded to the Content ID database by large corporate rights holders. Monetization is for the rights holder's benefit alone, even when the video contains material whose rights they do not hold, like a fan's unique editing or commentary (Tushnet 2014). That this technological control benefits industry tremendously can be seen from their willingness to set aside their distrust of digital platforms in the hope that Content ID "will obviate the need for fair use" (Tushnet 2014, 8), thus giving them total control. Perhaps ironically, Content ID itself infringes copyright. In addition to being abused by people without legitimate claims to copyrighted materials, Content ID is troublesome because "to the extent that a video has copyrightable elements that aren't owned by the claimant, the claimant has no legal right to exploit those elements. Though it might have the right to remove the video, that is different from having the right to monetize it" (Tushnet 2014, 10). The portion of a fan video contributed by its maker is certainly among the things usurped this way.

Content ID cannot possibly replace fair use because it does not measure any of the same things. In *Lenz v. Universal*, the Ninth Circuit expressly states that "the statute requires copyright holders to consider fair use before sending a takedown notification, and that failure to do so raises a triable issue as to whether the copyright holder formed a subjective good faith belief that the use was not authorized by law." Content ID thus routinely uses technological decision making to supersede law, like seizing revenue from "standard reviews and reporting—classic fair uses even when done for profit" (Tushnet 2014, 11). The decision in *Lenz* speaks highly of the potential for "computer programs that automatically identify for takedown notifications content where: '(1) the video track matches the video track of a copyrighted work submitted by a content owner; (2) the audio track matches the audio track of the same copyrighted work; and (3) nearly the entirety . . . is comprised of a single copyrighted work.'" However, it is not at all clear that such a technological system, which is much more careful than Content ID treating any match at all as determinative, could comply with fair use either. At best these systems can identify works for human review. As Tushnet (2014, 12) points out, the stakes are high because there is so much content on YouTube that even a small percentage of false positives would affect many people. In addition, because fair use involves actually using parts of copyrighted material, those pieces, including fan remix, are "disproportionately likely" to be false positives. Perhaps most damningly, Content ID cannot be contested in the way that accusations of copyright infringement could potentially be taken to court (Tushnet 2014). In its current form, the system allows shutting down reuse simply because the rights holder dislikes it, such as videos that are critical, because the criteria used to determine removal are not transparent. Given what research has shown about these systems, it is important to take seriously the notion that technological design decisions embody corporate beliefs about (il)legal fan behavior. The interpretation of the law authorizes designing the technology in a particular way.

Contracting the Possible through Contracts

However, even the way websites, technologies, and platforms are designed is different from their TOS as contracts. If industry often replaces the threat of the copyright cease-and-desist notice with an invitation to fans to come and play on official websites (Gray 2010; Johnson 2007; Scott 2011), this might seem like retracting the power of the law. However, Brooker (2002) shows that as early as 1997, Star Wars was inviting fans onto its official site specifically to replace fan activity with corporate control. Using these sites means agreeing to their TOS—a contract—whether or not fans are aware of it, as is noted in every iteration of "by using the Site, you agree to be bound by these terms and conditions" (SyFy). TOS are often more restrictive than what legislative or judicial formulations of law would impose (Benkler 2007; Postigo 2012; Tushnet 2014). The contract is a private form of law that does not carry the same restrictions or responsibilities as public law. It also governs a private space, the website, where the owner has much more control.

One particularly striking aspect of TOS is the distance between what sites establish as their rights regarding fan creative production and what rights fans have to use corporate materials. To take Star Wars as an example, it is instructive to put the two sections of the TOS side by side.[7] Their rights:

> Any use of any of the materials on this Site other than for private, non-commercial viewing purposes is strictly prohibited. The sale, auction, lease, loan, gift, trade or barter, or use of any of the materials contained herein, for any other purpose except as expressly permitted pursuant to these Terms of Use, in any form, media or technology now known or hereafter developed, including the use of any of the aforementioned materials on any other Web site or networked computer environment, without a prior written consent from Lucas, is expressly prohibited. Except as expressly provided for under the Terms of Use, the creation of derivative works based on the materials contained herein is expressly prohibited. You may download one copy of the materials on any single computer for your personal, non-commercial home use only, provided you keep intact all copyright and other proprietary notices. Modification of the materials or use of the materials for any other purpose is a violation of Lucas's copyright and other proprietary rights.

Your rights:

> If at our request you send certain specific submissions (e.g., postings to chats, surveys, message boards, contests, or similar items) or, despite our request that you not send us any other creative materials, you send us creative suggestions, ideas, notes, drawings, concepts, or other information (collectively the "Submissions") shall be deemed and shall remain the property of Lucas in perpetuity. By making any Submission, the sender automatically grants, or warrants that the owner of such material expressly grants, Lucas the royalty-free, perpetual, irrevocable, non-exclusive right and license to use, reproduce, modify,

adapt, publish, translate, and distribute such material (in whole or in part) throughout the universe and/or to incorporate it in other works in any form, media or technology now known or hereafter developed, for the full term of any copyright, trademark or patent that may exist in such material for any purpose that Lucas chooses, whether internal, public, commercial, or otherwise, without any compensation, credit or notice to the sender whatsoever. The sender waives all so-called "moral rights" in all Submissions. The sender further waives the right to make any claims against Lucas relating to unsolicited submissions, including, but not limited to, unfair competition, breach of implied contract and/or breach of confidentiality.

This is, as Russo (2010, 149) puts it in discussing the TOS at the site for *BSG*, "a remarkable catalogue of verbs enumerating everything that can or conceivably could be done to a media object," and it is also full of nouns and adjectives. Of course, they include this language, and so does every other website-running entity, so that someone cannot make an unsolicited submission and then sue them if something they create down the road looks like it, because there is a history of litigation over exactly that.[8]

However, the TOS do not just say, "Don't send us things, and if you do, it is not our fault if our stuff is like it." They do something different. They claim equal and opposite rights to those they assert over their own materials. You may not use their materials except privately and noncommercially. They can commercialize yours "throughout the universe." You may not trade, barter, or even gift theirs "in any form, media or technology now known or hereafter developed," but they have "royalty-free, perpetual, irrevocable" license to yours "in any form, media or technology now known or hereafter developed." They have control unless there is "prior written consent from Lucas." You lose your control simply by using their website. They can modify and adapt your work, but you are expressly forbidden from doing the same to theirs. Indeed, with a prohibition on any modification or use beyond that single personal copy, their TOS forbid fair use itself, and by declaring submissions their perpetual property, they disregard statutory limits of copyright. This, then, is indicative of their legal consciousness and sense of total entitlement to control, beyond the (believed to be) necessary protection against lawsuits.

Part of why rights holders can assert ownership over any creative works on their site is their belief in total control—the IP is theirs to benefit from, even if a fan adds something, because it is viewed as a derivative work they control by default. Whether or not fan activity is actually illegal (there is often a strong argument that it meets the requirements of fair use), the contemporary model defaults to assuming piracy (Jenkins 2006a), thereby constructing fans as lucky to get their sticky fingers on media texts at all. Moreover, sites can achieve expansive control just by asserting it, and legitimately so from the perspective of the law, because a website is a private space where they are choosing to provide a service. As Lessig (2006) notes, a private space does not guarantee even constitutional freedoms like the First Amendment.

However, as a thought experiment, what would it mean for a fan to say to ESPN, for example:

> You hereby grant us and our licensees, distributors, agents, [friends, social media followers], representatives, and other authorized users, a perpetual, nonexclusive, irrevocable, fully paid, royalty-free, sublicensable, and transferable (in whole or part) worldwide license under all copyrights, trademarks, patents, trade secrets, privacy, and publicity rights and other intellectual property rights you own or control to use, reproduce, transmit, display, exhibit, distribute, index, comment on, modify (including removing lyrics and music from any [broadcast material] or substituting the lyrics and music in any [broadcast material] with music and lyrics selected by us), create derivative works based upon, perform, and otherwise exploit such [broadcast material], in whole or in part, in all media formats and channels now known or hereafter devised (including on [our personal websites], on third-party websites, on our [Tumblr, Twitter, LiveJournal, Dreamwidth, Facebook], on physical media, and in theatrical release) for any and all purposes including entertainment, news, [criticism, fan fiction, vids,] advertising, promotional, marketing, publicity, trade, or commercial purposes, all without further notice to you, with or without attribution, and without the requirement of any permission from or payment to you or to any other person or entity.

This carries to its equal and opposite conclusion the idea embedded in TOS that when something is transmitted to you, it is yours to do as you please. Under contemporary notions of law, it is ludicrous to even imagine a fan making this pronouncement to industry. Industry condemns this as copyright violation and piracy when enacted by consumers, but I want to call attention to how unremarkable it seems when imposed the other way.

By comparison to broad assertions of control, then, other industry approaches look generous. Although at the Star Trek site they claim automatic right to license fan works, they follow up by saying, "We respect your ownership of User Submissions. If you owned a User Submission before providing it to us, you will continue owning it after providing it to us." However, the same TOS later says, "We may take any of the following actions in our sole discretion at any time and for any reason without giving you prior notice." The list includes "restrict or terminate your access to the Services" and "deactivate your accounts and delete all related information and files in your accounts." They thus assert no less control than other sites after all. ESPN, surprisingly, grants fans a license to make derivative works from their IP, but it is contingent on fans granting ESPN rights to the work they create, which would not be required if remix were considered transformative and fair use. These gestures, while clearly less repressive than standard approaches, remain merely gestures.

Ultimately, as Hector Postigo (2012) argues, contracts are increasingly used to short-circuit fair use. Benkler (2007) notes that contracts can really institute anything to which the parties agree. However, "agree" is somewhat misleading:

> Mass-market transactions do not represent a genuine negotiated agreement, in the individualized case, as to what the efficient contours of permissions are for the given user and the given information product. They are, rather, generalized judgments by the vendor as to what terms are most attractive for it that the market will bear. [. . .] This means there is likely significant information shortfall on the part of consumers as to the content of the licenses. (446)

Thus, it is important to take seriously that people are not necessarily assessing the terms presented and making a reasoned choice. Certainly the process does not include the ability to negotiate the terms. Putting these authors into conversation with each other shows that because it is not a contract between equals, and because consumers must accept the terms or not use the product at all, TOS, as contracts, enable more complete control than other forms of law. Even though they are produced by lawyers, they are still running on corporate legal consciousness, not the law itself, as they act to shape an idea of proper fandom.

PUBLIC RISK, PRIVATE GAIN

Although there is a lot of overreach and claiming greater control over fans than the letter of the law, the single most prevalent feature of TOS and privacy policy documents is a litany of disclaimers of risk and insistences that users bear all risk, which is actually more important. Site owners accept neither risk nor responsibility, but users must accept all risk and responsibility. Users are, for example, responsible for knowing about changes in TOS, but site owners have no responsibility to inform them. Instead, the terms "may be updated by CSTVO [College Sports TV Online] from time to time without prior notice to you. It is important for you to periodically refer to these TOS to make sure that you are aware of any additions, revisions, or modifications that we may have made to these TOS. Your use of the Website constitutes your acceptance of these TOS" (Purdue University Athletics). The Star Trek site deploys rhetoric reminiscent of former secretary of defense Donald Rumsfeld's commentary about unknown unknowns, requiring that users "acknowledge that you may be waiving rights with respect to claims that are unknown or unsuspected. Accordingly, you agree to waive the benefit of any law [. . .] that otherwise might limit your waiver of such claims." This is boilerplate, of course, but it is nevertheless interesting when sites so thoroughly refuse responsibility, and the assumptions animating these fan–industry relationships matter. These legal strategies, while not directly relating to copyright, show the through line in how the law works when industry approaches fans: attempting to inculcate a norm of offloading risk to the public while assuring gains remain private.

Gillespie (2007, 14) describes this conjunction as demonstrating copyright's "fundamental contradiction: that it aspires to serve the public good by constructing a property regime premised on private gain." However, in media industry legal frameworks, the formulation is bent or even reversed, where private gain becomes the public good in and of itself, at the public's expense. Turning creativity into property is one example of how this works. Holding property rights in creativity indefinitely, and so refusing to enrich the commons from which the property rights holder has benefited and keeping all benefits for itself, is a way contemporary constructions of copyright fail to make rights holders internalize the costs of their production (Boyle 2003). As a result, the public bears the cost while industry benefits, making industry's gains, in important senses, ill gotten. This ultimately is unproductive rent seeking, a demand for greater access to money rather than a quest to protect creativity, much like when college students and suburban moms are sued for hundreds of thousands of dollars for sharing music, or like when "Limewire was sued for $75 trillion," which is "more money than the entire music recording industry has made since Edison's invention of the phonograph in 1877, and thus in no way corresponds to the actual demonstrated damages" (Khanna 2012, 2). In these ways, private monetary benefit becomes the only yardstick for worthwhile copyright action.

Along with private gain at public expense, there is a shift toward private law. As Gillespie (2007) notes, the law is generally public—debated in public, made by people elected by the public to serve the public, and able to be questioned by the public—but the new paradigm lacks these checks and balances. Lessig (2006) says it is the government's responsibility to ensure values other than capital's are taken into account so we are not just given over to private law, but that does not happen in practice. This echoes what Saskia Sassen (2012) argues about financial capital as partially located in the nation and partially extranational, subject to national laws in some ways, but able to exert pressure on law toward its own interests. While copyright-holding entities do not have direct control over lawmaking in any simple way—witness a staff member for the fundamentally probusiness Republican Party arguing for limited, constitutional copyright as opposed to business über alles (Khanna 2012)—they do affect it profoundly. This can be seen in the DMCA as well as the Stop Online Piracy Act and PROTECT IP Act (Preventing Real Online Threats to Economic Creativity and Theft of Intellectual Property Act) of 2011, which were proposed but defeated after public outcry, and the negotiated but not ratified Trans-Pacific Partnership treaty (TPP).

All of these legal documents sought to protect corporate IP in ways that threatened the public's free speech, indicating where the balance of power lay, and in fact the TPP was notoriously negotiated with representatives of corporations and none from the general public.

This capture of law by industry, however imperfect, leads to court decisions restricting how technologies can be used, as in preventing sporting events from being streamed online even if the recipient could legally watch the broadcast (Boyle 2015). More dramatically, industry has sought to outlaw competing or emerging technologies to protect their market share (Boyle 2008; Gillespie 2007). In such ways, law serving corporate rather than public interests has actually impeded the development of new technologies and economic models (Benkler 2007). At times interventions are direct, such that industry figuratively or even literally writes their own laws, and legislatures and courts more or less rubber stamp them (Gillespie 2007), as when industry lobbyists shaped the 1994 General Agreement on Tariffs and Trade to "exact concessions that they had been unable to achieve domestically and effectively do an end run around elected bodies, national governments, and inconvenient judicial concerns with larger social interests" (Coombe 1998, 71n119)—which is also more or less how the (secret) text of the TPP has been described.

RECOVERING THE PUBLIC

In some ways, then, corporations are above the law—or at least there is different law for the powerful than for regular people. Coombe (1998, 6) draws attention to "the law's recognition and protection of some activities of meaning-making" while it calls others "piracy." In practice, whose creativity is protected and whose is free to exploit is not absolute but rather selective protection of authorship, often tilted not only toward corporations (Coombe 1998; Jenkins 2006a; Lessig 2004) but also away from less powerful groups like African Americans (Hesmondhalgh 2006; Schumacher 1995; Vaidhyanathan 2003) and indigenous peoples (Feld 1988; Seeger 1992; Tan 2013). Although clearly fans are not structurally oppressed, they get the short end of the law as well (Fiesler 2007; Tushnet 2014). "Under the current system, because other companies know how far they can push and are reluctant to sue each other, they often have greater latitude to appropriate and transform media content than amateurs, who do not know their rights and have little legal means to defend them even if they did" (Jenkins 2006a, 190). Tushnet (2014, 11) notes, for example, that when a rights holder monetizes a YouTube work in which only part of the content is its own, it is taking someone else's creation to benefit itself, "something that in other contexts the same claimants are very happy to call 'piracy.'" Some people's creative production, then, is fair game for other people's (re)use or commercialization, but not others.

In all of this, the public supposedly served by copyright is lost. Reuse of corporate property is approached as if only the corporation can be harmed (Gordon 1992), as opposed to harm because subsequent creators cannot create. The creativity coming into being with reuse is not considered at all; there is no assessment of the harm to that market or what is denied to the public by its prohibition. Rewarding creativity is supposed to serve the public interest by incentivizing production, but the term "public interest" has competing definitions (Bunker 2015; Coombe 1998). However, the dominant definition is a capitalist one. After all, IP litigation, and indeed legislation, happens without a representative of the public interest (Coombe 1998), even though the public interest is the supposed beneficiary of the entire enterprise. The measurement of public good must be expanded and reoriented away from capital if IP law is to support progress as intended.

In the end, the same action means something quite different depending on who does it. While the copyright system is meant to cultivate more "science and useful arts," it does not do that particularly well at this end of history but rather supports extraction of monetary value. To repurpose Christian Fuchs's (2012b, 141) argument about privacy, IP rights are at once "upheld as a universal value for protecting private property" when it comes to corporations and "permanently undermined" for everyday people "for the purpose of capital accumulation." Many scholars grappling with IP go back to John Locke, working through the implications of his contention that creators deserve the benefit of their labor (Fredriksson 2014; Gordon 1992; Roth and Flegel 2014; Toula and Lisby 2014). However, this relies on creativity having a beginning point, and in practice the raw material creators draw on is always someone else's labor. This is not unique to fans, but it affects them particularly. The labor–benefit framework and the fair use–public domain framework are incompatible. To say that all creativity is built on and gives back to the public is to disregard the labor of the person adding on to the commons. To say that creativity is labor and that people should therefore hold property rights in what they make is to disregard the labor of those who came before and prevent those who come after. These two beliefs cannot be satisfied simultaneously. They can, however, be satisfied sequentially. The intent of copyright can accommodate both models: reward for creativity, then paying the benefit forward. What might a legal system that returned to these principles allow in terms of new areas of creativity?

CHAPTER FIVE

FANDOM AND/AS LABOR

Although, as Chapter 3 shows, sometimes industry invites fans to interact but actually wants them to react and consume, other times industry does actually recruit engagement and productivity. The idea that fan production is now normative and encouraged is often explained as collapsing distinctions between producers and consumers, for better or worse (Andrejevic 2008; Deuze 2007; Jenkins 2006a; Pearson 2010). There is a lot of enthusiasm about technological change making it possible for people to make media who could not before; through the rise of the internet and cheap computing capacity, everyday people, formerly consumers or users, can now produce—and, perhaps more importantly, distribute (Fisher 2012; Murray 2004; Jenkins, Ford, and Green 2013)—their own media objects. Benkler (2007) notes that around a billion people globally have gained access to media production, a figure that has undoubtedly grown since he was writing, with 53 percent of households having internet access worldwide by 2017 (International Telecommunication Union 2017). The optimistic view, advocated by authors like Benkler and Chris Anderson, is that technology enables production of things that were not economical before, like niche content (Anderson 2008), and production by people who could not produce before (Benkler 2007). The expansion of production to new content and people is particularly exciting when it is groups not well served by mass media, like women, racial and sexual minorities, and people in the Global South.

In particular, media production becoming routine for users is understood as making fan media production, formerly considered somewhere between quirky and pathological, into routine media engagement. As Leora Hadas (2009, ¶ 3.4) notes, "In theory, the participatory logic of the

Web 2.0 ethos is the same one that has been driving fandom for as long as the concept has existed." Some authors contend that recent technological changes have shifted power toward the people formerly known as the audience (Jenkins 2006a; Murray 2004). Jenkins describes fans as "demanding the right to participate within the culture" and argues that fans are winning this battle for inclusion: "If the corporate media couldn't crush this vernacular culture during the age when mass media power went largely unchallenged, it is hard to believe that legal threats are going to be an adequate response to a moment when new digital tools and new networks of distribution have expanded the power of ordinary people to participate in their culture" (2006a, 24, 157–58). If industry cannot stop it, the argument goes, ordinary people must be powerful.

These fan activities look different viewed as labor. Seeing participation as inherently good short-circuits analysis. There is nothing else to say. The lens of labor, however, opens up the question of what fan productive activity means. If fans are a vital part of the new economy, then it is important to take the economy part as seriously as the vital part. A labor framework lets us ask who benefits from these fan activities, and in what ways. Importantly, even the most pro-industry discussions of fan participation acknowledge that it produces value for media companies (Baird Stribling 2013; Jenkins, Ford, and Green 2013). This chapter takes the following simple premises. First, fan activity adds value to the media object it works on. Second, fans do this work without receiving equivalent monetary value in return, producing a net benefit to industry. Third, this means fan activity produces what Marxist theory calls surplus value, and therefore it makes sense to view the recruitment of fan work as incitement to exploitative labor.

There is much disagreement over what constitutes exploitation in a technical Marxist sense. The definition I use returns to *Capital* (Marx 1978a) to explain exploitation as extracting surplus value from workers—making more money from their labor than you pay them, a usage shared by Brown and Quan-Haase (2012) and Nicole S. Cohen (2012). Indeed, as Fuchs (2010, 2012b) points out, as pay goes to zero, as is generally true of fan production, the rate of exploitation goes to infinity. Accordingly, activity that is invited by industry or encouraged by industry or takes place at official industry sites or benefits the industry in any way is always exploitation in the Marxist sense of surplus value extraction. This sets aside the question of whether fans feel exploited—as Bertha Chin (2014) and Bethan Jones (Chin et al. 2014) point out, they often do not—looking instead at exploitation as a structural relationship of value extraction.

Media studies scholarship has examined audience activity as labor. One of the first to use a labor framework for user activity on the internet was Tiziana Terranova (2000, 37), who says that in what she calls free labor, "knowledgeable consumption of culture is translated into productive activities that are pleasurably embraced and at the same time shamelessly exploited." In this tradition, Mark Andrejevic describes audience discussion at the Television Without Pity website (Andrejevic 2008) and YouTube use (Andrejevic 2009a) as forms of labor from which industry extracts value and which it exploits. Others make similar arguments about engagement with social networking sites (Fisher 2012; Fuchs 2012b). One of the clearest examples of harnessing user activity is reCAPTCHA, ostensibly used to prevent automated posts, but also spending human labor to correct badly scanned documents for optical character recognition. Megan Foley (2014, 374–75) notes that "reCAPTCHA solvers are currently working to digitize early issues of the *New York Times* and books from the Google Books Project, extracting labor products that can then be sold back to them." This exemplifies the way this labor does not feel like labor—it is being done for another purpose, after all—but it nevertheless extracts value from human action.

The labor approach has not been common in fan studies so far. There are good reasons why people have not used it, like the absence in fan production of the alienation associated with work and fandom's traditional structure as a gift economy, which I examine in Chapter 6. However, the perspective that fan activity can, should, or even must be considered as labor is currently emergent in fan studies. The novelty of the topic can be seen from the fact that fan studies journal *Transformative Works and Cultures* published a special issue on "Fandom and/as Labor" in March 2014, and *Cinema Journal* had an In Focus section on "Fan Labor and Feminism" in April 2015.[1] Common themes in this body of work include arguments that industry is stealing or co-opting fan labor (Lothian 2009, 2015; Busse 2015; Russo 2009, 2010)—and accordingly either that fans deserve compensation for their labor (De Kosnik 2009, 2012, 2013; Noppe

2011) or that fans work in a gift economy and so do not desire compensation (Chin 2014; Hellekson 2015). Those focusing on the fan–industry intersection, my point of interest here, all identify the financial benefits of fan work as flowing disproportionately to industry.

Industry's use of fan work is enabled because the internet does not just let people do work but also "make[s] the fruits of their labor readily accessible to the mainstream—and to producers themselves" (Andrejevic 2008, 25). Technology has made fan practices, many of which predate contemporary tools and platforms, more visible and easier to aggregate, allowing industry to try to capitalize on them (Helens-Hart 2014; Russo 2010). Clay Shirky (2008) argues that the Web 2.0 model of content production is "publish, then filter," as opposed to gatekeeping for quality before publication. In the case of industry and fans, this can be reframed as, "Let fans make a bunch of stuff and then we'll exploit the free content we like best." Accordingly, just because fans have access to the means of media production does not mean they control them.

Fans have always created value, particularly in terms of meaning, loyalty, commitment, and promotion. What is new is industry recognition, encouragement, and attempts to capture this value. Through various means, industry increasingly articulates, translates, or exchanges fan valuation for market value—as, indeed, all nonmarket values are becoming marketized under neoliberalism (Brown 2003). Given the explanatory power of a labor framework and industry encouragement of fan activity, it is important to look carefully at what fans are being invited to do. In this chapter, drawing on industry worker statements, representations of fans, and web design, I describe the forms fan labor takes in contemporary understandings of fans regardless of fan type: the work of watching associated with Dallas W. Smythe's (1977) audience commodity; promotional labor; content labor; and lovebor, the work of loving.

AUDIENCE COMMODITY WORK: CONTINUITIES AND CHANGES

As originally pointed out by Smythe (1977), one way audiences work is by watching the ads that support media they receive apparently for free. This labor generates direct monetary value for industry through ad sales as what Smythe calls the audience commodity. More recently, traditional audience commodity work has been altered by technological change, and measurements of user activity have value, turning audiences into a data commodity. Additionally, audiences are now called on to do the work of being watched, making their desires visible to industry. Fans are also recruited to make their own free lunch—that is, they produce the incitement that Smythe argues gets audiences to do the work of watching ads. In this section, I describe how each form of labor functions in the contemporary fan context.

The Audience Commodity

As the quip goes, if you're not paying for media, you're the product. Despite rhetoric about a new era of audience power, the objectifying logic of buying and selling people's attention—which Jenkins, Ford, and Green (2013, 1) describe as "eyeballs in front of a screen (in television terms), butts in seats (in film or sports terms), or whatever other body parts media companies and brands hope to grab next"—is still in current use. Although calling this the "audience commodity" obscures the labor, the chiding and hand-wringing around using a DVR to skip advertisements on TV or installing ad blockers in web browsers make it clear that audiences are called on to do something in exchange for consuming media. Ad-avoiding audiences are imagined to be taking the payment of media without doing the work of watching ads. In fact, Jonathan Beller (2011, 125) suggests watching as working may have even been intensified: "The cinematic century posited that looking could be treated as value-producing labor; the digital age presupposes it." Certainly access to ad-viewing user-workers is worth a lot of money; witness the more than $545 million (93 percent) drop in the value of MySpace as users abandoned it in droves (Brown and Quan-Haase 2012).

The audience commodity is built into the fan–industry relationship. Industry workers use this terminology when they talk about fan activity. Steve at Campfire explicitly defines fans as an audience commodity, contending, "A movie starts or a TV show starts, you know, brands emerge and a Tumblr community starts immediately, and new technologies are creating fan bases around themselves. Sometimes the fan base is their *product*." In the season 6 DVD extra "*Buffy the Vampire Slayer:* Television with a Bite," WB network executive Gail Berman directly frames the issue economically: "The show had made an enormous impact on the WB. It increased the revenue of how much the WB could charge for a 30-second commercial spot" because it was so popular. These statements articulate the audience commodity exactly: they are the product, and their value is gauged in advertising dollars.

Accordingly, industry workers try to produce the best audience commodity possible, whether through the quantity of viewers they gather or through their specific qualities. Steve from Campfire argues, "If a franchise doesn't get in new audiences, it's kind of going to die away with that small hard-core [group]," pointing to quantity-related struggles. However, if shows die without enough of an audience, it is also true that a solid audience can resuscitate them, as when David Germain (2008) of the AP reports, "Cast and crew are game for more *X-Files* movies if fans still believe strongly enough to convince distributor 20th Century Fox that the audience is there." With a robust audience, a media object can be not just continued but started back up, as demonstrated by revitalization of shows like *Family Guy* and *Arrested Development* as well as the 2016 revival of *The X-Files*. Myles McNutt argues that the 2013 Kickstarter campaign for a movie based on TV show *Veronica Mars* was not actually about funding; rather, "They needed [fans'] money as a symbol of their fandom which would convince Warner Bros. the movie was viable" (Chin et al. 2014, ¶ 2.6). Sometimes instead of a bigger audience, industry wants a broader audience, rather than only one with niche appeal. Campfire's Merrin describes the "balancing act" of her work: "Because sometimes there are clients that do really want to engage the fans, but they want to make sure that they're presenting the piece of entertainment in a really open way, so [as to] get that broader audience. [. . .] You don't want to be so hard core, insular, that you're going to be turning off people who wouldn't identify as being, like, a genre fan." While Merrin's point is about inclusivity, she also gestures toward the ongoing negative stereotyping of fans that I discuss in Chapter 2.

Closely related to fears of audiences being too niche is concern for ratings and demographics. For example, "*Buffy the Vampire Slayer:* Television with a Bite" proclaims, "Although Buffy wasn't topping the ratings, the upstart WB network was delighted by the young audience the series was drawing" because this was a valuable demographic group. Industry values the work of watching ads in aggregate, with the demographics of the laborers determining the price (Fisher 2012; Lee 2011). Valuable audiences are explicitly segmented by age, gender, race, and income in measurements like the Nielsen ratings (2017), although the most commonly discussed measures are age and gender alone, as in "Hollywood's ongoing allegiance to 16–34 year-old young men as their target audience" (Scott 2011, 34).

However, Arvidsson and Bonini (2015, 162) describe the way ads target even "specific psychographically defined lifestyle segments. What counted was not simply eyeballs watching, but the ability of a specific program to create engagement in or influence the selected target group." In particular, Eleanor Baird Stribling (2013) argues, advertisers have an interest in "audiences whose enthusiasm is believed to translate to more awareness of and receptivity to product placement and commercials. How much more 'engaged' and receptive this new audience is than the older, bigger one was considered crucial in setting a price." The prototypical engaged and receptive audience of course comprises fans. Certainly during the Save Our Show campaign for *Chuck* that Christina Savage (2014, ¶ 6.4) describes, one selling point was that the audience, although relatively small, "was loyal to both the show and the advertisers. Advertiser loyalty was key, as product placement became a more effective way to advertise in television to avoid viewers who were fast-forwarding through commercials or viewers watching in nontraditional methods." Additionally, industry has since tried to quantify nontraditional viewing. Arvidsson and Bonini (2015, 165) note that a Nielsen Twitter rating was developed to "measure the total audience for TV-related conversation on Twitter, including both people who comment and people who are exposed to their comments." Although the characteristic to be valued varies, the logic that some fan workers have more value than others remains.

That ratings are fundamental in cultural common sense around audience work may be clearest when they show up in media objects themselves. For example, Krusty the Clown complains in *The Simpsons* episode "The Itchy & Scratchy & Poochie Show" (1997), "Your *Itchy & Scratchy* cartoons are stinking up my ratings!" Krusty then shows a chart and exclaims, "That crater is where your lousy cartoon crash-landed. It's ratings poison!" This anxiety around losing attention during Krusty's broadcast, precisely measured, (re)produces the quantification and qualification of audiences as normative and unremarkable, showing the pervasiveness of the audience commodity. Despite claims of a changed relationship to audiences in general or an embrace of fans in particular, audience commodity logics are still essential in fan–industry relationships.

The Data Commodity

The audience commodity is a long-standing framework for advertising-supported media, but in the internet era it has undergone modification and expansion. One key driver of this shift is that, as opposed to laborious and contested measurements of audience activity like Nielsen ratings—with or without Twitter changes—digital platforms are designed to make users shed data constantly, like skin cells. As Andrejevic (2012, 149) puts it, "If the ability to track online behavior started out as somewhat seren-dipitous—the by-product of the convenience offered by a strand of code that allowed websites to remember previous visitors, now monitoring is being designed into the system," which he describes as "one of the dominant business models for the online economy." Users giving up their data is the cost of free online services (Ross 2009; Scholz 2012), just as watching ads has been the cost of free television.

The sports side of the industry has been (maybe conspicuously) absent so far. That is partially because sports organizations have a different relationship to audience commodification; leagues generally sell media audiences to networks rather than advertisers, so things do not work the same way as for nonsports media. However, the sports industry still wants to commodify audiences, and both sports and speculative media organizations participate in the data trade through their websites. Data commodity audience work is normalized because it is the default; the sites are based in the United States, where that is legal.[2] The Seattle Mariners website, for example, notifies users in its privacy policy that it collects data via "automatic methods":

> Examples of the information we collect and analyze using such meth-ods include, without limitation, the Internet protocol (IP) address used to connect your computer to the Internet; e-mail address; login

name and password; operating system type, version and computer platform; purchase history, which we may aggregate with similar information from other customers; the full Uniform Resource Locator (URL) clickstream to, on, and from our Website, including date and time; cookie information; and products you viewed or searched for. We may also use software tools to measure and collect session information, including page response times, download errors, length of visits to certain pages, page interaction information (such as scrolling, clicks, and mouse-overs) and methods used to browse away from the page.

Automatically collecting this kind of information as aggregate, anonymous data is standard because users as data is fundamental to contemporary web logics.

Additionally, websites may collect "personally identifiable information" (and aggregate it, or not, with anonymous data). MLS's site says, "In consideration for our granting you access to these features of the Site and Services, you hereby expressly agree to provide true, accurate, current and complete information about yourself as requested and as necessary for our provision of, and/or your registration for the use of, those features of the Site and Services." The data commodity's value is specifically precision and comprehensiveness. Sites try to ensure information can be collected, including having to opt out rather than in. In fact, even if users opt out, they are warned, as at the SyFy site: "If you prefer, you can set your browser to refuse cookies or to alert you when cookies are being sent, but it is possible that some parts of the Site will not function properly if you do so." Both default collection and appeals to getting the full experience normalize user data producing value for site owners.

All these ways of collecting data and all this difficulty in refusing collection suggest how important data is to industry. Organizations use data to sell advertising in a new version of the old audience commodity (Andrejevic 2009a; Ross 2012). As ESPN describes, sites use data to "provide you with advertising based on your activity on our sites and applications and on third-party sites and applications." Knowing the audience in order to sell it to advertisers is the same model as older media. However, the web allows advanced audience commodification, where data has value beyond providing ads to their own users and can be sold in itself (Andrejevic 2012; Ross 2012). SyFy, like other sites, says they "reserve the right to share Personal Data with our affiliates." Data's value shows most clearly in statements like CalBears.com's: "The Site or CSTV [College Sports TV] Online, Inc. may be sold along with its assets, or other transactions may occur in which your personally identifiable information is one of the business assets transferred." User data as a "business asset" is an audience-commodity framework, but a new version amplified by technology.

User data is their asset. Although user labor generates it—so if users stopped doing things it would dry up—site owners have total control of data. As Carolin Gerlitz and Anne Helmond (2013) note about Facebook likes, not only do users not own them, but also they cannot look at the list of things they have liked, although it is part of what algorithmically determines which ads are seen and what users' news feed looks like. The ways data is both opaque and consequential is a general concern across platforms. Precisely what data sites collect is not transparent, although Gerlitz and Helmond's (2013) analysis of the "like economy," while specific to Facebook, is one of the most comprehensive examinations. Data collection includes aggregate demographic data, which is not terribly different from Nielsen ratings; additionally, and perhaps disturbingly, "the Like button cookie can also trace non-users [of Facebook] and add the information as anonymous data to the Facebook database" (Gerlitz and Helmond 2013, 1353). Importantly, the platform captures action and both ties it to specific people and aggregates it (Gerlitz and Helmond 2013; Postigo 2016). These are thousands of tiny actions with personal meaning to people, abstracted into valuable data points and packaged for use or sale. Like the old audience commodity, value is extracted from people's leisure, without their clear assent. It is important to pay attention to the mechanisms of this new mode of audience commodity labor.

The Work of Being Watched

However, alongside labor extracted from leisure, there is recruitment to new action. In the internet era, Andrejevic (2009b) points out, audiences, like reality TV stars, are called to the work of being watched. Audiences are asked to actively make their preferences knowable and visible (Andrejevic

2008, 2011). Looking at the specific tactics used with fans in particular, we see that rather than moving fans into a new role as collaborators, as the optimistic interpretation says, interactivity makes the audience measurable, much as I note in Chapter 3, with interactivity really facilitating consumption. Commonly, fans are incited to be watched by being invited to connect using social media. The basic invitation to participate is the website button to "like" or "become a fan" on Facebook or to "follow" on Twitter. As Gerlitz and Helmond (2013, 1358) point out, such simple actions have larger impacts: "A click on the Like button transforms users' affective, positive, spontaneous responses to web content into connections between users and web objects and quanta of numbers on the Like counter." If, as boyd and Ellison (2008) argue, a social networking site functions by users explicitly articulating connections, then the invitation to "like" asks fans to articulate a connection between themselves and objects of fandom and become visible. More intensively, fans can use their Facebook account instead of registering for the ESPN site or add the Mariners to their Google+ circles, giving industry more access to these platforms' data about them. When StarTrek.com uses Facebook to host an entertainment poll about the franchise's aliens, its invitation to "log in to see what your friends like" also inevitably means, "Log in so we can see what you like." It is a call to an action making fans visible.

Industry workers framed social media's value as visibility. Elizabeth of BMU, when asked what she meant by active fans, says, "Social media has allowed us to kind of see, to hear more of those *active* fans," defining "active" through social media visibility. Industry's expectation of social media visibility might be clearest in concerns about its absence. Merrin from Campfire describes a challenging situation where a client had too great an expectation of transparency:

> I think the client was concerned because they weren't seeing as much activity on their Facebook page as they wanted. They didn't see that visibility. But that was never where the conversation was meant to take place. We always wanted the conversations to be taking—taking place in the established communities. So from a client perspective it probably would have served us better to host a forum on our website as well, just to help so *they* could see stuff, because they weren't dig-

ging around in the different communities necessarily. And they were looking to their Facebook page to be where this conversation was going to take place, but that's where the broad audience was engaging with it rather than the niche audiences that we were tasked to engage with.

Social media is thus strongly associated with fan visibility for industry, reasonably or not.

Location-based invitations to participate turn encouragement to be visible into quasi-surveillance. This can be seen, for example, by the Mariners' invitation to "check in at the Ballpark" using the MLB At the Ballpark app. Similarly, Elizabeth at BMU is excited about the success of "a 'stripe the stadium' promotion," where they asked fans in alternating sections to wear different colors. "And then we did a fan cam, so they actually took a picture of everybody in the stadium and they could actually go back after the game and prove they were there by tagging themselves, and we did some giveaways on there." In this way, "tell us who you are" (demographics) becomes "tell us what you like" (psychographics), and even at times "tell us where you are" (geographics).

The work of being watched sometimes becomes fans doing industry's market research for them by making their feelings known. Lee McGuigan (2012) refers to feedback as something industry "harvests." In fact, if the *Veronica Mars* Kickstarter was about proving there was an audience (Chin et al. 2014), then industry workers asking fans to participate are recruiting them to make themselves visible. Savage (2014, ¶ 2.3) describes fans trying to save imperiled TV shows as doing "the labor of selling the size and desirability of the audience." In particular, with *Chuck*'s Save Our Show campaign, organizers told fans writing letters that "they should write about their own connection to the show; that they should provide some demographic information about themselves; and that they should tell the network how they watch the show especially if they watched in a nontraditional way" (Savage 2014, ¶ 5.7)—that is, they told fans to do the audience research legwork for industry, because traditional measurements did not capture *Chuck*'s audience. Most explicitly, there was "a Twitter campaign called #NotANielsenFamily. Each week, while watching the episodes live, fans would tweet to sponsors based on advertisements that aired during the episode" (Savage 2014, ¶ 7.3), emphasizing that the Nielsen ratings were not accounting for them. All of this labor makes fans visible on industry terms, benefiting industry—and it was encouraged by *Chuck*'s production staff (although they did not direct the campaign). Incitement to market-research oneself can also be straightforward: "SyFy wants to know what you think! Take part in surveys to share your opinions" is a direct call to visibility. In these ways, audience segmentation into markets is outsourced to audiences themselves (Fisher 2012).

Fans doing the work of being watched also allows going beyond quantitative ratings to have industry choices qualitatively validated. This unexpected use of fan visibility seems to happen only with speculative media. This is perhaps unsurprising because their validation is fuzzier than a win–loss record. However, these workers' consistent habit of commenting on how much fans liked things only makes sense considering the work of being watched. Over and over in DVD extras, industry workers describing the production process mention how much fans like things they did. *Kick-Ass* director Matthew Vaughn, for example, comments, "I've learned this: the braver we've been with this film, the better it's become, and the more people've liked it." In such ways, the idea that fan preferences should be visible and visibility has value is well integrated into industry beliefs and practices.

Making Your Own Free Lunch

Finally, building from Smythe's (1977, 5) argument that television programming is a free lunch to entice audiences to do the work of watching ads, industry now often either encourages fans to make their own free lunch or capitalizes on existing practices of fans making their own free lunch. Fans do the work of watching and being watched. However, through their fan activity, they also make the object of fandom more involving to themselves or to others. Customizing or reworking an object of fandom, like writing fan fiction, making remix videos, or engaging in fantasy sports, is making a free lunch, because these practices make media more fun to consume, or they keep people consuming despite frustration—when the writing goes downhill on a favorite TV show or a favorite team is having a bad season, for example.

Industry invitations to talk to other fans, engage with materials, or vote for favorite episodes or players incite fans to make their own free lunch and make doing audience and data commodity labor more enjoyable. This gives fans more to do and extends the shelf life of media products (De Kosnik 2012; Postigo 2003; Jenkins, Ford, and Green 2013). Free lunch production drives web design at SyFy.com, which includes a discussion forum for every show the network has, past and present. The page uses a question and/or imperative verb inciting participation for each forum, as in "Stargate Universe: When a band of soldiers, scientists and civilians find themselves on an unmarked path headed toward the unknown, what do you think they'll encounter? Discuss it here in the forum." MLS similarly has many invitations to participate, like scavenger hunts, predictions of game outcomes, or tailgate recipe contests. In the documentary *We Are Wizards,* Harry Potter fan and fan-site runner Melissa Anelli, both a fan and someone who has fans, describes her role as "giving the fans the stuff to obsess about, the stuff to do, the way in which they can most enjoy being a fan during this specific time in Harry Potter history." This moment indicates that fans themselves (although as mediated by filmmakers) believe fan work makes the object of fandom fun, and it also makes this idea more normative by putting it in the documentary. Particularly for media with complex narratives, fan work to collect pieces of the story and background information, either as resources like wikis or for collective interpretation, facilitates participation (Jenkins 2006a; Ross 2009; Scolari 2013). This too is making your own free lunch.

Sports fans are also encouraged to participate and make being a fan interesting because fans are fundamental to the stadium experience. As Crawford (2004, 37) notes, "Sports supporters play an important role in creating the atmosphere, spectacle and entertainment of the 'live' sports venue." It is fan activity, in part, that makes sports audiencing worthwhile. BMU workers repeatedly mention that a bloc of wealthy, older donors who are not "loud" is a challenge to the atmosphere they wanted fans to produce. Elizabeth explains, "We just want to create this environment that you don't want [to miss]—[don't] not want to be a part of." The way fans appear in fictional representations shows that fans producing atmosphere is essential for sports; they are always there, even when the narrative is about the players. Fans often exist only as noise, abstracted from people cheering either because they are not shown or because there is way more noise than the small number of people shown could generate. The non-diegetic sound suggests how essential fan participation is to being at a game; it is just part of the landscape. Moreover, fans are always there even when irrelevant to the plot, whether it is a handful at a driveway game of fictional sport BASEketball, a kids' soccer or hockey game, or a huge crowd at a major sporting event. Representations therefore construct fan free lunch labor as integral to sports. Free lunch logic is thoroughly embedded in the contemporary mediascape. In all of these ways, the audience commodity described by Smythe (1977) persists today, and it is important to recognize contemporary tactics' kinship with it as well as recognizing these forms of activity as work.

PROMOTIONAL LABOR: BUZZ, SHARING, AND FREE ADVERTISING

Beyond laboring as the audience commodity, fans are incited to pro-motional word-of-mouth work. Given that fans produce and circulate promotional content (Reinhard 2011; Russo 2010), we should recognize that "media industries can co-opt fan labor for their own promotional gain" (Scott 2015, 172) and parse its mechanisms. Promotional work con-sists first of simply discussing the object of fandom publicly. As BMU's Elizabeth puts it, "In marketing, we realize no press is bad press really, because that means they're talking about you, which is good." Getting the word out has value in itself. Next comes generating interest, or buzz, commonly described as a vital kind of audiencing (Bechmann 2012; De Kosnik 2012, 2013; Jenkins 2013; McCracken 2013). AP stories consis-tently describe Comic-Con as a place to generate buzz through telling fans about upcoming releases or previewing them. News sources also routinely explain social media traffic as buzz or how interest in a media object builds through networks, further demonstrating how thoroughly promotional labor is incorporated in industry practice. This is a product of both the architecture of platforms—Facebook tells users about their friends' likes, thus spreading information (Gerlitz and Helmond 2013)—and explicit intent—as when Fox ran "the Biggest Gleek Challenge on

Facebook, offering a prize to the fan who most frequently and vigorously discussed [*Glee*] in their Facebook profile" (Stork 2014, ¶ 2.6).

In the "Frequently (Soon to Be) Asked Questions" section of the *Dr. Horrible's Sing-Along Blog* site, creator Joss Whedon explains the means and value of promotional labor at length in answering the question, "What can WE do to help this musical extravaganza?"

> What you always do, peeps! What you're already doing. Spread the word. Rock some banners, widgets, diggs . . . let people know who wouldn't ordinarily know. It wouldn't hurt if this really was an event. Good for the business, good for the community—communitIES: Hollywood, internet, artists around the world, comic-book fans, musical fans (and even the rather vocal community of people who hate both but will still dig on this). Proving we can turn Dr Horrible into a viable economic proposition as well as an awesome goof will only inspire more people to lay themselves out in the same way. It's time for the dissemination of the artistic process. Create more for less. You are the ones that can make that happen. Wow. I had no idea how important you guys were. I'm a little afraid of you.

Whedon's explanation emphasizes that promotional labor can have huge effects and is often vital to the success of media objects. This was especially necessary for *Dr. Horrible* because it was produced outside the Hollywood system and without its promotional capacities, but it is routine for productions big and small.

Alternatively, promotional labor creates value by distributing industry-made promotional content, which capitalizes on fans' access to the means of media distribution for industry's benefit. As Sam Ford and Xiaochang Li both argue, circulating content is a form of creative labor (Stein 2014). Fan distribution is the whole model of Campfire's work; they produce marketing content that they hope fans will like enough to share. At a basic level, placing social media buttons conveniently on websites incites and facilitates promotional labor, spreading content about the show or team to social platforms. Promotional labor also takes more surprising forms, like *BSG*'s widget letting users put videos of the show on their own website, defying IP protectivism in the interest of promotion—although of course fans could not really take the videos unless they defeated the security features.

StarTrek.com even has a heading called "Viral Distribution" in their Terms of Use: "We may expressly authorize you to redistribute certain Content for personal, non-commercial use. We will identify the Content that you are authorized to redistribute and describe ways you may redistribute it (such as via email, blogs, or embedded players, or by producing Mash-Ups)." Giving fans access or content specifically so they can retransmit it—or be the carrier wave, as Steve of Campfire puts it—underscores how integrated promotional labor is within industry norms.

More intensively, fans do promotional work to convince others to like or participate in the object of fandom. As Campfire's Steve puts it,

> After that level of education there is participation, which is a deeper engagement, which usually includes sharing, ideally. Because at that point then you want to turn your participants into evangelists. If you can convert fans—fans like to evangelize, but sometimes they often lack the tools or lack the network or the system to do so. So enabling fans to evangelize is definitely the next layer.

Steve speaks repeatedly of fans as evangelists, leading me to call this recruitment "efangelism." The notion of wanting fans to love something so much that they bring other people in is echoed by his colleague Mike. News coverage of Comic-Con also takes the position that fans recruit, as when fannish web guru Harry Knowles says, "Because of the 'Net and the permissive editorial nature of it, we can champion films before they've ever been picked up for distribution and get people excited about them way in advance" (Rowe 2007). With *Chuck,* efangelism was explicit and intentional to support the show by increasing the audience (Savage 2014), but fans telling all their friends about their favorite television show or sports team is also a routine practice for fans that is being co-opted and optimized for industry ends. This is why one fundamental aspect of social analytics is "valuing users according to their ability to engage with other users and make them endorse and re-transmit their communications" (Arvidsson and Bonini 2015, 165).

Fan promotional labor clearly sometimes substitutes for paid labor, either because they directly replace workers or because industry gets work for free that it would otherwise choose not to pay for. Certainly fan work would cost a lot. When fans responded to a cease-and-desist letter from Universal Pictures over their promotional activities around the film *Serenity*, Jenkins (2013) says, they added up "all the time and labor (not to mention their own money) put into supporting the film's release" and then "sent Universal an 'invoice' for more than $2 million, as represented by their 28,000 'billable hours.'" Steve at Campfire notes, "All our work is aimed, designed to be carried by fans, fans are the carrier wave as they do [things]. If we create a world that fans didn't enjoy, it would wither on the vine and die, right? There's no budget to throw $5 million into media. So our business model is based around creating things that fans enjoy." The idea that their business model relies on fan distribution because Campfire cannot do large media buys is telling. In fact, discussing Disney's proprietary Comic-Con–like D23 event, Michelle Rindels (2009) of the AP explicitly says, "Over the long run, strengthening the relationship between the company and its fans online can create self-perpetuating marketing, where eager fans can promote Disney products online without the company incurring further costs." Tama Leaver (2013, 168) points out that if the fan promotion incited by Joss Whedon above was "done through traditional, paid advertising strategies, then the advertising costs would almost certainly have outweighed the entire *Dr. Horrible* production budget." Scott (2015, 169) describes this as fans acting "as (unpaid and unaffiliated) ambassadors for their object of fandom." Busse (2015, 113) more harshly describes such campaigns as taking "free fan content to use as advertisements to get fans to buy more stuff."

However, using fans in place of paid promotion, although expected and sought, is rarely simple. As Merrin from Campfire puts it,

> It's almost like—I feel like there was probably a point at which everyone was going—It's just like social media with all clients. They go, "Oh my god, free media! This is great! This is fantastic! They're going to do all the work for us, we don't have to buy, you know, TV commercials," la la la. They think they're going to save money; they think they're going to get something for nothing. And then they kind of started figuring out, "Oh well actually they have a mind of their own, and they're going to say what they want and do what they want, and we can't control them, and it's not really free media." It's kind of a different—it's a problem, a different communication problem.

Campfire workers discuss using "earned media" rather than "paid media"; they rely on producing good content that fans want to circulate. Related to earning distribution, some conceptualize fan promotional labor as something "money can't buy," as in AP writer Sandy Cohen's (2008a) assessment that "the annual [Comic-Con] convention, now in its 38th year, draws the most avid fans around[,] the kind who will blog about what's cool and generate online attention that money can't buy." Thus, fan promotion is labor, and although it is easily exploitable for financial gain, it carries important complexities.

CONTENT LABOR FROM PARATEXTS TO COLLABORATIONS

Third, fan work contributes to producing media objects themselves. The idea that fans produce content is so normative that most websites in my archive discuss it in their TOS even when they do not have affordances that allow submissions. The MLS site, which does not have a way for fans to submit fan works or even a way for fans to talk to each other, mentions that users might be able to contribute, and they should do so responsibly. More often, as at the sites of SyFy and Star Wars (which do afford on-site production of content), Star Trek (which affords discussion but not submissions), or Cal, ESPN, and the Mariners (which have no affordances for participation), the TOS assert that submitting your content grants a license to the site, indicating how assumed it is that fans make stuff and will send it by any means necessary. Alternatively, or sometimes simultaneously, several sites have disclaimers forbidding fans from making derivative works. Cal's statement runs: "Website users shall not reproduce, prepare derivative works based upon, distribute, perform or display the Materials without first obtaining the written permission of CSTVO [College Sports TV Online]." Both TOS standards assume that fans produce content and desire to regulate it into docile, productive forms.

Theorizing the value of user-generated content takes us back to Marx, who points out that workers put the value into a product (Marx 1978a, 1978b), but value is alienated and fetishized so it seems to be inherent in the object (Marx 1978b). Accordingly, user-generated content engaging media gets value from fans' labor—not solely, as prohibitionist IP regimes argue, from the raw material they draw from (which of course gets its value from the labor that went into it). From one angle, fan content labor around the original or official media object creates value. If meaning is thought of as a semantic value, then Gray (2010) points out that paratexts produce much of the meaning of texts. Certainly fan character Paul Aufiero in football drama *Big Fan* actively works to shape the meaning of his beloved New York Giants through his paratextual activity, calling in daily to a sports radio talk show. Paul's work, which he spends all day at his paid job preparing, interprets team or player failures as insignificant and successes as substantial to produce a meaning he desires while also benefiting the team's brand value.

However, semantic value ties deeply to economic value. The Seattle Mariners value fan paratextual activity—like support during MLB All-Stars voting—enough that their website urges, "Vote Mariners" no fewer than twenty-one times, because having All-Star players is good for brand value. Industry's fear that fan content labor could destroy value also shows its relationship to value. Elizabeth says of BMU's athletics Facebook page that fans "can post to things that we post, so they can put a comment to anything that we post, but we don't actually allow anybody anymore [to post independently]; they shut that off. Because of, you know, we get the occasional person that just wants to vent and be negative." Steve at Campfire describes the tension: fan activity "can be a little *scary* to brands because they lose control. But at the same time, they do *appreciate*—Some of those shows, they appreciate the fan base and what they do." He uses the example that "a fan will take the DVDs and then cut every swear word that's in *The Sopranos* and put it up online," saying, "It's something that HBO could never endorse, something which they could never *do* themselves. They love that fans do them—they have to be seen to take them down, but at the same time they love that they go up. So it's almost, kind of, often it's about kind of placid discouragement, if that makes sense." HBO loves the engagement but not the means, showing how fan content labor focusing on the titillation of blue language endangers the value of *The Sopranos* as so-called quality TV. Fan content labor impacts semantic value, and industry tries to keep that impact positive.

Fans also routinely contribute to the object of fandom, not just its meaning, through content labor. Fan content labor made many contributions to web series *The Guild,* which is discussed by the actors, directors, and producers in DVD commentaries. Fans produced the second season opening credits, appeared as unpaid extras, did translations, and sent in humorous videos applying to join the diegetic role-playing game guild as freely provided content for an upcoming episode. Similar recruitment of fan video for the official media object also occurred with the Nickelodeon show *iCarly* (Ross 2009) and *Dr. Horrible* (Jenkins 2013; Leaver 2013); fans also contributed to DVD extras for the *Veronica Mars* movie (Hills 2015). In one of the more blatant instances, Comedy Central series *Tosh.o* collects web video through its site that may or may not be featured on the televised show but can be put on the website regardless, thus keeping a continual stream of content without expending its workers' labor while encouraging fans to stay on the site viewing ads (Helens-Hart 2014). Video game modding is a similar content labor practice that generates additional levels or scenarios for a game (Deuze 2007; Fuchs 2010; Jenkins 2006a; Poderi and Hakken 2014; Postigo 2003). In such ways, fans are invited to produce content so industry does not have to do as much labor, or so that the object of fandom is more expansive than would otherwise be possible.

Indeed, fans often drive media innovation through content labor (Bechmann and Lomborg 2013; Potts et al. 2008), and particularly, as Fast, Örnebring, and Karlsson (2016, 974) argue, "lower its costs of production and spread its risky business." As Daren C. Brabham (2012) points out, these supposed amateurs are often trained and paid professionals in their formal working lives, meaning that what the content industry gets for free is precisely as good as what they get from formal, paid channels, but without payment or recognition of their authorship.[3] Importantly, industry receives this content without any obligation to use it (Helens-Hart 2014). As Hector Postigo (2016, 346), puts it, relying on user-generated content is like being "a bettor at a roulette table who is in the happy position of betting on all the numbers, where the payout *in aggregate* outweighs what appears to be an otherwise wild investment. Some numbers don't pay, others pay a little, and some pay a lot." Letting fans take all the risk and co-opting any benefit has been documented particularly well with video game fans (Poderi and Hakken 2014; Zhang and Fung 2014). Importantly, top-down extractive practices are different from crowdsourcing because there is no shared control between the entity getting the labor and the crowd. Fan content labor, then, is work, and it benefits industry substantially.

LOVEBOR: THE WORK OF (SHOWING) LOVE

Finally, fans are recruited to do lovebor, the work of loving the object of fandom and showing that love. I coin the term "lovebor" here, although it is neither elegant nor euphonious, because there are as many definitions of "affective labor" as scholars who use the term (cf. Federici 2011; Gregg 2011; Hardt 1999; McRobbie 2011), plus "emotional labor" (Hochschild 1983), "labor of devotion" (Campbell 2011), and "affective economics" (Jenkins 2006a). Yet none of them describes the reciprocal relationship between work and love I identify with fans. On the one hand, as Karen Hellekson (2015, 125) says, "the impetus that drives fannish activity remains independent of the platform of expression: fan activity remains a search for community, a way to unabashedly love something"—being a fan precisely is love. On the other hand, as Busse (2015, 113–14) notes, "fan labor is particularly vulnerable to being co-opted [. . .] because by its very nature, it is based on and driven by love and passion," which situates fan action as motivated by love. Lovebor lies in the space between these positions.

It is first vital to recognize love as having value. Particularly, affective attachments produce value for industry (Arvidsson and Bonini 2015; Banks and Humphreys 2008; De Kosnik 2012). As Jenkins, Ford, and Green (2013, 104–5) note, "Fans appreciate media properties, in the sense that they like them and thus make them a site of emotional investments. Fans might then 'appreciate' the material in an economic sense as well, increasing these artifacts' potential value by expanding their shelf life and opening them up to new potential markets." Lovebor is also a contention that love itself has value. Arvidsson and Bonini (2015, 159) point out that part of industry's goal is to "situate audiences so that their desires and preferences—their passions—can be rendered predictable" in order to extract the labor of their love in a profitable form, much like my concept of domestication. In a football context, Peter Kennedy and David Kennedy (2012, 33) argue that "fan identity is a rich seam that revenue-hungry clubs are eager to mine." Cases like donating to the

Veronica Mars Kickstarter campaign show fans themselves converting their love into a monetary valuation (Hills 2015). Arvidsson (2005, 237) refers to attachment to brands as generating "an *ethical surplus*—a social relation, a shared meaning, an emotional involvement that was not there before"—and (taking the next analytic step) under capital surpluses are ripe for extraction. Given the existence of a surplus to exploit, then, we have to look at the production and extraction of love.

Although lovebor does produce value, it does not always do so quantifiably. Mike from Campfire notes,

> Marketers'll go, like, "Engagement's bullshit 'cause I can't quantify it," you know what I mean? And so there's like, there's a lot of discussions here but I think—I think it's interesting that a lot of people are starting to go with their gut and realize, like, "But there's something there. We can't quantify it now," and a lot of people struggle to understand it, but they recognize there's a difference there in what's happening.

It is clear that understanding lovebor is still uneven among industry workers, but developing. Mike and his colleague Steve both speak of sometimes trying to manage fan love. As Steve puts it, "Sometimes advertising is about taking a product that people hate and making them love that product. That is a much steeper challenge for us to do than working with fans that already love a property to celebrate and harness that." In these ways, Campfire understands love has value, and they are prepared to create love to get that value if necessary.

Given that people do something that generates value, it is important to recognize lovebor as work. In particular, lovebor builds from the tradition of taking seriously women's reproductive labor as work and not just love, highlighting that it requires work to extract, package, and transmit affect rather than being a free outpouring of feelings. Additionally, equal emphasis on work and love resists defining work involving affect as natural, which has historically been used to devalue this work's skills (England and Folbre 1999; Nussbaum 1998) as well as to justify not paying for this work to (allegedly) protect it from being demeaned by commodification, usually expressed around sex and sex work (Nussbaum 1998; Schaeffer 2012; Zelizer 2000). Both reproductive labor and lovebor can be seen as rooted in some fundamental human capacity to connect to others, which is why they are not seen as labor or as skilled even though they take effort to produce in socially normative forms. This leads to them not being negotiated in most cases (let alone compensated), and there is no opportunity for recognition. Lovebor therefore stakes a claim that this is valuable, skilled labor that deserves recognition and compensation.

Fans do several related forms of lovebor. First, fans work by loving and showing love generally. One clear instance is the standing, yelling, and singing that the workers at BMU mention across the board as something they work hard to get fans to produce, and the absence of which they lament, as when Lisa identifies baseball as "more of a chill sport," but notes that she can manage the affective climate and generate demonstrations of love because "they will get up on their feet for—if I'm tossing out shirts or things like that." Lovebor animates the norm shown in the pictures fans can download at the Mariners website, where stadium shots are common and fans are always standing and cheering. Indeed, the idea that fans love their team so much they cheer or stand means that they appear in representations doing this lovebor even when they are not at the stadium producing the free lunch. Fans work to show their love when watching games on television in *Game 6* and *Big Fan* as well as separated from economics when the sport is not a business, like children's games, high school games, or other nonprofessional events.

In addition to producing affect, lovebor also produces affective ties, or community. Campbell's (2011) discussion of commercial women's web portal iVillage notes that user labor produces both content and community. As Fast, Örnebring, and Karlsson (2016, 968) argue, "Maintaining affective ties and community links are keys to the creation and maintenance of the highly desired category of engaged or active consumers." Importantly, this is reproductive labor (Fast, Örnebring, and Karlsson 2016; Lothian 2015)—the work that happens behind the scenes that enables other work but that is rarely recognized as work. Producing, showing, and managing feelings and producing and maintaining community underpin all other fan labor, but they often go unrecognized as work in much the same way that traditional women's work is not recognized as work. Naming this as lovebor seeks to render it visible and its value recognizable.

Another kind of lovebor is producing tangible expressions of love. The work of showing love on one's body, for example, manifests in the near ubiquitous use of face or body paint in represented sporting events and industry practitioner beliefs as well as the idea that fans get tattoos of their object of fandom.[4] Fans also do extensive work to make costumes (as distinct from consumption if they buy them). Actor Bruce Campbell links work and love in costuming when he asks in his documentary *Fanalysis,* "Why are they fans to the extent that they'll spend forty weeks making a costume that's going to walk across the stage for four seconds?" The work that goes into homemade costumes appears in discussions of both sports and speculative media fans. AP writer Sandy Cohen (2007a) describes what went into one Comic-Con outfit:

> Wayne Sullivan traveled all the way from Albuquerque to show off his beloved Batman suit. The 43-year-old university staffer said he spent "a couple years" getting the outfit just right. He refurbished the rubberized pants himself and ordered a custom-made cowl from Australia. He carried a golden grappling gun (really a "cut and painted Nerf gun") and hand-cut pointy bats to throw at villains.

Although more often associated with speculative media through the tradition of cosplay (costume play), sports fans also do the lovebor of making homemade costumes. As Andrea Adelson (2006) reports in her Super Bowl coverage, "One [Pittsburgh Steelers] fan made an interesting fashion statement. She had a top and skirt made with Terrible Towels," the quintessential material expression of being a Steelers fan. Importantly, these modes of lovebor have a fuzzy and attenuated—but real—relationship to economics in a way similar to the subconsumption that I discuss in Chapter 3.

Fans also work to make other things that show love but that have no clear route to monetization. Homemade signs supporting one's team are a staple of sports film and television. In fact, it seems impossible to have a crowd watching a sporting event without signs they created to support a player or the team, or to deride the opponent. Homemade player T-shirts or jerseys work the same way. Beyond sports, character Hutch in Star Wars comedy *Fanboys* made an R2-D2 to attach to his van, mimicking using such robots as rear-seated copilots in the series' X-wing ships. Similarly, fans' live-action role-playing in *Supernatural* have made a cardboard ghost detector like the one used by their heroes. Lothian (2015, 141) contends that "crafted costumes [..] and other objects show the labor of fannish hands as both self-expression and free advertising," and there is definitely also a link to promotional labor. Although this production is undeniably work, it is not clearly articulated to economic value, although fans' love for the object of fandom clearly motivates buying as well as promotional or content labor or showing up to be the audience commodity. Similar to how desire is seen as potentially hazardous in consumption, the aspect of emotional ties in lovebor leads to devaluing it and not being willing to recognize it as work.

The final kind of lovebor I call coercive positivity—the demand that fans produce love and only love. This is closely related to how Arlie Hochschild (1983) describes "emotional labor" among customer-facing workers, who are compelled by both norms and policy to always be positive, cheerful, and pleasant, regardless of what they might feel under other circumstances. That what is demanded from fans is love is clear because critical discussion or negative opinion is framed as its opposite, hate: "don't be a hater," "don't hate," and so on are common responses from industry workers (and fans who have accepted the norm) to even the most benign and civilly stated criticism. Lovebor is also built into platforms, with the "like" as the one-click response option on Facebook from 2009 to 2016 (and still the default because of habits formed during that era), as well as Twitter changing its star symbol for "favorite" into a heart for "like" in 2015. There is no "dislike" button on these platforms, even with Facebook's expanded options. Only love is built in, even as "dislike" might be convenient to discourage the algorithm from providing similar content. In Gerlitz and Helmond's (2013, 1362) analysis, "the Like economy is facilitating a web of positive sentiment in which users are constantly prompted to like, enjoy, recommend and buy as opposed to discuss or critique"; this structure "enables only particular forms of social engagement and creates specific relations between the social, the traceable and the marketable, filtering them for positive and scalable affects." In the end, although Russo (2010, 183) correctly notes that "as commodities themselves become increasingly immaterial, the affective labor of desire, identification, and meaning-making accrues greater economic value," how lovebor becomes economic value is indeterminate, making it a quite different sort of labor, but it is one that, as I discuss in Chapter 6, underpins resistance to seeing fan work as labor.

OUT OF EXPLOITATION?

The norm industry seeks to instill both assumes and recruits fan labor. They are asked to work as the audience commodity by watching the ads that support "free" media, generating direct monetary value for industry through ad sales. Fans also normatively produce value as the data commodity, where information about users has value. They are expected and invited to work to make themselves seen and known, the work of being watched, as well as produce the free lunch that is supposed to get them to show up to do the other work. Fans also normatively do promotional labor. Content labor helps produce media objects themselves, whether paratextually or directly through adding more content so industry does not have to. Last but not least, fans are assumed and encouraged to do lovebor—the work of loving and demonstrating love that generates value for industry. All this work is unpaid and benefits industry disproportionately, and so is exploited in the technical Marxist sense. In the domestication model, this is selecting stock that can produce more for industry. It is also unevenly available to fans on the basis of how much time they have free from other labor to do it. Therefore, as it becomes a norm, middle-class fans, who are disproportionately white, and those with fewer demands on their nonwork time, commonly men who do little reproductive labor in the home, are those most able to meet the norm. Of course, it is important to recognize that fans also love what they do—an important valence of lovebor. Although it is labor, and it is exploited, fans are unlikely to form labor unions or go on strike anytime soon.

However, other routes out of exploitation are possible. As with the example of fans billing Fox for their work promoting *Serenity* (Jenkins 2013), when industry's behavior is particularly egregious, fans can and do push back. Moreover, the idea that fan labor could be paid, although unfamiliar in the US context, is routine in Japan. On the fan work website that Nele Noppe (2015) analyzes, fans not only sell their work but can also sell at any price, without paying the copyright holder. Although this does probably technically break Japanese law, Japanese rights holders have always thought that fan work benefits them (unlike the recent realization in the United States), so fans can be paid. Additionally, more direct pushback on media industry co-optation of labor may happen without traditional labor organizing. Brett Caraway's (2016, 914) analysis of the Organization United for Respect at Walmart (OUR Walmart) campaign frames the organization as "a resistance commons, a resource for the collective translation of fear and indignation into hope and action. The sharing of grievances fosters an awareness of the collectivity and a sense of togetherness." Those same resources of community produced by under-valued lovebor, then, may be the key for valuing everything that fans do, providing the potential for something like class consciousness to emerge.

CHAPTER SIX

ENCLOSING FANDOM

Labors of Love, Exploitation, and Consent

It is difficult to think of fan practices and labor as anything other than apples and oranges. Fans freely do these things; certainly, unlike formal labor, they are not coerced by the intractable need to earn a living. Fans enjoy doing these things. Therefore, it seems like it is not really labor, and fans do not require payment because enjoyment is enough. This theoretical chapter argues that this view is insufficiently structural, inattentive to both the unequal position from which fans choose to do this work and how being a fan on industry's terms fundamentally differs from traditional fandom by and for fans. Because questions of labor and production are rarely studied with sports fans, this chapter primarily focuses on how these practices work for speculative media fans, drawing analogies as appropriate; however, the larger trajectory of enclosure that I examine here holds as an industry logic regardless of the different experiential meaning of the labor. I first describe the contemporary labor system against which fans should be analyzed, arguing that the convergence of labor-cost reduction by industry, rejection of capitalist projects by many fans, and the contemporary blurring of work and leisure produces a perfect storm that allows exploiting fan labor. I then argue that given these circumstances, we should interrogate fan willingness to participate for the potential distance between what fans agree to do and what industry extracts from them. Ultimately, industry embrace of fans is a privatization of fandom that turns fans into a workforce for industry's benefit.

Fan Labor in the Time of Precarity

As Brooke Duffy (2015) points out, the media production that consumers or users do is usually studied separately from formal work in the media industries; however, as with her example of fashion blogs, it is helpful to examine both kinds of production in the case of fans. Fan productivity should be considered first against larger labor patterns. One key trend is the casualization of labor and increase of precarious work—work that could end at any time. While it is true that looking at all of capitalism across space and time, Fordism and its stable, career-long employment is the exception rather than the rule, for much of the last century, cobbling together enough work from various sources was largely contained to marginalized people like the working poor, (disproportionately) people of color, and workers in the Global South. After World War II, skilled, white, middle-class workers, primarily men, had decades of relative employment security that has only recently eroded, perhaps predictably producing resentment among white men (Rodino-Colocino 2012) as similar shifts in other sectors did in the 1980s (Savran 1998) and 1990s (Kusz 2001). With the rise of precarious labor and flexible labor—work that could expand or contract in scope or pay at any time—women are often seen as ideal workers precisely because this kind of adaptation has been required of them for a long time (McRobbie 2011; Ross 2012). Temporary and contract work without the benefits accorded to full-time employment has become the norm for increasing numbers of workers.

These broader shifts in employment also affect media labor practices. Hollywood has traditionally been, as Amanda D. Lotz (2007) points out, much more unionized than many economic sectors. Although some work has been project based for a long time, and although Camille Johnson-Yale (2015) contends that the power of unions began to diminish from the 1948 Paramount decision that broke up the studio system, precarity now encroaches on media labor that used to be insulated from it. However, Nicole Cohen (2012) notes that this growing precarity is camouflaged by framing moves from project to project and employer to employer as desired by creative workers rather than because of inconsistent work. Additionally, recent years have seen a marked increase in what used to be called runaway production and is now maybe just production, with TV series in particular filming in Canada and films increasingly being made in New Zealand. In the same period, there has been intensive deployment of unscripted television formats like reality TV. Both location change and unscripted series employ writers, actors, directors, and other personnel in ways that skirt the terms of union contracts to lower industry's labor costs (Lotz 2007). The rise of digital production and consumption, which has, as I discuss in the previous chapter, incited fans to produce content, has simultaneously changed professional media labor. For instance, one major issue in the 2007 Writers' Guild of America (WGA) strike was that industry classified web content as promotion, which creators are contractually required to do for free, while the WGA argued it was creative work, eligible to be paid at the rate for creative content (Gray 2010; Leaver 2013; Russo 2010). Perhaps inevitably, as soon as WGA writers won compensation for digital work, it became the job of marketing, so it was still not something that needed to be paid on top of existing salary.

This larger desire to suppress labor costs matters for fan labor. The kinds of digital content that were at stake in the WGA strike are what is generated by what Chapter 5 calls promotional and content labor, and turning to fans rather than paid staff for this work is great for the bottom line in sports as well. Even in relation to declining union power in Hollywood, fan work is a bargain, and being replaced by unpaid labor undermines paid professionals much more than just not having steady employment. Indeed, Brabham (2012) finds that amateur production—in the form of crowdsourcing—is often framed precisely as harming professional workers. Andrew Ross (2012) notes that unjust labor conditions are visible as a departure from the relative protection provided by the unionization of Hollywood, but digital production has no such protection of workers, and the inclusion of exploitable amateurs is routine. This emerging slippage between professional and amateur labor echoes and amplifies one between work and leisure. On the one hand, digital production framed as amateur is often in fact done by trained professionals in their spare time (Brabham 2012; Duffy 2015). On the other hand, always-on internet and mobile devices mean we are never entirely away from work, and leisure hours blur into work hours, or are filled with play that is hard to distinguish from work (Deuze 2007;

Driscoll and Gregg 2011). At a time when these trends move away from compensated labor, unpaid and freely given fan labor provides one viable alternative mode of production.

Official producers get paid—although they have to fight to secure it —while prosumers, a portmanteau of "producer" and "consumer" popularized by George Ritzer and Nathan Jurgenson (2010), produsers, a combination of "producer" and "user" popularized by Axel Bruns (2008), and playborers, those who intermingle "play" and "labor" (Kücklich 2005), do not. Unpaid or underpaid labor is "over-exploited by capital in the sense that such jobs would cost much more capital if they were performed by regularly employed wage labour" (Fuchs 2010, 143). Relying on fan work not only acquires loyalty or attachment that money perhaps can't buy (Campbell 2011; Hamilton and Heflin 2011) but also, and more insidiously, cuts the costs of paid labor (Brabham 2012; Dyer-Witheford and de Peuter 2009), a point acknowledged in discussions of user-generated content but hardly considered in the specific context of fans. Importantly, although Marxism argues that capitalism exploits all workers, it does not exploit them equally or in the same way, and fan production's distinct characteristics should be taken seriously. Indeed, fans may be particularly disempowered in relation to creative labor. Because high-skill workers like creative professionals cost more to train and are in short supply and high demand, they tend to receive as compensation more of the value they produce compared to people whose work is seen as unskilled, like fans. This unequal exploitation intersects in unfortunate ways with the expansion of the means of media production to increasing numbers of people and the well-attested "anyone can write" ethos of fandom, for while fan work certainly requires skill (often equal to or greater than that of paid professionals), it is ideologically defined as amateur and low quality.[1] Additionally, for a variety of structural reasons, workers who are imagined to be more easily replaceable and low skilled are also more likely to be from socially devalued categories (white women, people of color, immigrants), another important factor in their uneven exploitation.

Some fans do this work to launch or further careers as professional, paid workers—a trajectory normalized in representations of fans and industry statements about fan production. Fandom can serve as a training ground for new talent (Deuze 2007; Jenkins 2006a). However, not everyone can have a deliberate, intentional relationship with industry and join it using fan work as a "calling card" (Jenkins 2006a, 132). One has to have enough economic capital for professional-quality equipment and the time free from other obligations (including paid labor) to do the often intensive work of production (Duffy 2015), which are both unevenly available on the basis of not only class but race. Moreover, the potential for fans to join the industry is deeply gendered: game modders[2] and documentary and/or satire fan filmmakers are candidates for professionalization—and often deliberately produce with that intention (Busse 2009a; Scott 2011)—and fan film, at least, is a genre dominated by men.[3] On the other hand, vidding, or editing pieces from televisual texts to music to tell a new story (Coppa 2008, 2009; Scott 2011), and fan fiction (Derecho 2006; Hellekson 2009) are understood as dominated by women, or even as distinctively feminine ways of seeing; these laborers both are not courted by industry in the same way and tend to be less interested in joining it (Busse 2009a; De Kosnik 2009), with some exceptions from fan fiction authors seeking to be published. Similarly, the ways fans of color tend to be doing transformational, critical work to center their experiences also does not bode well for their incorporability. Thus, career trajectories toward becoming professional media workers do not necessarily mitigate the extraction of unpaid labor. Moreover, these forms of training-ground labor add a second shift of playbour (Kücklich 2005) to ever-expanding groups of people—and they either add a third shift for both the people (disproportionately women) already doing what Arlie Hochschild (1989) calls the second shift of work as caretakers (Ouellette and Wilson 2011) and those working multiple shifts of paid labor, or exclude them from participation altogether. Additionally, doing amateur work for experience or exposure in the name of the possibility of formal media work, usefully described as hope labor by Kuehn and Corrigan (2013), has itself been decried as an exploitative model.

Ultimately, one key context for contemporary fan labor is that media industries, like many industries, are trying to have fewer full-time, regular employees in favor of a contingent workforce that can expand and contract on short notice. At the same time, technological change makes the means of production and distribution of media readily available to regular people, allowing production comparable in quality to professional work—and, as I will discuss in more depth below, fans are often eager to do it. Work produced by formal, paid workers is thus increasingly like that of informal, unpaid ones.

The Gift Economy, Lovebor, and the Commonsense Test

Calling these activities "labor" produces some trouble from the fan side, because "work" does not tend to describe people's experiences of being fans. Being a fan in general, and fan productivity in particular, is a leisure and pleasure activity. Fans have their own specific use values—what need an object satisfies for an individual—distinct from exchange value— what an object is worth, usually monetarily, in a market economy. Fans do the work they do for personal gain (Leaver 2013; Stork 2014), for the joy of the hobby (Lee 2011; Scott 2011) or out of strong desire to create (Boyle 2003; Tushnet 2009). Specifically, the opportunity to accrue fan cultural capital, gained by participating in ways valued by the fan community, is one key driver of fan activity. Thus, people make stuff freely because they personally benefit from it.

Fan work's benefits are often relational. Tushnet (2007a, 152) notes that when she discusses practices of giving authors credit for their work in fandom, "credit here works, among other ways, as a financial metaphor. Creators are paid not in cash, but in credit." The reward fans get is recognition from others, which has value. Similarly, when Robert Moses Peaslee, Jessica El-Khoury, and Ashley Liles (2014) note that fan labor at film festivals produces social capital—the store of relationships with others that a given person has available to draw on—this both benefits the individual fan and forges community ties when done by many fans. Fan labor is often communitarian in scope, circulating between and among people contributing in different ways to that larger cultural formation (Jones 2014b; Turk and Johnson 2012). At times this work is even explicitly undertaken toward serving the community (Chin 2014; Peaslee, El-Khoury, and Liles 2014). Taking all of these specific instances, it becomes clear that producing, circulating, and discussing forge the social bonds of fan community.

This combination of desire for status and producing in and for community is why the non-market-oriented value system of speculative media fandom has usually been described as a gift economy.⁴ Participants in gift economies use gift giving, as opposed to the market exchange used under capitalism, to circulate goods and services. This economy is not a simple, friendly, voluntary thing in the way we colloquially understand gifts as free expressions of affection, but actually is quite structured. Giving in a gift economy is, first, hierarchical; in fandom, as in the Indigenous North American practice of potlatch (Mauss 2000; Hyde 2010), giving more produces status. Accordingly, producing a lot of stories, fan vids, essays, or pieces of art is perceived as a great contribution to the community and provides fans with status. The person who provides effusive feedback on fan contributions is also seen as a good contributor, whereas the person who either writes only sporadically or begins a story and does not finish it has less status.

Additionally, giving and returning gifts is obligatory in a gift economy. Karen Hellekson (2009, 114–15) argues that "fan communities[,] as they are currently comprised, require exchanges of gifts" as "the gift of artwork or text is repetitively exchanged for the gift of reaction." Under fandom social norms, the gift of creative production obligates feedback, and this is why the "lurker" who reads but does not write can be seen as a freeloader or "leecher" (Jenkins, Ford, and Green 2013, 63). Although reciprocation is not direct quid pro quo but a fuzzy exchange where authors are understood to deserve feedback from the community but not from every single member, the obligation to give and keep giving highlights another place where stratification is built in. Fan gift economies rest on leisure time free from paid labor, which is unevenly available on the basis of race, gender, and class. One of the important norms of response to fan labor is that feedback should be positive or at least constructive—and sometimes, if the fan work is in short supply or difficult to produce, appropriately grateful (Švelch 2013). However, the counterpart to constructive criticism is that as fan producers incorporate it to improve, their work ceases to be solely authored by them. As Bethan Jones (2014b) shows, this was one driver of backlash to *Fifty Shades of Grey*. E. L. James incorporated feedback into the fan fiction that became the book, but she not only did not acknowledge fans' contribution but also refuted its fannishness after publication. To put this in the terms of the gift economy, this is giving, receiving reciprocation, and then taking back the gift. As Tisha Turk (2014, ¶ 3.2) notes, "Community, therefore, is not just an abstract byproduct of the fannish gift economy but a recipient within that economy."

In a gift economy, gifts produce obligations, which produce reciprocation, which produces relationships between and among people. From multiple and continually reconstituted relationships of giving comes community. Indeed, as Roberto Esposito (2009, 5) reminds us, etymologically, "community" is from *cum* (with) and *munus* ("the gift that one gives because one *must* give and because one *cannot not* give"). These affective ties are a major component of the traditional distinction between fandom's economy and the market economy. The fan community comes into being as continually recirculated giving or as performatively constituted through acts of (obligatory) bonding. Communities exist in being repetitively enacted. The gift-built relationship therefore differs categorically from the contract or the market exchange, which is set, defined, and contained: I provide *x* and you provide *y*. Market exchange contains immediate cause and effect, and the relationship only necessarily exists as exchange itself. Gift-built relationships are indeterminate because the relationship between the gift and the reciprocation is norm based, often asymmetrical, not immediate, and not guaranteed. This is the second valence of Tushnet's (2007a, 152) credit metaphor: "A credit-based transaction necessarily implies a continuing relationship between the parties."

In these ways, fandom has historically had a value system distinct from capitalism's. At a basic level, fan monetary valuation often differs substantially from market valuation—that is, both sports and speculative media fans value things like collectibles more than they would otherwise be worth (Hellekson 2009; Hills 2002). Fans have also often explicitly distanced the use value of their work from exchange value because noncommercial use is perceived to be safer from legal action over IP infringement (Hellekson 2009; Scott 2011). Fandom's separation from the market also appears in the norm that it is inappropriate to monetize work done on a fan object for one's own benefit. However, lovebor—which I describe in Chapter 5 as the work of loving and demonstrating love, because love is a form of work and not a free outpouring of feelings— lurks here. Resistance to monetization often arises from the belief that, like other forms of love or intimacy, being sullied with money demeans fan love.[5] Ironically, the outcome is that fan work cannot be financially rewarded and is therefore devalued anyway.

This refusal of monetization rests in part on the fact that, as Noppe (2011) argues, fans have not only avoided the market economy because they cannot access it but also because they do not like it, and they do like the gift economy. Because contemporary gift economies are alternative to capitalist distribution in general, and because fan gift economies often resist industry in particular, it is often seen as inappropriate to enmesh the two (De Kosnik 2012; Jenkins, Ford, and Green 2013). Moreover, this anticapitalist ethos discourages seeing commonalities with industry production, recognizing fan works as benefiting industry, or interpreting fan works as something either industry or other fans might pay for (De Kosnik 2012). Accordingly, Hellekson (2009, 118) describes fandom has having its own "field of value" that "specifically excludes profit, further separating their community from the larger (male-gendered) community of commerce." Russo (2010, 226) puts it more strongly, describing a "repugnance to many fans" of assuming "equivalences between market price and value, between value and public recognition, and between recognition and hierarchical authority."

For these reasons, framing fan productive activity as labor exploitation tends not to pass the commonsense test from a perspective internal to fandom. To modify the open-source software saying "free as in free speech, not as in free beer," fan work is "for free as in a gift, not for free as in without pay." Or, in De Kosnik's (2013) framing, "'Free' fan labor (fan works distributed for no payment) means 'free' fan labor (fans may revise, rework, remake, and otherwise remix mass-culture texts without dreading legal action or other interference from copyright holders). Many, perhaps even most, fans who engage in this type of production look upon this deal very favorably."

To Play, Perchance to Work

Fandom's long-standing prioritization of motives other than financial gain and embrace of production for the joy of it resemble in important ways the recent emphasis on pleasurable work as a widespread or even normative phenomenon in the creative industries. Since the rise of industrialization, there has been an "identification of leisure with life, work with drudgery" (Meehan 2000, 76). Because of this rigid separation, pleasurable labor often does not register as labor at all, and if pleasurable work does not feel like work in the formal economy, pleasurable production especially does not feel like work in the fan economy. In Banks and Humphreys' (2008) case study, the language of labor only appears when video game modders' free labor becomes drudgery. Moreover, in contrast to formerly strict managerial control over production, contemporary white-collar labor often provides more autonomy, which is frequently interpreted as worker freedom. In these ways, this is work that is not alienated, allowing the "possibility to express oneself, to control one's production process, to objectify one's essence and connect and communicate with others" (Fisher 2012, 173). Rather than the alienation of labor historically the hallmark of capitalism, where the work you did was not yours to keep, was not yours to control, was not tied to you in any way but rather strictly separated, a lack of alienation is seen as common or even endemic in contemporary white-collar labor (Cohen 2012; Postigo 2009), with a concerted effort to tie work to workers' identities (Hermes 2015). When work is not alienated—not separated from one's personhood—it often does not feel like work. Thus, while fan work has not generally been alienated, increasingly neither is paid white-collar work. This is part of what makes the boundary between the two porous.

Importantly, while the term "exploitation" colloquially involves exactly that affective condition of alienation, in the sense described by Marx (1978a), it means only the extraction of surplus value from workers—that is, making more money from their labor than you pay them. While people resist the language of exploitation when the labor in question does not feel bad, when using that formal definition it is quite possible to have exploitation even without alienation. Indeed, Eran Fisher (2012) argues that nonalienated work facilitates more exploitation. This is the idea that people will sacrifice material comfort for things they love, whether out of an artistic (Cohen 2012; Lloyd 2006) or academic (Ross 2000) calling or for their personal relationships (England and Folbre 1999; Ross 2012). People are willing to accept drudgery because of those emotional ties, reflecting our collective "training in the habit of embracing nonmonetary rewards—mental or creative gratification—as compensation for work"

(Ross 2000, 22). Even when nonalienated work feels exploitative, as with Hector Postigo's (2009, 465) analysis of AOL volunteers, there remains "a tension between a discourse of passion or love for one's work and needing the discourse of labor to legitimate [creative workers'] demands for fair treatment in an admittedly exploitative relationship." These things are not supposed to go together, so where there is passion, the language of labor fears to tread. Lovebor is helpful to explain this labor because it ties together love as work and working out of love, letting us see that this is actually work even when it does not seem to be, so the fact that we enjoy it does not mean compensation should not be an option.

This convergence of cultural and economic factors facilitates exploiting fan labor. Industry seeks free labor; fans enjoy and are socialized to give free labor; white-collar labor in general is increasingly framed as an enjoyable expression of the self. The colloquial sense of exploitation as hurting people, forcing them, or taking things away is often absent from these relations of media production even as they include labor exploitation in the sense of surplus value extraction. The great complication of fan labor in the contemporary mediascape is that these things are both true at once. The work is "simultaneously voluntarily given and unwaged," "pleasurably embraced and at the same time shamelessly exploited" (Terranova 2000, 33, 37). The phenomenon fundamentally cannot be understood without acknowledging both.

Yet how can pleasure, affect, and nonmarket values happen alongside exploitation and surplus value? This can be true because fan activity is a nonrivalrous good: taking it for profit does not mean fans have less.[6] Fan production exists in multiple economies or value systems simultaneously, which the single-level focus of political economy on the structural conditions of user labor or that of cultural or fan studies on the experiential pleasures of being a fan creator has prevented us from recognizing. Fans' work is often oriented toward sociality, community, or recognition in their own motivations as well as deployable for profit or more abstract industry interests like engagement. Between the media industry's increased interest in alternative sources of labor, fan traditions of nonmarket production, and the blurring of work and life, the exploitation of fan labor becomes the logical outcome from multiple directions simultaneously.

These multiple economies mean that a single object or act or person can carry different value in each of them at the same time. Hills (2015, 191) puts this in terms of use value and exchange value; there are tensions because any given item has "exchange value (which cannot wholly anticipate poachers' use values) and use value (which cannot wholly evade capitalist exchange value)." These different values are both distinct and never able to be completely separated. The same work means one thing to capital and another thing to fans (Jones 2014b; Postigo 2016). People themselves also exist in multiple economies at once. Göran Bolin (2012, 801) warns against "confus[ing] the statistical aggregate (the audience commodity) with the social subjects who watch (or read or listen to) the specific media texts." The aggregate of fan actions is exploited, but as social subjects, they pleasurably interact with texts. This is why the fact that people enjoy these activities does not mean they aren't work, and that people choose to participate does not mean they aren't exploited in an economic sense.

Recognizing the multiple economies in play also lets us avoid reenacting the exaltation of capitalist values that devalues fans as foolish people freely giving away things they could (and should) sell. Tushnet (2007a, 138) contends that copyright misunderstands fan motivations because "putting marketplace production ahead of other sources of creativity [. . .] has unduly dominated our ideas," making the nonmarket fan values described above unintelligible as reasons people might produce creative work. More bluntly, David Hesmondhalgh (2010, 278) argues, "Without denying for a moment the fundamental importance of a living wage, it seems dangerous to think of wages as the only meaningful form of reward." It is therefore important to recognize the validity of fans' nonmarket motivations even while we critique uneven distribution of market-based reward.

The ways that fan productivity is harnessed for industry's benefit capitalize on the existing gap between fans' use value and exchange value, as well as fans' mixed attitudes toward exchange value, to convert fan work into exchange value on terms that benefit industry. The fan culture framework and the market framework are not particularly compatible, which often causes tension when fan activities explicitly overlap both (Jones 2014b; Postigo 2016). Ultimately, however, capital can benefit whether fans seek market participation or not. As Postigo (2016, 335) points out, "All forms of cultural practice traversing through architectures framed by algorithms and affordances are similarly captured," regardless of what they mean to people who do them, and regardless of the fact that sports and speculative media fan cultures are quite different. Thus, at a variety of levels, fan actions both serve fan motivations and happen on industry's terms. Therefore, pleasurable fan activity coexists surprisingly comfortably with exploitative extraction of value from fan labor.

IF LABOR IS PASSED OFF AS PLAY, CAN THE FAN CONSENT?

This mismatch between what fans are experientially doing and what they are structurally doing is why industry benefit from fan labor is troubling. It also raises the question of whether fans truly consent to these relationships with industry. My theory of consent, which draws from work on sexual consent (Cowling and Reynolds 2004), has two components: in addition to not being coerced, people have to know what they are agreeing to. Andrejevic (2012, 153) notes, "Rejoinders to critiques of exploitation in such contexts typically involve both the lack of coercion and the pleasures of participation," which indeed is the response when people reject the notion of fan exploitation in particular (Chin 2014; Hills 2015). Fans are clearly not directly coerced to participate in labor bene-fiting industry; neither violence nor economic need compels them. It is also clear that fans choose to participate because they want the benefits of this work described above. However, fans are structurally constrained toward participation, and the gap between fan motivation to participate and industry's capture of value matters.

Much like the trouble with bringing our everyday understanding of gifts as free expressions of affection to the gift economy, the nonco-erced nature of fan practices is overinterpreted as meaning they are free practices rather than deeply socially constrained. In considering how fans may be structurally coerced, I begin from the feminist insight that unequal circumstance makes the "free" status of choices shaky (Brown 1995). De Kosnik (2012, 108) points out that the history of seeing fans as mentally ill "has undoubtedly set a low bar for what fans can hope to define as their rights vis-à-vis larger society," and such low expectations have consequences. This situation therefore calls for a more nuanced examination of the conditions of fan participation.

The wildly narrowed range of choice promoted by industry incorporation can be described as follows: participate on terms that benefit industry, or not at all. Would-be participants have no capacity to negotiate beyond simply leaving the deal. At a basic level, it must be taken seriously that opting out of digital platforms where large swaths of contemporary interaction take place carries a social cost (Brown and Quan-Haase 2012; Scholz 2012). This is, in some ways, a choice between accepting exploitation and losing the ability to be heard in culturally central "networked publics" (boyd 2007), although this social coercion is endemic to these platforms rather than particular to fans. Looking specifically at media industry action regarding objects of fandom, TOS say submissions are automatically licensed to the site's owners at Star Trek, Cal, and the Mariners. Even more dramatically, the TOS say creative materials automatically become the site owners' property at SyFy, Star Wars, and ESPN. The idea that anything transmitted to you becomes yours to do with what you please—of course and ironically—is exactly what industry condemns as copyright violation and piracy when enacted by consumers. The reaction to one direction of appropriation, unsurprisingly, differs substantially from the other. Indeed, as Jenkins (2006a) notes, corporations can get away with greater theft generally because they have the legal firepower to push all the way to or even past the limits of the law. Using the same logic for opposite ends avoids a hopeless contradiction with the assumption, discussed in Chapter 4, that industry has, and should have, all control. Moreover, fans do not always constitute an organized bloc, which undermines their capacity to fight for their interests. Football supporter groups in Europe are one key exception, and their relative success in pushing back on team owners underscores how little power fans have when atomized. For any given fan who decides not to provide free labor for industry, there are ten more in line behind her ready to do so because they are not thinking of their work as labor.

The legal gray area occupied by fan work also contributes in important ways to exploiting fan labor. This builds from the insight that sex work is dangerous because it is illegal and denies workers access to legal protections (rather than being illegal because it is dangerous to its practitioners) (Nussbaum 1998; Rubin 2011; Sullivan 2004). Doing legally troublesome work makes it hard to be protected as a worker. Although, as I argue in Chapter 4, much fan activity has a good case to be fair use, the contemporary model defaults to an assumption of piracy (Jenkins 2006a), with fans construed as "lucky" to be allowed to work with or on media texts. This is a model where, when fans work with IP, industry allows it but could equally at any time shut it down as (actually or assertionally) illegal. This is the inevitable result of an IP model that assumes all value is in the raw material worked by the fan, which lets industry desire and benefit from fan labor but also deny its value. These structures undercut fan demands for fair treatment as workers by defaulting to shutdown and framing anything else as generous. To build on Jenkins's (1992) famous metaphor of the fan as a poacher who absconds with mass media, if fans are poaching, industry is turning a blind eye to it because it benefits them is not the same as legitimating fan activity. The selectiveness of being permissive, as well as the underlying unequal division of power, divide structurally identical uses of copyrighted material into legitimate and illegitimate, producing a norm beneficial to industry (Coombe 1998) as it frames itself as generous and as granting "amnesty" for transgressions if fans play nice (Johnson 2007, 295). These examples vividly demonstrate the insight from feminism that choices between bad options cannot be considered free (Hochschild 2003; Nussbaum 1998). Compared to legal censure or not being able to participate at all, fans might be willing to accept almost anything. In these ways, structural coercions make it easy for fans to contribute free labor and difficult to opt out.

Turning to the second component of consent, we must also consider whether fans know what they are agreeing to in these activities. At the level of what I describe in Chapter 5 as the audience commodity (selling audience attention to advertisers) and the data commodity (selling data to brokers), one factor is that unlike paid work, when people sell themselves to capital and are exploited, audiences are sold by the media producer to third parties. Of course, the intractable need to earn a living makes paid work deeply coercive and not freely chosen either, but people tend to at least be aware that they are having to bow to that coercion in a way that audience labor goes unnoticed. In agreeing to the TOS of Twitter, one may formally agree to the use of one's data, but there is low awareness of the extent of use. Awareness is even lower that every tweet, positive or negative, can be measured as social engagement to benefit the object of fandom's corporate owners. Fans are not choosing to do this work—they might, if they were asked, but they are not asked—so this is not consent.

In a more philosophical way, there is justifiably a lot of resistance to the suggestion that fan participation is duped into existence or the product of false consciousness, in that models of unquestioningly devoted fans are what fan studies has contested for decades. I am certainly not arguing that fans have false consciousness, but neither do I believe that industry mechanisms are fully transparent to fans. False consciousness is the wrong framework. Fans undoubtedly have an awareness of the economy in which they intend to work, but only some understand media industry business models, labor frameworks, and digital measurement strategies. Thus, a blanket argument that fans strategically engage in market economies (Chin et al. 2014; Hills 2015) reproduces the deeply neoliberal assumption that all people act solely out of market-based cost–benefit analysis (McGuigan and Manzerolle 2015). The mismatch between fan and industry values matters. Fans generally are not freely doing work for industry. They are freely creating for themselves or one another, and industry either happens to also benefit or sets the conditions to allow itself to benefit. When fans freely give something to their favorite team, that act of love is not an agreement to do work for free that would ordinarily be paid, even as industry repurposes it as exactly that. To respect fans here is not to maintain that they must be using the same frameworks as industry, but rather to insist on respecting what this work experientially means.

In these ways, as Andrejevic (2012, 153) points out, criticizing labor exploitation "is neither to disparage the pleasures of workers nor the value of the tasks being undertaken. To argue otherwise is to stumble into a kind of category confusion: an attempt to reframe structural conditions as questions of individual pleasure or desire." Individual pleasure and desire are powerful and valuable, regardless of marketization. We should fight tooth and nail for the continuation and legitimacy of fan pleasure while also criticizing its exploitation for profit. People willingly do these things, but the leisure or pleasure framework does not provide complete knowledge from which to decide. Without awareness, it cannot be a free choice. Indeed, as with the concept that letting fans do anything at all is generous, it seems that while fans may have access to the means of production of media, industry still controls those means—and recent moves point toward gaining sway over the means of production of fandom itself.

EMBRACING FANS AS ENCLOSURE, OR THE INDUSTRY'S ARMS ARE MADE OF FENCES

Peaslee, El-Khoury, and Liles (2014, ¶ 1.2) describe the media industry as "increasingly decentralized and user-powered, though not user-owned." This gap between labor and ownership is the one that fundamentally drives capitalism. In the broadest strokes, the landless laboring class that made capitalism possible was created when formerly public arable land was enclosed as the property of the nobility and made unavailable for peasant use. Enclosure, in privatizing the means of production, produced nonowner people who then had to survive by having their labor appropriated for a wage (Andrejevic 2009b; Dyer-Witheford 2010). Here I argue that a parallel distancing of ownership and labor is occurring with industry's embrace of fans and bring enclosure to bear as an explanatory framework. If, in Jenkins's (1992) terms, fans are poaching from the private property of media corporations—or, perhaps more appropriately agricultural, stealing corporate seeds and taking them off to plant their own fields—then the property dimension and labor dimension of the enclosure of fandom can be described as building out the fence to make property of existing fan practices and extracting surplus value off the top of existing fan labor. These levels are combined in the emerging practice of building official platforms that attempt—extending the enclosure metaphor—to implement a form of sharecropping as the approved model of being a fan.

The enclosure model is often used to make sense of IP. These analyses argue that, as I discuss in Chapter 4, copyright and other IP law were originally intended to feed the public domain as a commons (property owned in common by all) by establishing incentives to creativity, but have instead been deployed to fence off public culture into private IP (Boyle 2003; Hyde 2010). Mass culture was therefore produced by fencing off the commons of folk culture, and—in Lessig's famous quip—the constant extension of copyright terms sets out to ensure that "no one can do to the Disney Corporation what Walt Disney did to the Brothers Grimm" because Disney's IP will never return from property to commons by entering the public domain. These scholars worry that enclosure stifles further creativity by privatizing the raw material of ideas (Boyle 2003; Rose 1998). Here I want to build on this work as well as work that discusses enclosure in a fan context only briefly (Lothian 2009; McCourt and Burkart 2007; Scott 2011) to examine the full implications and insights afforded by the concept of enclosure for being a fan.

Enclosure, first, turns the commons into private property. As James Boyle (2003, 37) describes contemporary enclosure of IP, "Things that were formerly thought of as either common property or uncommodifiable are being covered with new, or newly extended, property rights." Correspondingly, the commons of fan content produced for love and status is being made into property when industry appropriates this commons for its own benefit (what Chapter 5 calls promotional and content labor), moving it into the market economy as user-generated content. Although the production of cultural objects may have been unpaid for most of human history (Hesmondhalgh 2010), it was not always producing profit. Similarly, there have been productive forms of leisure like knitting and painting for a long time, but they were not always used for capitalist ends. There is slippage here because of the dual meanings of both public and private: leisure is of the private sphere and it is being commodified and made public, but also the former public good of fandom is being privatized. The new public/private is different than the old public/private, but they both tend toward private property. What we see in fandom is similar to open-source software: a communitarian mode of production that has been swept up into the market (Bechmann and Lomborg 2013; Kelty 2013). When Rose Helens-Hart (2014, ¶ 1.1) talks about fan practices being "imported" by industry and when Carlos A. Scolari (2013, 416) says fan contents are "taken over," they are describing the privatization part of enclosure. Importantly, while not every fan action is profitable for industry, the strategy is like, in the metaphor used by Postigo (2016) about YouTube, betting on every space in the roulette wheel. By treating all of it as theirs to use, they benefit no matter which content becomes popular or profitable.

The second characteristic of enclosure, which is rarely examined, is turning workers into labor. Nick Dyer-Witheford (2011, 279) notes, "Primitive accumulation was an accumulation not just of territories, but of a proletariat." Although there might (justifiably) be resistance to considering largely middle-class fans a proletariat, it is useful to recall Dyer-Witheford's (2010, 492) other point that "class is defined by who appropriates surplus value from whom." Structurally, fans are made proletarian through being subject to appropriation. Fans are produced as laborers in that structural way any time their labor benefits industry. This is turning the fan-held means of production to serve industry ends. As Lothian (2009, 135) contends, shifts toward incorporating fan production "can also be understood as an inversion in the direction of fannish theft. Rather than fans stealing commodified culture to make works for their own purposes, capital steals their labor."

This model suggests why Terranova (2000, 36) identifies the gift economy as increasingly important to "late capitalism as a whole." If fandom has often been described as a gift economy, then leveraging gifts made in the fannish economy for surplus value in the market economy has usefully been termed a regifting economy by Suzanne Scott (2009, 2011), as work that fans are doing for gift economy motivations is skimmed off the top into user-generated content for industry's benefit. The most notorious version of regifting came from FanLib, a company that sought to be the conduit between the fan economy and the for-profit economy but fundamentally misunderstood the fan side, offering prizes like T-shirts and "proximity to the participating shows['] producers," accepting only specifically prompted fan fiction, and requiring that fans surrender their IP rights (Scott 2011, 199).[7] Although FanLib was poorly executed and ultimately rejected by fans, the idea that fan productivity can and should be turned to profit is ongoing. This happens particularly on third-party platforms like Facebook and Twitter where fans go to engage in conversations with like-minded individuals but have their leisure captured as industry-benefiting labor given platform partnerships with Nielsen for ratings and as what Chapter 5, following Andrejevic (2002), calls the work of being watched.

Turning fandom into property and a proletariat are both means of capitalizing on work fans already do. The two combine in the third strategy of enclosure, which encourages fans to enter and labor in new enclosures of proprietary space, which I frame as sharecropping. In the era of zines and personal websites, fandom was produced in fan-owned spaces. With the rise of third-party internet platforms such as LiveJournal, Twitter, and Tumblr, fans still usually produced fandom by and for themselves even as they used privately owned platforms. Indeed, this often involved using the platforms in ways they were not intended, although when corporate policy decisions harmed fans—like deleting Harry Potter fan fiction as child pornography in what came to be called Strikethrough 2007—there was concern about fans not owning their community infrastructure. This gave rise to one battle cry at the formation of the nonprofit fan advocacy group Organization for Transformative Works: "I want us to own the goddamn servers!" (Busse 2009b). The sharecropping model intensifies attempts to maximize and formalize fan labor's benefit for industry; it is what drives offering fans official, sanctioned places to be fans (Ross 2009; Scott 2011). "Encouraging audiences and fans to work their fields, rather than despoiling them and moving on to cultivate their own land," as Scott (2011, 154) describes it, is a sharecropping model. Fans are given access to a place to grow fandom under the assumption that doing this officially is better, but if they take the deal, they not only have to abandon fan traditions of critique and gift economies but are also asked to put themselves under industry control and work on perpetually disadvantageous terms.

These forms of enclosure differ greatly from how the gift economy articulates labor and ownership in a commons model. All members of the community have free use of the commons, which is completely different from how capital exploits the commons (Fuchs 2010). Like a common piece of land, everybody has a stake in maintaining the commons of fandom. At its best, fandom is public, in the sense of the public interest or public broadcasting. Fandom is public the way that public infrastructure or public spaces like parks and libraries are public. Fandom is public like the public domain, a public good for the public good. Fandom is public in the sense of the public or the citizenry. The fan gift economy is productively understood as what Carol M. Rose (1998, 144) calls "limited common property": "property on the outside, commons on the inside." It is not a pure commons because not everybody may exploit it, but those within the community holding it in common can make use of it however the norms of the community allow. Leon Tan (2013) gives an example of a similar structure when he calls for an understanding that when an indigenous group like the Maori acts to prevent others from using their cultural heritage, they are not fencing off part of a universal commons that rightfully belongs to all humanity. Instead, there are different commons, and this commons is a Maori commons, free on the inside and restricted on the outside. In the limited common property of fandom, everybody in the community has shared access to everybody else's stories, vids, essays, or whatever other intangible goods—tangible goods tend to function differently (Jones 2014b), not least because they have scarcity—but their circulation through the bond-forming gift economy means there is often a protective attitude in relation to outsiders. Limited common property explains how people can seemingly share things freely and at the same time have a right to freedom from appropriation by capital.

I do not want to romanticize the commons. Fan culture was never some utopian space any more than there were nothing but happy peasants in ye olden times before the Inclosure Act. Fans have conflict and inequality, as all human communities do. What matters is that a commons mode of production makes things possible that other modes do not. Benkler (2007, 20) proposes to "treat property and markets as just one domain of human action, with affordances and limitations," and the commons would be another domain with different affordances and limitations. The commons as a way to organize ownership and labor affords communitarian and gift economy uses and relationships because its resources are "available to anyone who wishes to participate" (23).

We should therefore ask what happens when fandom is enclosed and made private rather than common. Other scholars have raised concerns about privatization of the public internet in general (Dyer-Witheford 2010; Scholz 2012) and the privatization of people's personal data in particular (Andrejevic 2012; Terranova 2012). These questions need to be asked about fandom too. As Russo (2010, 224–25), using FanLib as an example, explains, "To FanLib, the vast commons of freely exchanged fanworks perhaps appeared as if it simply lacked a businessperson with the savvy to privatize it. But in fact, creative fandom has a rich tradition of conceptualizing its labor in ways that reject financial profit as a criterion for value." But FanLib only stood out and produced a backlash because it was clumsy. As Chapters 5 and 6 demonstrate, many other initiatives, great and small, funnel fan productivity toward industry coffers.

One challenge to analyzing industry embrace as enclosure is that the practices of being a fan may feel the same to fans inside these new property and labor regimes, like peasant lives may not have changed overnight. Fans are often still experientially in the gift economy, producing and sharing out of love. However, enclosure produces a structural difference. A model conceptualizing fan production as user-generated content or inviting fans into proprietary spaces orients fans toward a vertical relationship between a user and a media product and beyond that the industry. The gift economy thinks of fan activity as a contribution to a community and produces horizontal bonds between fans, although they are not necessarily egalitarian relationships; recall that gift economies run on status. If, following Sara Ahmed (2006, 3), we understand "orientation" spatially, it becomes clear that "orientations shape [. . .] 'who' or 'what' we direct our energy and attention toward." The directions we face "make certain things, and not others, available," because in facing one thing we have to turn away from other things (14). Thus, as fans orient toward industry, they cannot orient to each other. This gives urgency to Brabham's (2012, 405) question, "Can crowds organize against unfair labor practices?" The answer is probably no precisely because a crowd is an aggregation of individuals rather than having community bonds. To the extent that these attempts to domesticate fan communities into crowds and orient them toward the market economy and the media company succeed, they threaten the very existence of fandom as produced through exchanged gifts. Labor exploitation and the gift economy can and do coexist, but these different orientations are fundamentally incompatible. Capital may be killing the very thing it seeks to monetize.

Thinking back to questions of consent, the enclosure of fandom can only be freely chosen if fans know it could be otherwise. This is the danger of the regifting economy, which presents "a narrowly defined and contained version of 'fandom' to a general audience" that is "unfamiliar with fandom's gift economy" (Scott 2011, 202, 205). To make a choice, fans must know the regifted version is not the only option. As Noppe (2011, ¶ 3.5) notes, "Fannish practices and mindsets are just as susceptible to change as those of companies, so the fact that certain concerns have been dominant among fans up to now does not mean they will always remain so." Study after study in recent years has shown fans beginning to adopt the industry logics developed in the period examined by this book. Lin Zhang and Anthony Y. H. Fung (2014) find this tendency with gamers in China; Matthias Stork (2014) traces a similar process with *Glee* fans; Suzanne Scott (2015) finds it in the *Veronica Mars* Kickstarter campaign. David Kennedy's (2012, 350–51) study of soccer fans contends that "the emerging common sense appears to be eroding the status of those holding traditional feelings of emotional solidarity between supporters in their collective attachment to the club and encouraging more individualistic, instrumental and quantifiable forms of attachment" to the team. Traditional, strongly noncommercial, communitarian models of fandom are increasingly existing alongside, or even in some cases being superseded by, market-oriented and individualistic ones. As these new forms gain ascendancy, old forms may fall out of use and cease to be an option, particularly if fans do not know it could be otherwise, which is encouraged by the construction of narrow subsets of fandom as "proper" or "official" by industry. Under these circumstances, fans cannot make an informed decision about which kind of fandom they want to have.

NONALIGNED INTERESTS, MEANINGFUL CONSENT, AND FAIR COMPENSATION

Although these changes to the means of production of fandom may seem innocuous and may produce no immediate experiential changes, they have serious implications. Sometimes the interests of industry and fans align, and sometimes they do not. Interests align when people want to gain access to the industry or to relate to it as a customer. They do not align when fan production is oriented toward other values. To assume what is good for industry is good for fans is fundamentally wrong. However, it is also fundamentally wrong to assume that what is good for industry is bad for fans.

Fan motivations to work are skewed relative to the industry's motivations to have fans work. They do not align because they are on a different plane, not because they are fundamentally opposed, so the choice between them is not zero sum. Indeed, precisely because fan and industry desires lie in different planes, and because there are multiple economies at work, both can be satisfied at once. Banks and Humphreys (2008) and Noppe (2011) both suggest that these different value systems can coexist. Kristen Barta and Gina Neff (2016, 519), studying the quantified self movement, show a case where the motivations of everyday people to engage in self-measurement rub up against industry attempts to commodify or make gadgets for these practices, but they contend that this is managed with "a détente that helps to keep commercial values and community values both in play"—neither value system has to be discarded. This is a useful precedent for fandom.

The relevant question in assessing exploitation is whether "the benefit constitutes adequate compensation for the work" (Campbell 2011, 506). "Adequate" may mean something other than a monetary reward (Bruns 2012; Postigo 2009), particularly given the traditionally nonmarket values of fandom, although in earlier work Postigo (2003, 605) notes that while such laborers might get benefits other than money, the fact that they are working for companies with billions in revenue suggests "they should gain more than a good reputation." Ultimately fans can cease to be exploited labor despite industry benefit if they are compensated in a currency they value in a way they consider sufficient and are not alienated from their labor by draconian TOS and copyright measures in the process.

TWO FUTURES OF FANDOM

The overall tendency of industry engagement with fans from 1994 to 2009 was toward domesticating fandom, making it useful, and constructing it in narrow ways that exploitatively benefit industry. In industry logics, fans are constructed as white men, and being a fan is framed as normal by linking it to children and family. This mainstreams fans, bringing the benefits of inclusion but also shifting marginality onto less socially powerful fans. At other times, ideas about fans seem opposite, with being a fan constructed as involving failed masculinity and whiteness through failed adulthood and heterosexuality, but this includes a redemption narrative that both reinforces the cultural common sense of privilege as a natural property of white, heterosexual masculinity and produces being a fan as white. Industry also attempts to manage fan desire and tie it to consumptive modes, including transmedia Consumption 2.0 that seems to invite participation but still assumes passive consumers should shut up and buy. Consumption is both constructed as an essential fan desire and actively facilitated. Moreover, industry legal action and rhetoric chronically overreach the letter of the law toward private gain at the public's expense. Fans are sometimes incited to act through being both assumed and recruited to do several forms of labor—although industry extracts surplus value from, and therefore exploits, these actions. Industry embrace of fandom is an enclosure of the commons that seeks to turn fans into a workforce for industry ends, which calls for greater attention to how the benefits of fan work are distributed. Overall, in the period this book examines, industry produces a norm of being a fan as a narrow range of practices and people that complies with industry desire in both behavior and demographics, setting up the right way to be a fan as what is right for industry.

What I have found about the norms of being a fan in the internet era has been troubling. However, there is a subtle counterdiscourse within the broad propensity for domesticating fandom that appreciates and even respects wild fans, seeing them as valued stakeholders owed consideration. If this book tells how we got to today, where does it go from here? The positive (maybe utopian) outcome would be industry realizing fans do benefit them and should be taken into account. The negative outcome would be excluding fans from participation completely through backlash against the minor gains they have made. There are thus two futures of fandom, and in what follows I will describe the seeds of both of them in turn.

BACKLASH: THE DARK FUTURE OF FANDOM

This book began with one conversation about the fan–industry relationship in 2016; the one it ends with is both similar and different. Arguments that fans are entitled have accumulated in recent years and erupted in summer 2016; they are a sign of a backlash that could potentially roll back the (limited) progress of fan inclusion. In this section, I analyze the "entitled fan" argument in news stories and blog posts as it proliferated in summer 2016, supplemented with earlier examples cited in those essays. On its face, the fan entitlement genre is strange. Authors run together wildly disparate fan actions: petitioning for inclusion of women, people of color, and LGBTQ+ folks is blended with demanding media regress to less inclusion of those groups; critical analysis is equated to death threats. It makes no sense—except that the common theme across the disparate examples lumped together is that fans are seeking input into how media is made. That this is the through line, and that it is framed as entitlement, reveals an underlying anxiety about whether industry will continue to have sufficient control. Although as the rest of this book has shown the shift in power has been small at best and entirely illusory at worst, the response to it is dramatic and deeply disproportionate. The reaction also casts media industries as victims of monstrous fans. In these ways, the backlash against fans has all the key features of a moral panic.

A moral panic, according to Stanley Cohen's (1972, 122) early and influential model, "starts off with the perception by some people of a condition which is trouble-making, difficult, dangerous or threatening and requiring action: 'something should be done about it.' A specific rule is deduced from the general value which is felt should be protected or upheld, and, if appropriate, a method of control is suggested." People are disproportionately distressed in a moral panic because the perception of danger is disproportionate to the actual threat (Cohen 1972; Marwick 2008). Moral panics happen through extrapolation from particular instances of (mis)behavior to a larger threat, "a consensus that the beliefs or actions being denounced were not isolated entities ('it's not only this') but integral parts of the society or else could (and would) be unless 'something was done'" (Cohen 1972, xi). This model is useful for explaining fan entitlement as a contemporary fear.

What is perceived, unreasonably, as a broad and fundamental threat is fans talking back to industry and wanting media made differently. This "threat" is made both disproportionate and existential through a flock of false equivalences: suggestions are deemed to be the same as demands, and distinctions among criticism, harassment, threats, and violence are hopelessly muddied. This slippage shows in how professional fannish commentator Chris Hardwick, in discussing what constitutes appropriate fan criticism, slides quickly from describing correct criticism as "walking up to someone and telling them rationally why you did or didn't like something" to comparing critique to "walking up to them and hitting them in the face with a frying pan." He says, "Those are two different things," but he constructs them as a single category by yoking them together in the sentence (Martens 2016). The urgency of fans' alleged threat is amplified in fan entitlement essays by emphasizing the most violent examples of fan behavior—creators' need to install bulletproof glass (Martens 2016); attempted suicide as the result of harassment (Elderkin 2016); doxing (Bramesco 2016); racist invective (Martens 2016; Child 2016; Hess 2016); death threats (Martens 2016; Child 2016; Adams 2016a, 2016b; Faraci 2016); and terrorism (Faraci 2016).

Fan entitlement essays are driven by beliefs that fans think of themselves as far too powerful. One journalist laments that "artists, especially genre artists, like to tell fans that they are the lifeblood of the operation—that they are the reason these movies get made, that these shows stay on the air, that these books keep getting published. This kind of PR line is its own, almost insultingly direct form of fan service. Moreover, it also provides a kind of false empowerment, which in turn can lead to a very real sense of entitlement" (Hassenger 2016). Not only is the flattery empty, Hassenger suggests, but, more importantly, it encourages fans to get above themselves. Another writer is similarly distressed by the demise of "the old respect for the film-making process that once ran through geek culture, at least in the blogosphere" (Child 2016). Again, the worry is fans not being appropriately respectful—or subordinate. Fans perceiving themselves as powerful is particularly galling when industry thinks fans do not have informed opinions, as when—in the only sports example of this phenomenon—a sportswriter takes fans to task for incorrectly thinking the San Francisco Giants' general manager makes bad trades, detailing why they are in fact smart trades (Sillanpaa 2014). Similarly, another journalist criticizes fans demanding sequels, saying they request them because they do not understand previous installments of things they love didn't sell well (Mendelson 2013).

As the above lament for "the old respect" already suggests, moral panics are often "acting on behalf of the dominant social order," and in particular they "often entail looking back to a 'golden age' where social stability and strong moral discipline acted as a deterrent to delinquency and disorder" (McRobbie and Thornton 1995, 562, 561). Therefore, moral panics are predominantly conservative—and this one is conservative in two ways. First, at a content level, it is conservative because interest in social justice is never more than a gesture; inclusion is then actively dismissed through either indirect or direct equation to harassing campaigns for change: "While the intentions come from a better, more inclusive place, insisting that Elsa [of Disney's *Frozen*] should be given a girlfriend by popular demand is not so different than insisting that ghostbusting ought to be a male profession, to better conform to childhood memories" (Hassenger 2016), as a vocal group of men fans did in response to the 2016 all-women *Ghostbusters* remake. Second, moral panics are structurally conservative, seeking to conserve the status quo—where industry makes things and fans buy them and shut up—against a (greatly inflated) threat that this division may diminish.

If there is a threat, it is to someone, and if fans are bullies (Hess 2016; Bramesco 2016), then industry becomes their victim. As Cohen (1972, xii) notes, a moral panic requires "a suitable victim," often someone socially valued. Fans have wrested control away from poor industry workers, the story goes. Joss Whedon—yes, the same Whedon discussed earlier as fan friendly—notes that "there is definitely a sense of not just 'We know better,' but also 'We should have the right to dictate'" (Martens 2016). This is terrible, according to the panic, because industry should keep control: "What is disconcerting is how seriously they are taken by the media at large, and in turn how often they seem to get their way through luck or happenstance" (Mendelson 2013). "We're now living in a movie culture driven by the whims of diehards," one journalist laments, comparing this to cancer as something that has "metastasized" (Bramesco 2016). Commonly, fan input is resisted through appeals to art. Fans should respect the creative vision (Martens 2016; Faraci 2012, 2016) and not dictate how art is made: "They shouldn't be bringing a bucket of paint to the museum to take out some of the blue from those Picassos, you know?" (Faraci 2016). In a startling contrast to the reality of media industries, Whedon rejects fan suggestions because "you can't create by committee" (although TV and film are created by committee), and author Neil Gaiman insists authors do not work for fans (although creators have jobs because the market commodities they make sell, and so in some ways they do; Martens 2016). This perspective casts industry workers or industry itself as a victim of fans. Those poor white actors being criticized for taking roles of characters of color! (Hill 2016). Industry workers "genuinely just want to tell stories to entertain people and uplift them" (Martens 2016), the poor things! Those fans—they're scary! "Over the past year or so, the fan has revealed himself to be no kind king. He is a mad despot, issuing demands from on high and sputtering with rage when defied" (Bramesco 2016).

If the fan as a bully, as harming a disempowered industry, as protean in its ever-changing but ever-threatening forms, seems like a convenient foil, that is because it is. The objects of moral panics are "folk devils: visible reminders of what we should not be" (Cohen 1972, 2). The folk devil, like the broader category of monster, does cultural work. The etymology of "monster" is useful here: in both Old and Middle French and Anglo-Norman, its "derivations articulate transfigurations of the human form, and the term's evolution from classical Latin" into its iterations in the modern Romance languages "impl[ies] a warning [. . .] embodied in the monstrous form" (Boon 2007, 33). Monsters are humans gone awry meant to warn us. Moral panics deploy monsters or folk devils as "a means of orchestrating consent by actively intervening in the space of public opinion and social consciousness" (McRobbie and Thornton 1995, 562). That is, "discourses that would mobilize monstrosity as a screen for otherness are always involved in circuits of normalizing power as well" (Puar and Rai 2002, 119). Therefore, pointing to something as "don't be that" always also tells us what we actually should be. The folk devil of a moral panic needs to be a "*suitable enemy:* a soft target, easily denounced, with little power and preferably without even access to the battlefields of cultural politics" like the ability to speak for themselves in the media (Cohen 1972, xii). This is because "moral panics can be defined as the efforts of a particular group to exert collective moral control over another group or person" (Baker 2001). Fans serve this need particularly well because as a threat "they are *new* (lying dormant perhaps, but hard to recognize; deceptively ordinary and routine, but invisibly creeping up the moral horizon)—but also *old* (camouflaged versions of traditional and well-known evils)" (Cohen 1972, vii–viii). Long-standing ideas of fans as violent and pathological are dormant and ready to activate, but the new twist is provided by industrial and technological change.

The fan as a folk devil or monster is why the rhetoric in backlash articles is downright ominous. This can appear narrowly, as word choices that fans and their attitudes are "strange" (Martens 2016) or "deeply troubling" (Faraci 2016). However, fans are often (still) described as mentally ill, invoking the trope of mental illness as inherently threatening (Martens 2016; Bramesco 2016; Faraci 2012). Fan monstrosity is also linked to violence. The soft version is through the use of metaphors of violence that, as George Lakoff and Mark Johnson (2003) note in their study of metaphor, are so routine we may no longer recognize them as metaphors of violence, such as commentary that fan objects are "loved so ardently that those who demur come under fire" (Child 2016). The rhetorical link to violence can also be entirely conscious and intended, as when blogger and antifan of fandom Devin Faraci (2016) argues "creators can be trapped, bullied and tortured" by the "most dedicated, most rabid fanbases."

In particular, the anxiety of fannish influence—to riff on Harold Bloom's (1973) term—is what Alice E. Marwick (2008) calls a technopanic, a form of "moral panic as a response to fear of modernity as represented by new technologies." The moral panic around fans is a technopanic in focusing particularly on how these risks are caused or facilitated by the internet, especially social media. Because of technology, fans now have access to their industry "victims": "These people now have the megaphone known as the Internet," one journalist notes (Mendelson 2013). Faraci (2016), characteristically more dramatic, says, "Twitter is the match that has been touched to this powder keg, and all of a sudden the uglier parts of fandom—the entitlement, the demands, the frankly poor understanding of how drama and storytelling work—have blown the fuck up." Technology is also blamed for making fans more vicious. We are told that "only since the advent of social media has the vocal minority found a lively breeding ground for their unsolicited, vicious attacks—mostly of the personal variety with an intent to damage another person's well-being" (Scott 2016). Ivan Reitman, director of the initial films in the Ghostbusters franchise, notes, "The popularization of the internet and the opportunity for any person to give an opinion have created a certain level of criticism and a kind of vulgarity that certainly wasn't around in the '80s" (Glasner 2016). Technology is therefore to blame for the problem the moral panic panics about.

Obviously I am not condoning the terrorism visited on many by the most extreme instances of fan harassment. From *Ghostbusters* to Gamergate, some fan behavior has been indefensible, but the fact that people behave reprehensibly online is not in itself interesting. (The causes and effects would be interesting.) What is interesting is the strange ways fan behavior is talked about. The fan entitlement discourse focuses around the fan monster and industry victim through both taking a handful of dramatic instances as typical fan action and actively conflating nonviolent advocacy with them. This shows that it is not about the content or format of the complaints at all, thus demonstrating the larger backlash formation at work. Fans are imagined as scarier and more powerful than they are—I've just spent a whole book arguing that their power is largely illusory, after all—because it serves the interests of industry workers, including journalists, to frame these gains as attacks to roll them back and reaffirm industry's power.

However, alongside the management, normalization, domestication, and scapegoating, there is something different. The ideas that fans matter, that industry owes them something, and that they are people of value and worth considering also show up repeatedly in my archive. The belief that industry has an obligation to fans is not a major thread as the contemporary discourse of the fan developed; it crops up a few dozen times, compared to hundreds for more prominent concepts. However, there is a consistent muted refrain of positivity within the general trend toward constricted possibilities in the period this book examines. Saying fans matter may even be disingenuous, but at least industry thinks it should say fans matter, indicating they think fans cannot be entirely controlled or disrespected. Thus, these instances may signal the potential for something more to exist in the fan–industry relationship.

Arguments that fans deserve something are one manifestation of this belief. At the end of the parodic comedy *My Name Is Bruce,* when the monster pops out after being defeated, what fans deserve is invoked:

BRUCE: Stop, stop. *[Steps in front, looking out and breaking the fourth wall]*

DIRECTOR: What's the problem, Bruce?

BRUCE: Look, I'm sorry, but these shock endings are a rip-off. I mean, we just killed the creature, like, thirty seconds ago, and now it's back? The fans deserve better.

Related to this idea of deserving something is a sense that, as Jenkins, Ford, and Green (2013, 61) argue, industry is "obligated to learn from and respond to fan expectations, not the other way around, since fans do not owe companies anything," so fans should be thanked for their support since they could just as easily withhold it. One fan in the sports documentary *Mathematically Alive* comments of New York Mets catcher Mike Piazza, "He always said thank you to me for being a fan. And you don't hear that enough from a ballplayer. You're spending your hard-earned money to go to games, and watching ballplayers, and you don't hear thank you from them enough." While a fan says this, including it within the documentary in a straightforward way legitimizes her argument. Sometimes it is even argued that industry has an ethical obligation to reward fan loyalty. After a 2007 fan campaign saved CBS show *Jericho*, executive producer Carol Barbee notes, "It was incumbent upon us to tell a great story for these people who saved the show." More expansively, actor Skeet Ulrich says, "The only reason most of us came back was for the fans. [. . .] We wanted to make episodes for them because they certainly deserved it after all the effort they put in. I couldn't imagine turning tail on them after everything they'd done'" (Littlejohn 2008).

In opposition to the moral panic framing, fans are also sometimes treated as having informed opinions and valuable knowledge. Discussing the rise of sites like movie review aggregator Rotten Tomatoes, Merrin of Campfire describes this belief that fan views carry weight:

> MERRIN: You know, "What does this fan think about—what does an influential fan think about this movie? 'Cause if a fan doesn't like it, what's—Is there a chance that as a newcomer to the franchise I will?" Or, this kind of tension of, "I'm not a fan of that, but what does a fan think?" And wanting to know that it's satisfying them as well.
>
> INTERVIEWER: Fans as knowledgeable, like, experts in a field?
>
> MERRIN: Yeah, that's kind of the way I see things happening.

Similarly, although *Xena: Warrior Princess* episode "Send in the Clones" makes fun of fans who can cite episode and scene by having those characters be bumbling idiots within the text, it structurally rewards having seen all the episodes because it is a clip show—one that recycles old footage to save money, relying on viewers' knowledge of the context of the initial scene when it is reused. In general, intense serialization in 2000s TV demands corresponding fan practices of amassing intensive and extensive knowledge formerly considered niche or even marginal. With complex and long-term narratives of this sort, as Sharon Ross (2009, 45) notes, "viewers must be devoted in order to understand their shows' universes."

More specifically, there is a sense that what fans want matters. In the sports thriller *The Fan*, a sports radio host describes player Bobby Rayburn as the "hopes and dreams of the fans," authorizing fan expectations as legitimate to try to meet. There can also be more specific or content-based obligations to provide for fan desires. As Merrin of Camp-fire puts it, "There's no kind of like, 'Do x, y, and z and you're going to get this result.' It's always, I think it's, you know, based on intuition and what you know about the community but then what you know about human beings. [Laughs] And being realistic about, you know, who would actually do this? Would they actually do this? Would I actually do this?" Concerns about what actual fans want underpin Merrin's approach as opposed to the standardization of a formula. Similarly, Allen Graf, foot-ball coordinator for film The Express, says in a DVD special feature that the football movies he has done "have the realism. It's really important to me because I know there's a lot of football aficionados out there who are just looking to see: How is this football played out, and how does it look?" Graf identifies satisfying those aficionados as a primary goal.

Prioritizing fan desires sometimes becomes the idea that industry will or must alter its practices to suit fans. Steve from Campfire sums up the priorities of his work: "You have to understand the needs of the audience as much—and probably more so than the needs of the brand"—a somewhat unexpected emphasis. More intensively, sometimes fan needs even take precedence over financial concerns. Putting fans before money is rare, but for it to happen at all is noteworthy. Importantly, industry workers on the business side never take this position, only people whose motivations do not begin and end with money (although they generally do, of course, include it). Thus, in the Jericho revival example mentioned above, "Sacrifices were also made. 'It was different for different people, depending on what their initial contracts were,' notes co-star Lennie James, 'but everybody, in one way, shape or form, took a pay cut in order to come back to Jericho'" (Littlejohn 2008). Here actors' sense of duty to fans outweighs desire for maximum payment.

Fans are particularly constructed as owed something through the de-ployment of three characters: the (falsely) entitled celebrity, the innocent (and therefore deserving) child fan, and the adult fan hero. These three images, often painted in broad strokes to the point of caricature and oper-ating as symbols, usefully illuminate how "good" fans are conceptualized. My Name Is Bruce is as much a send up of the misbehaving celebrity as a narrative about an overly invested kidnapper fan. The character of Bruce Campbell, played by actor Bruce Campbell, sets the bar for rude, telling fans they smell, treating townspeople in need as country bumpkins, and displaying terrible table manners. He even actively harms others to benefit himself: he shoves a wheelchair-using military veteran into traffic for annoying him and carjacks an elderly woman to escape the film's monster. One common version of the mean celebrity is the greedy sports star. Sports comedy *The Replacements* depicts professional football players who have gone on strike for higher pay as avaricious specifically at fan expense. A reporter asks one player, "There are a lot of angry fans out there tonight that feel the players are being too greedy with their demands. Anything you'd like to say to that?" The player insists $5 million may seem like a lot of money, but he has to pay 10 percent to his agent and 5 percent to his lawyer—that is, he generally misses the point. Another player, even more out of touch, cuts into the conversation to demand, "Do you have any idea how much insurance costs on a Ferrari, motherf—" before being cut off. Aside from the troubling antiunion politics of the film, the players are incredibly unsympathetic.

Industry personnel who behave badly toward children are even less likeable. Baseball player Ricky in the comedy *Major League II* blows off a party thrown in his honor by underprivileged children, leading one of them to gripe, "What a pukehead. He didn't even have no cake." Worse, Roger Meyers Jr., chairman of the studio that produces diegetic cartoon *The Itchy & Scratchy Show* in *The Simpsons*, shouts at a focus group of eight- to ten-year-olds after they have given contradictory answers, "You kids don't know what you want! That's why you're still kids! 'Cause you're stupid! Just tell me what's wrong with the freaking show!"—an outburst that causes Ralph Wiggum to cry. These instances of showing children's reaction to industry misbehavior particularly underline its inappropriateness.

This behavior is troublesome because of the simultaneous construction of a special duty to children. *Spider-man* series director Sam Raimi describes himself as having a "great responsibility to tell the story of this character that kids look up to as this great hero. Certainly you don't want to make anything that isn't worthy of their admiration" (Cohen 2006). That kids deserve role models produces a scene in the nerd sports comedy *The Benchwarmers* when one of the nerdy, fannish adults who have been standing up to the bullying athletic kids on behalf of the nerdy, fannish kids is revealed to have been a childhood bully himself. A journalist comments, "That's too bad. Those guys inspired a lot of really nice kids." One of the bullied contemporary children says, crying, "I can't believe I looked up to you."

In these scenes, child fans always legitimately deserve attention from their object of fandom and are never framed as troublesome. Particularly, young fans who might just as easily be considered obnoxious—and surely would for the same behavior as adults—are treated as somewhere between neutral and endearing. Seven-year-old blond boy-child Darius in the Harry Potter fan documentary *We Are Wizards* is a fan musician who makes terrible music that seems to consist of him shouting "Dragon rock rules!" tunelessly, but the audience within the documentary nevertheless cheers him on. The perfect encapsulation of the child fan as a worthy figure occurs in a news story about the 2002 Super Bowl:

> Bobby Brady stood at attention outside the Superdome on Sunday, his hand raised to the brim of his New England Patriots baseball cap in a snappy salute for the soldiers standing on the street corner. "He loves football players, but now he says he wants to be a soldier," said the 5-year-old's mother, Carolyn Brady. "Isn't this great? He gets the best of both worlds today." The Bradys, not related to Patriots' quarterback Tom Brady, were decked out in red, white, and blue team outfits that reflected the patriotic theme of the Super Bowl. (Foster 2002)

As the first Super Bowl after the September 11, 2001, terrorist attacks, this one celebrates America even more than the Super Bowl baseline, but the trifecta of boy-child, sport, and nation illuminates particularly clearly how all three are normatively unquestionably "good," putting being a fan in the most culturally valued of company.

As little Bobby Brady, the shiny symbol, begins to suggest, at times kids are constructed as so pure and special that they act as saviors for industry workers, showing them the error of their ways. In football film *Any Given Sunday*, there is an almost Socratic dialogue between player Julian "J-Man" Washington and a young African American boy-child fan:

FAN: What's up, J-Man?

WASHINGTON: What's up, little man?

FAN: Is it true you makin' 10 million a year? [*Washington smiles and nods]* That true, then, about you not blockin' no more either? It's part of your contract? That's what my dad says. He says you don't have to catch no passes over the middle either 'cause you don't want to get hurt? It's also in your contract—right, J?

WASHINGTON: Yeah, your dad's got it down, kiddo.

Because of this conversation, Washington realizes he should not put his own financial gain over the good of the team. He changes his ways to play more aggressively and less safely.

This child-as-savior narrative resembles how adult fans sometimes are not just redeemed into normativity, as is described in Chapter 2, but are also positioned as heroic. Suzanne Scott (2011, 38–39) argues, "Refashioning the fanboy as a visible romantic protagonist, or an (often reluctant) action hero or superhero, the fanboy's recuperation into Hollywood's hegemonic demography has been coupled with his representational recuperation into hegemonic masculinity." Importantly—as with the redemption narrative, and as suggested by the preponderance of boy children among pure, worthy fans—not everyone has access to the hero narrative. As Busse (2013, 81) puts it, "The fan hero remains relentlessly gendered. While the fanboys are often clearly caricatured, their portrayals nevertheless tend to be more lovingly tongue-in-cheek than the respective fangirl characterizations. Fanboys are allowed more agency and can become heroes." The fan hero is somewhat more inclusive in that boys and men who save the day do not have to be white or even heterosexual—so it does not follow the same line as the redemption narrative and must be considered different rather than an extension. However, seemingly being a boy or man is not optional.

One key aspect of the fan hero is that the narratives tend to "frame the fanboy's affective relationship with geeky media properties as an intrinsic part of his charm" (Scott 2011, 285), like fans who save the day precisely through their fannishness. In spy comedy *Chuck,* Chuck's knowledge of fannish things facilitates being a secret agent, as when his familiarity with video gaming lets him be guided through flying a helicopter or his practice with military-style games means he can describe an imaginary strike force well enough to bluff an enemy agent. Chuck does not believe in his own capacities, noting to real CIA agent

Sarah, "I don't think I'm really cut out for a job where you disarm a bomb, steal a diamond, and then jump off a building." However, Sarah replies, "Well, you could have fooled me," thus marking his heroism as up to professional standards.

The fan hero figure also appears when fans are noble and try to be brave even when failure at their manly duties seems certain. Importantly, in these few cases of the symbolic fan hero, the command to straighten up and fly white is lifted. *Heroes* frequently positions Japanese character Hiro Nakamura as heroic, as when the narrator solemnly intones, "For all his bluster, it is the sad province of man that he cannot choose his trials. He can only choose how he will stand when the call of destiny comes, hoping that he'll have the courage to answer" against a visual of Hiro looking determined and noble. Similarly, Hiro insists, in the face of his friend Ando's quite reasonable question, "If there's a nuclear explosion, shouldn't we be running away from the bomb?" that "A hero doesn't run away from his destiny." This heroism sits uneasily alongside his goofy, childish, excessive enthusiasm, such that it is almost inconsistent characterization, but he is able to achieve heroism despite being neither white nor hegemonically masculine (itself a category of whiteness).

In *Supernatural,* fans doing live-action role-play as real heroes Sam and Dean save the day in the episode "The Real Ghostbusters." These fans want to help even though they know there is real danger and not just the mystery game they signed up for. The fan dressed as Sam notes, "If all these people are seriously in trouble, we gotta do something," despite their fear, because, as the fan dressed as Dean says, "That's what Sam and Dean would do." In the end, the fans save not only all the other people at the fan convention but the heroes, Sam and Dean, themselves, who are trapped and fighting for their lives until the fans dispel the evil spirits. Here again the hero diverges substantially from the redemption narrative, as these two men are a couple. Being white men may be what allows them to be gay and still heroes, or perhaps the pressure of *Supernatural*'s fan base being so queerly invested in a Sam and Dean romance (Schmidt 2010; Tosenberger 2008) makes nonincestuous gay men safe by comparison. With the fan hero narrative, fan knowledge or a fannish value system is a benefit. Thus, the misbehaving star, the child fan, and the fan hero all articulate being a fan to the good, whether directly or by contrast. It is relatively rare, but it is there, and it should be taken seriously as the possibility of a good outcome even as it goes against the grain of the overall picture.

CODA

A few years ago, I was guest lecturing in someone else's course, talking about the research that ultimately became Chapters 5 and 6 of this book, and a student pushed back on the idea that there was anything to be concerned about in the practice of extracting labor from fan activity. "That's just the way it is," he said. After a few back and forths, what finally got him to understand my point was this: "But no one asked you. No one asked if you wanted to trade your attention on advertisements and your personal data for free digital content. It just happens when you use the internet."

Industry is not asking fans whether they want to be domesticated. It is easy to see the benefits of industry's offer: stigma has been diminished (although not erased), access and information have been expanded, and legal strictures have been relaxed. It is hard—because we are not accustomed to thinking systemically, but also by design—to see the costs they require: normalizing into a narrow and exclusionary model of fandom, performing uncompensated labor, and abandoning the critical traditions of fandom. Industry certainly has more power than fans do, and they have a full array of tools to both incite and coerce fans toward behaviors that benefit them, but whether domestication succeeds will, in the end, be up to fans. Although this is not a book about fans as people or fandom as a culture, I do hope that it can nevertheless serve fans and fandom through its accounting of exactly what is on offer in the new era of fan friendliness. Fans have been offered deals that, much like TOS, have a lot of fine print. Maybe fans will find the terms acceptable; maybe they won't. But before fans can make that assessment, the terms need to be made much more transparent, and this book has sought to do just that—not because fans are dupes or lack agency, but precisely to enable the true agency of well-informed choice.

Film and TV Sources

Title	Year	Fiction or Nonfiction	Medium	Object	Sport
30 Rock—Season 1	2006–7	Fiction	TV	Speculative	
30 Rock—Season 2	2007–8	Fiction	TV	Speculative	
30 Rock—Season 3	2008–9	Fiction	TV	Speculative	
40 Year Old Virgin, The	2005	Fiction	Film	Speculative	
Any Given Sunday	1999	Fiction	Film	Sports	Football
BASEketball	1998	Fiction	Film	Sports	BASEketball (fictional)
Benchwarmers, The	2006	Fiction	Film	Sports	Baseball
Big Bang Theory, The—Season 1	2007–8	Fiction	TV	Speculative	
Big Bang Theory, The—Season2	2008–9	Fiction	TV	Speculative	
Big Fan	2009	Fiction	Film	Sports	Football
Buffy the Vampire Slayer—Season 6	2001–2	Fiction	TV	Speculative	
Chuck—Season 1	2007–8	Fiction	TV	Speculative	
Chuck—Season 2	2008–9	Fiction	TV	Speculative	
Cobb	1994	Fiction	Film	Sports	Baseball
D2: The Mighty Ducks	1994	Fiction	Film	Sports	Hockey
D3: The Mighty Ducks	1996	Fiction	Film	Sports	Hockey
Double Dare	2004	Nonfiction	Film	Speculative	
Express, The	2008	Fiction	Film	Sports	Football

continued on next page

Title	Year	Fiction or Nonfiction	Medium	Object	Sport
Facing the Giants	2006	Fiction	Film	Sports	Football
Fan, The	1996	Fiction	Film	Sports	Baseball
Fanalysis	2002	Nonfiction	Film	Speculative	
Fanboys	2009	Fiction	Film	Speculative	
Fever Pitch	2005	Fiction	Film	Sports	Baseball
For Love of the Game	1999	Fiction	Film	Sports	Baseball
Forgetting Sarah Marshall	2008	Fiction	Film	Speculative	
Friday Night Lights	2004	Fiction	Film	Sports	Football
Friday Night Lights—Season 1	2006–7	Fiction	TV	Sports	Football
Friday Night Lights—Season 2	2007 8	Fiction	TV	Sports	Football
Friday Night Lights—Season 3	2008–9	Fiction	TV	Sports	Football
Galaxy Quest	1999	Fiction	Film	Speculative	
Game 6	2005	Fiction	Film	Sports	Baseball
Guild, The—Season 1	2007–8	Fiction	Web series	Speculative	
Guild, The—Season 2	2008–9	Fiction	Web series	Speculative	
Guild, The—Season 3	2009	Fiction	Web series	Speculative	
Happy Gilmore	1996	Fiction	Film	Sports	Golf
Heroes—Season 1	2006–7	Fiction	TV	Speculative	
Heroes—Season 2	2007	Fiction	TV	Speculative	
Heroes—Season 3	2008–9	Fiction	TV	Speculative	
Horror Fans	2006	Nonfiction	Film	Speculative	
Hurricane Season	2009	Fiction	Film	Sports	Basketball

Title	Year	Fiction or Nonfiction	Medium	Object	Sport
Invincible	2006	Fiction	Film	Sports	Football
Knocked Up	2007	Fiction	Film	Speculative	
Leatherheads	2008	Fiction	Film	Sports	Football
Longshots, The	2008	Fiction	Film	Sports	Football
Looking for Kitty	2004	Fiction	Film	Sports	Baseball
Major League II	1994	Fiction	Film	Sports	Baseball
Mathematically Alive: A Story of Fandom	2007	Nonfiction	Film	Sports	Baseball
Mighty Macs	2009	Fiction	Film	Sports	Basketball
My Name Is Bruce	2007	Fiction	Film	Speculative	
Mystery, Alaska	1999	Fiction	Film	Sports	Hockey
New Guy	2002	Fiction	Film	Sports	Football
O.C., The—Season 1	2003–4	Fiction	TV	Speculative	
O.C., The—Season 2	2004–5	Fiction	TV	Speculative	
O.C., The—Season 3	2005–6	Fiction	TV	Speculative	
O.C., The—Season 4	2006–7	Fiction	TV	Speculative	
Replacements, The	2000	Fiction	Film	Sports	Football
Rookie, The	2002	Fiction	Film	Sports	Baseball
Simpsons Movie, The	2007	Fiction	Film	Speculative	
Simpsons, The—Season 10 (selected episodes)	1998–99	Fiction	TV	Speculative	
Simpsons, The—Season 11 (selected episodes)	1999–2000	Fiction	TV	Speculative	
Simpsons, The—Season 12 (selected episodes)	2000–1	Fiction	TV	Speculative	

continued on next page

Title	Year	Fiction or Nonfiction	Medium	Object	Sport
Simpsons, The— Season 13 (selected episodes)	2001–2	Fiction	TV	Speculative	
Simpsons, The— Season 14 (selected episodes)	2002–3	Fiction	TV	Speculative	
Simpsons, The— Season 15 (selected episodes)	2003–4	Fiction	TV	Speculative	
Simpsons, The— Season 20 (selected episodes)	2008–9	Fiction	TV	Speculative	
Simpsons, The— Season 5 (selected episodes)	1993–94	Fiction	TV	Speculative	
Simpsons, The— Season 6 (selected episodes)	1994–95	Fiction	TV	Speculative	
Simpsons, The— Season 7 (selected episodes)	1995–96	Fiction	TV	Speculative	
Simpsons, The— Season 8 (selected episodes)	1996–97	Fiction	TV	Speculative	
Simpsons, The— Season 9 (selected episodes)	1997–98	Fiction	TV	Speculative	
Star Trek: Voyager— Season 2 (selected episodes)	1995–96	Fiction	TV	Speculative	
Star Trek: Voyager— Season 6 (selected episodes)	1999–2000	Fiction	TV	Speculative	

Title	Year	Fiction or Nonfiction	Medium	Object	Sport
Star Trek: Voyager—Season 7 (selected episodes)	2000–1	Fiction	TV	Speculative	
Summer Catch	2001	Fiction	Film	Sports	Baseball
Superbad	2007	Fiction	Film	Speculative	
Supernatural—Season 4 (selected episodes)	2008–9	Fiction	TV	Speculative	
Supernatural—Season 5 (selected episodes)	2009–10	Fiction	TV	Speculative	
To Save a Life	2009	Fiction	Film	Sports	Basketball
Trekkies	1997	Nonfiction	Film	Speculative	
Trekkies 2	2004	Nonfiction	Film	Speculative	
We Are Wizards	2008	Nonfiction	Film	Speculative	
West Wing, The—Season 4 ("Arctic Radar")	2002–3	Fiction	TV	Speculative	
Winning Season	2009	Fiction	Film	Sports	Basketball
Xena: Warrior Princess—Season 3	1997–98	Fiction	TV	Speculative	
Xena: Warrior Princess—Season 4	1998–99	Fiction	TV	Speculative	
Xena: Warrior Princess—Season 6	2000–1	Fiction	TV	Speculative	
Xena: Warrior Princess 10th Anniversay Collection	2005	Nonfiction	TV	Speculative	

INTRODUCTION

1. Fans also, in a topic I will return to in the Conclusion, used that collective might for aggressive attacks on the show, the writers, the network, and especially showrunner Jason Rothenberg in the aftermath, including an obsession with diminishing his number of Twitter followers, a desire to see him fired, and writing threats and detailed descriptions of violence.

2. Shipping, derived from "relationship," describes fans who enjoy and/or advocate for romantic relationships between particular characters, whether currently in a romance in the text or not.

3. I use the term "speculative" to encompass all media types grounded in not being realistic, whether horror, comic books, science fiction, or fantasy, because these types of media are represented and understood similarly, because fans of one genre are often fans of one or more of the others—and because many media objects in fact do not easily belong to a single one of the genres.

4. Proponents of the argument that fans are now normative media consumers include Henry Jenkins (2006a, 2007; Jenkins, Ford, and Green 2013), Cornel Sandvoss (2005), and Paul Booth (2010; Booth and Kelly 2013).

5. See, for example, advocacy of the democratization argument by Jenkins (Jenkins and Carpentier 2013; Stein 2014).

6. For a critique of how this narrative encourages conflating media participation with political participation, see Ouellette and Hay (2008).

7. See Schimmel, Harrington, and Bielby (2007). One notable exception is Sandvoss (2005).

8. Throughout the book, I use "fan" to refer to people or the discourse and reserve "fandom" for the community because this is the distinction that I argue is vital. One exception to this is the phrase "object of fandom."

9. For the foundational model of performativity, see Austin (1975).

10. The one exception to this is industry's intermittent cease-and-desist letters or lawsuits for illegal downloading under the 1998 Digital Millenni-

um Copyright Act (DMCA), but even then, the goal has been to make an example of those individuals for the larger population of downloaders.

11. To give him his due, Mark Andrejevic (2008, 44) also refers to "domesticated interactivity," but only in passing rather than following through on the implications of the metaphor, as I do here. Others who use "domestic" to discuss fandom refer to domesticity or the domestic rather than constructing a metaphor of agricultural selective breeding.

12. Whedon's position has subsequently been complicated by revelations of sexual misconduct with actresses who worked for him (Cole 2017). However, as of July 2018, a spate of announcements of new projects suggests an industry perception that Whedon is still a bankable auteur.

13. The time period of this study does not encompass the purchase of the Star Wars franchise by Disney, although Disney's policies are equally, if not more, controlling.

14. For a complete list of these texts, see the Appendix.

15. Moretti has also been accused of sexual misconduct (Mangan 2017). My use of his theories should not be taken as an endorsement of his behavior.

16. This is similar to Sandvoss's (2005) approach, which also expands past self-identified subcultures.

CHAPTER ONE

1. The Puppies had actually run two previous campaigns, but it was not until the 2015 edition—likely as a result of Gamergate happening in the meantime—that there was substantial attention outside the people closely involved. There was also a campaign in 2016.

2. Pseudonyms for the sports practitioners, who all requested anonymity, were selected from the most common names in the United States.

3. The list of other characteristics where trouble might arise, of course, similarly identifies the site's main population as members of the dominant category with respect to these structures.

4. While this is clearly not the only or necessarily the primary draw, and neither is it disqualifying from being a "real fan," Abby Waysdorf (2015b) shows that eroticizing men athletes in football through slash fan fiction is an activity with a substantial following.

5. The commentary tracks generally have six to eight commentators, nearly always all men. Although all participants introduce themselves at the beginning of the commentary, I find it impossible to differentiate so many

similar voices given the ever-changing roster—except Groening himself, who is consistently present in DVD materials, and the women who intermittently participate.

6. The exception to discussing only fanboys came with the Twilight fandom, but these fans were specifically marked off as not regular attendees—and in fact not "real" fans at all.

7. Though one could argue the cultural tendency to privilege men might mean that all sites default to male, so this doesn't indicate who designers expect, an informal look at some sites with a primary constituency of women demonstrates this is not the case: Disney and Victoria's Secret both have "female" as the more easily found option, and After Ellen, while not asking about gender, has "lesbian" as its first drop-down choice for sexuality, indicating a tailoring of these options to the particular user base.

8. Though, as Rahman (2011) argues, as men athletes have become understood as celebrities, they have been incorporated into the objectification and sexualization endemic to celebrity as a system, which is generally seen as incompatible with hegemonic masculinity.

9. The fact that this pattern persists in *The Guild*, a web series made by self-identified fans and by some estimates intended to be more of an inside joke than anything, shows how much these stereotypes are what "fans" means in the popular imaginary, even to the sympathetic.

10. In practice, this law tends to result in Terms of Service forbidding people younger than thirteen from registering, as sites are unwilling to allow users who can't be turned into data.

CHAPTER TWO

1. Interestingly, on the one hand, this comment seems to privilege fans by apologizing for disappointing their view of Jonathan as potentially heroic. On the other hand, it misuses the fan term "shipper," which does not mean an advocate of a single character, as Fury uses it here, but rather as a shortened form of "relationshipper," which indicates a fan who advocates a romantic relationship between two or more characters.

2. For early listings of these stereotypes, see Jenkins (1992) and the essays collected in Lewis (1992b), especially Jensen (1992).

3. For early iterations, see the Combahee River Collective (1981), Moraga and Anzaldúa (1983), and Collins (1990). The term "intersectionality" was coined by Crenshaw (1991).

4. This desire to be a superhero is treated as an understandable result of youth for Micah, an interesting counterpoint to treating Black children (Micah is biracial but as a result of hypodescent, or the so-called one-drop rule, would generally be classified as Black in the American racial system) as prematurely adult. Hiro's childishness, on the other hand, plays on tropes of Asian men as boyish rather than manly.

5. In Zaboo's case, tropes about fans as immature intersect with tropes about South Asian Americans as controlled by their parents.

6. Cosplay is a portmanteau of "costume play." It refers to dressing up as a character of whom one is a fan. Two of the characters in *Supernatural* turn out to be gay men in a relationship with one another, but the others fit this pattern.

7. Slash fiction is based in interpreting same-sex desire from characters who are not identified as queer in the text.

8. See, for example, Crawford (2004), Forsyth and Thompson (2007), Gosling (2007), and Wedgwood (2008). This is mostly heterosexual women eroticizing men athletes, although Klugman (2015) describes a fascinating practice of ostensibly heterosexual men proclaiming sexual desire for men who are sports stars.

9. Of course, in order to make that large amount of money from his collectibles, someone else had to buy them and value them so highly, undermining the surface-level contention that this is a waste of time. Thanks to Paul Booth for pointing this out.

10. In an interesting parallel, fan Darryl Frazetti has also "become a man" between the two *Trekkies* films, but through transitioning from female to male. The documentary does not explicitly address Frazetti's changed presentation, so it is difficult to know how the distinctive scratchy transman voice reads to someone unfamiliar with the changes a transitioning body undergoes; it may be that to the average viewer puberty just seems to have come late for this particular fan—which would, of course, be consistent with the overall narrative of fan arrested development and masculine failure.

CHAPTER THREE

1. *Dr. Horrible* links to third-party vendors like iTunes rather than selling on site.

2. James used "revenue" specifically to mean sports that turn a profit—foot-

ball and men's basketball—to the explicit exclusion of net-loss sports like volleyball and women's basketball that charge for admission to games, such that "sales" often coexists with "nonrevenue" at BMU.

3. The focus on individual players is also how fantasy sports serve as a character-driven form of transmedia dimensionality, giving fans more to explore with the player as the common element tying platforms together.

4. For similar linking of affirmational fandom to proper fandom, see Hadas and Shifman (2013) and Kohnen (2014).

CHAPTER FOUR

1. Given that whether a reuse of someone else's intellectual property has an effect on the market for the initial text is one of the factors courts use to determine whether the use is fair, noncommercial use might actually be safer (Tushnet 2007a), although of course it is only one factor, and noncommercial uses can be judged unfair.

2. This belief system, challenged and eventually replaced by the Romantic author, was on the wane in the late eighteenth century but was at work in the framing of the Constitution; see Hyde (2010).

3. However, Cox (2012) argues that broadcasting actually makes more money than it loses in ticket sales.

4. Safe Harbor protects internet service providers from liability for the copyright infringement of their users if they take the material down promptly when notified.

5. All direct quotations in this and the next two paragraphs come from *We Are Wizards*.

6. The competition ran from 2002 to 2011, then returned in 2014.

7. This refers to the site as captured in 2009, before Lucasfilm was purchased by Disney.

8. This includes, in the case of Star Trek, *Segal v. Paramount Pictures* (1993), over Samuel Segal's submission of an unsolicited script that a later film ended up resembling.

CHAPTER FIVE

1. As one of the coeditors, I named the issue; I have chosen to use the same title for this chapter.

2. In the European Union, in contrast, sites may not collect data unless

users opt in (Fuchs 2012a).

3. For a discussion of industry workers treating fans as inferior producers lacking knowledge, see Russo's (2010) analysis of *The L Word*'s "You Write It" contest.

4. On fandom and tattoos, see Jones (2014a, 2014c).

CHAPTER SIX

1. On the role of technological shifts in making fan production easier and more visible, see Coppa (2008).

2. Modders make homemade modifications to games, to give them additional features or levels or put a story into a new setting.

3. Given that hard-core gamers, the population from which modders are drawn, is disproportionately made up of men, modding is likely also dominated by men as a production practice, but I have found no studies that assess gender in the modding community.

4. The organization of labor in sports fandom as a culture has not yet been studied, and such a study of fan practice is beyond the scope of this book. It does, however, seem safe to say that sports fan culture has an integral system of status like a gift economy.

5. For analysis of the problem of separating familial, romantic, or sexual intimacy and commerce, see England and Folbre (1999), Nussbaum (1998), Schaeffer (2012), and Zelizer (2000).

6. In this framing, my thinking is informed by Tushnet's (2009, 529–30) discussion of slash fan fiction as being "about nonrivalrous pleasures," such that the same set of "characters, stories, and plots" can be used by all, in contradictory ways, without preventing other uses.

7. As noted at the Fanlore.org wiki ("FanLib"), the "lib" in FanLib is often thought of as standing for "library," but it actually refers to Mad Libs—a fitting model for the limited, fill-in-the-blank kinds of fan fiction the site solicited.

Abercrombie, Nick, and Brian Longhurst. 1998. *Audiences: A Sociological Theory of Performance and Imagination*. London: Sage.

Adams, Sam. 2016a. "It's Easy to Paint Fan Culture as Out of Control and Entitled. But Is It Really So Bad If Fans Have a Say in What Happens in Hollywood?" *Slate*, June 3, 2016. http://www.slate.com/.

Adams, Sam. 2016b. "The Anti–Rotten Tomatoes Movement Is Key to Understanding Angry Comic Book Fan Culture Overall." *Slate*, August 5, 2016. http://www.slate.com/.

Adelson, Andrea. 2006. "Harris, Swann Draw Biggest Cheers as Past Super Bowl MVPs Honored." *Associated Press State and Local Wire*, February 6, 2006.

Ahmed, Sara. 2006. *Queer Phenomenology: Orientations, Objects, Others*. Durham, NC: Duke University Press.

Ahmed, Sara. 2012. *On Being Included: Racism and Diversity in Institutional Life*. Durham, NC: Duke University Press.

Anderson, Chris. 2008. *The Long Tail: Why the Future of Business Is Selling Less of More*. New York: Hyperion.

Andrejevic, Mark. 2002. "The Work of Being Watched: Interactive Media and the Exploitation of Self-Disclosure." *Critical Studies in Media Communication* 19 (2): 230–48. https://doi.org/10.1080/07393180216561.

Andrejevic, Mark. 2008. "Watching Television Without Pity: The Productivity of Online Fans." *Television and New Media* 9 (1): 24–46. https://doi.org/10.1177/1527476407307241.

Andrejevic, Mark. 2009a. "Exploiting YouTube: Contradictions of User-Generated Labor." In *The YouTube Reader*, edited by Pelle Snickars and Patrick Vonderau, 406–23. Stockholm: National Library of Sweden.

Andrejevic, Mark. 2009b. *iSpy: Surveillance and Power in the Interactive Era*. Lawrence: University Press of Kansas.

Andrejevic, Mark. 2011. "The Work that Affective Economics Does." *Cultural Studies* 25 (4–5): 604–20. https://doi.org/10.1080/09502386.2011.600551.

Andrejevic, Mark. 2012. "Estranged Free Labor." In *Digital Labor: The Internet* as *Playground and Factory,* edited by Trebor Scholz, 149–64. New York: Routledge.

Arewa, Olufunmilayo B. 2013. "Making Music: Copyright Law and Creative Processes." In *A Companion to Media Authorship,* edited by Jonathan Gray and Derek Johnson, 69–87. New York: Wiley.

Arvidsson, Adam. 2005. "Brands: A Critical Perspective." *Journal of Consumer Culture* 5 (2): 235–58. https://doi.org/10.1177/1469540505053093.

Arvidsson, Adam, and Tiziano Bonini. 2015. "Valuing Audience Passions: From Smythe to Tarde." *European Journal of Cultural Studies* 18 (2): 158–73. https://doi.org/10.1177/1367549414563297.

Asquith, Kyle. 2015. "Knowing the Child Consumer through Box Tops: Data Collection, Measurement, and Advertising to Children, 1920–1945." *Critical Studies in Media Communication* 32 (2): 112–27. https://doi.org /10.1080/15295036.2014.1000351.

Associated Press. 2009. "NYC Pop Culture Show Draws TV and Sports Celebs." October 17, 2009.

Associated Press State and Local Wire. 2009. "Billings Church Hosts Men-Only Superbowl Party," February 2, 2009.

Aufderheide, Patricia, Peter Jaszi, and Elizabeth Nolan Brown. 2007. *The Good, the Bad, and the Confusing: User-Generated Video Creators on Copyright.* Washington, DC: American University.

Ault, Aaron, James V. Krogmeier, Steven R. Dunlop, and Edward J. Coyle. 2008. "EStadium: The Mobile Wireless Football Experience." In *Third International Conference on Internet and Web Applications and Services,* 644–49.

Austin, J. L. 1975. *How to Do Things with Words.* 2nd ed. Edited by J. O. Urmson and Marina Sbisà. Cambridge, MA: Harvard University Press.

Bacon-Smith, Camille. 1991. *Enterprising Women: Television Fandom and the Creation of Popular Myth.* Philadelphia: University of Pennsylvania Press.

Baird Stribling, Eleanor. 2013. "Valuing Fans." In *Spreadable Media: Creating Value and Meaning in a Networked Culture,* edited by Henry Jenkins, Sam Ford, and Joshua Green. New York: New York University Press. http:// spreadablemedia.org/essays/stribling/#.UbEZZpzqOZQ.

Baker, Paul. 2001. "Moral Panic and Alternative Identity Construction in Usenet." *Journal of Computer-Mediated Communication* 7 (1). https:// doi.org/10.1111/j.1083-6101.2001.tb00136.x.

Banks, John, and Sal Humphreys. 2008. "The Labour of User Co-Creators: Emergent Social Network Markets?" *Convergence* 14 (4): 401–18. https://

doi.org/10.1177/1354856508094660.

Barta, Kristen, and Gina Neff. 2016. "Technologies for Sharing: Lessons from Quantified Self about the Political Economy of Platforms." *Information, Communication and Society* 19 (4): 518–31. https://doi.org/10.1080/1369118X.2015.1118520.

Baudrillard, Jean. 2000. "Beyond Use Value." In *The Consumer Society Reader*, edited by Martyn J. Lee, 18–30. Malden, MA: Wiley-Blackwell.

Bechmann, Anja. 2012. "Towards Cross-Platform Value Creation: Four Patterns of Circulation and Control." *Information, Communication and Society* 15 (6): 888–908. https://doi.org/10.1080/1369118X.2012.680483.

Bechmann, Anja, and Stine Lomborg. 2013. "Mapping Actor Roles in Social Media: Different Perspectives on Value Creation in Theories of User Participation." *New Media and Society* 15 (5): 765–81. https://doi.org/10.1177/1461444812462853.

Beer, David, and Roger Burrows. 2010. "Consumption, Prosumption and Participatory Web Cultures: An Introduction." *Journal of Consumer Culture* 10 (1): 3–12. https://doi.org/10.1177/1469540509354009.

Belk, Russell. 2014. "You Are What You Can Access: Sharing and Collaborative Consumption Online." *Journal of Business Research* 67 (8): 1595–600. https://doi.org/10.1016/j.jbusres.2013.10.001.

Beller, Jonathan. 2011. "Cognitive Capitalist Pedagogy and Its Discontents." In *Cognitive Capitalism, Education and Digital Labor*, edited by Michael A. Peters and Ergin Bulut, 123–49. New York: Peter Lang.

Benkler, Yochai. 2007. *The Wealth of Networks: How Social Production Transforms Markets and Freedom*. New Haven, CT: Yale University Press.

Berkshire, Geoff. 2015. "Inside the Office of The CW's Mark Pedowitz." *Variety*, June 4, 2015. http://variety.com/.

Bloom, Harold. 1973. *Anxiety of Influence: Theory of Poetry*. New York: Oxford University Press.

Bolin, Göran. 2012. "The Labour of Media Use: The Two Active Audiences." *Information, Communication and Society* 15 (6): 796–814. https://doi.org/10.1080/1369118X.2012.677052.

Bonilla-Silva, Eduardo. 2003. *Racism without Racists: Color-Blind Racism and the Persistence of Racial Inequality in the United States*. Lanham, MD: Rowman & Littlefield.

Boon, Kevin Alexander. 2007. "Ontological Anxiety Made Flesh: The Zombie in Literature, Film and Culture." In *Monsters and the Monstrous: Myths and Metaphors of Enduring Evil*, edited by Niall Scott, 33–44. Amsterdam: Rodopi.

Booth, Paul. 2010. *Digital Fandom*. New York: Peter Lang.

Booth, Paul, and Peter Kelly. 2013. "The Changing Faces of Doctor Who Fandom: New Fans, New Technologies, Old Practices?" *Participations* 10 (1): 56–72.

Bourdieu, Pierre. 1984. *Distinction: A Social Critique of the Judgement of Taste*. Translated by Richard Nice. Cambridge, MA: Harvard University.

boyd, danah. 2007. "Why Youth □ Social Network Sites: The Role of Networked Publics in Teenage Social Life." *John D. and Catherine T. MacArthur Foundation Series on Digital Media and Learning*, 119–42.

boyd, danah, and Kate Crawford. 2012. "Critical Questions for Big Data: Provocations for a Cultural, Technological and Scholarly Phenomenon." *Information, Communication and Society* 15 (5): 662–79. https://doi.org/10.1080/1369118X.2012.678878.

boyd, danah, and Nicole B. Ellison. 2008. "Social Network Sites: Definition, History, and Scholarship." *Journal of Computer-Mediated Communication* 13 (1): 210–30.

Boyle, James. 2003. "The Second Enclosure Movement and the Construction of the Public Domain." *Law and Contemporary Problems* 66 (1/2): 33–74. https://doi.org/10.2307/20059171.

Boyle, James. 2008. *The Public Domain: Enclosing the Commons of the Mind*. New Haven, CT: Yale University Press.

Boyle, Raymond. 2015. "Battle for Control? Copyright, Football and European Media Rights." *Media, Culture and Society* 37 (3): 359–75. https://doi.org/10.1177/0163443714567020.

Brabham, Daren C. 2012. "The Myth of Amateur Crowds: A Critical Discourse Analysis of Crowdsourcing Coverage." *Information, Communication and Society* 15 (3): 394–410. https://doi.org/10.1080/1369118X.2011.641991.

Bramesco, Charles. 2016. "How 'Suicide Squad' Showcases Nasty Side of Fandom in 2016." *Rolling Stone*, August 9, 2016. http://www.rollingstone.com/.

Brennan Center for Justice. 2005. "Will Fair Use Survive? Free Expression in the Age of Copyright Control." Brennan Center for Justice at NYU School of Law. http://www.brennancenter.org/sites/default/files/legacy/d/download_file_9056.pdf.

Bridges, Elizabeth. 2016. "Elyza Lex™, Riot Grrrl, and Creativity in the Face of Grief: A Fandom Love Letter." Uncanny Valley, March 15, 2016. http://www.uncannyvalley.us/.

Brock, André. 2011. "Beyond the Pale: The Blackbird Web Browser's Critical Reception." *New Media and Society* 13 (7): 1085–1103.

https://doi.org/10.1177/1461444810397031.

Brooker, Will. 2002. *Using the Force: Creativity, Community, and Star Wars Fans*. New York: Continuum.

Brown, Brian, and Anabel Quan-Haase. 2012. "'A Workers' Inquiry 2.0': An Ethnographic Method for the Study of Produsage in Social Media Contexts." *TripleC* 10 (2): 488–508.

Brown, Wendy. 1995. *States of Injury*. Princeton, NJ: Princeton University Press.

Brown, Wendy. 2003. "Neo-liberalism and the End of Liberal Democracy." *Theory and Event* 7 (1). https://doi.org/10.1353/tae.2003.0020.

Bruns, Axel. 2008. *Blogs, Wikipedia, Second Life, and Beyond: From Production to Produsage*. New York: Peter Lang.

Bruns, Axel. 2012. "Reconciling Community and Commerce? Collaborations between Produsage Communities and Commercial Operators." *Information, Communication and Society* 15 (6): 815–35. https://doi.org /10.1080/1369118X.2012.680482.

Bryant, Jennings, and Andrea M. Holt. 2006. "A Historical Overview of Sports and Media in the United States." In *Handbook of Sports and Media*, edited by Arthur A. Raney and Jennings Bryant, 22–46. Mahwah, NJ: Lawrence Erlbaum.

Bunker, Matthew D. 2015. "Mired in Confusion: Nominative Fair Use in Trademark Law and Freedom of Expression." *Communication Law and Policy* 20 (3): 191–212. https://doi.org/10.1080/10811680.2015.1051915.

Buraimo, Babatunde, and Rob Simmons. 2009. "A Tale of Two Audiences: Spectators, Television Viewers and Outcome Uncertainty in Spanish Football." *Journal of Economics and Business* 61 (4): 326–38.

Burdsey, Daniel. 2006. "'If I Ever Play Football, Dad, Can I Play for England or India?' British Asians, Sport and Diasporic National Identities." *Sociology* 40 (1): 11–28. https://doi.org/10.1177/0038038506058435.

Busse, Kristina. 2006. "My Life Is a WIP on My LJ: Slashing the Slasher and the Reality of Celebrity and Internet Performances." In *Fan Fiction and Fan Communities in the Age of the Internet: New Essays*, edited by Karen Hellekson and Kristina Busse, 207–24. Jefferson, NC: McFarland.

Busse, Kristina. 2009a. "Introduction." *Cinema Journal* 48 (4): 104–7. https:// doi.org/10.1353/cj.0.0131.

Busse, Kristina. 2009b. "The Organization for Transformative Works: I Want Us to Own the Goddamned Servers." Kristina Busse (blog), August 2009. http://www.kristinabusse.com/.

Busse, Kristina. 2013. "Geek Hierarchies, Boundary Policing, and the Gendering of the Good Fan." *Participations* 10 (1): 73–91.

Busse, Kristina. 2015. "Fan Labor and Feminism: Capitalizing on the Fannish
Labor of Love." *Cinema Journal* 54 (3): 110–15. https://doi.org
/10.1353cj.2015.0034.

Busse, Kristina. 2016. "Beyond Mary Sue: Fan Representation and the
Complex Negotiation of Gendered Identity." In *Seeing Fans: Representations
of Fandom in Media and Popular Culture*, edited by Lucy Bennett and Paul
Booth, 159–68. New York: Bloomsbury Academic.

Busse, Kristina. 2017. "Fan Fiction Tropes as Literary and Cultural Practices."
In *Lesen X.0: Rezeptionsprozesse in Der Digitalen Gegenwart, Reihe Digilit.
Literatur Und Literaturvermittlung Im Zeitalter Der Digitalisierung*, edited
by Sebastian Böck, Julian Ingelmann, Kai Matuszkiewicz, and Friederike
Schruhl, 127–43. Göttingen, Germany: V&R Unipress.

Busse, Kristina, and Karen Hellekson. 2006. "Introduction: Work in
Progress." In *Fan Fiction and Fan Communities in the Age of the Internet:
New Essays*, edited by Karen Hellekson and Kristina Busse, 5–40. Jefferson,
NC: McFarland.

Butler, Bethonie. 2016. "TV Keeps Killing Off Lesbian Characters: The Fans of
One Show Have Revolted." *Washington Post*, April 4, 2016. https://
www.washingtonpost.com/.

Butler, Judith. 1990. *Gender Trouble: Feminism and the Subversion of Identity.*
New York: Routledge.

Butler, Judith. 1993. *Bodies That Matter: On the Discursive Limits of "Sex."* New
York: Routledge.

Campbell, Colin. 2000. "The Puzzle of Modern Consumerism." In *The
Consumer Society Reader*, edited by Martyn J. Lee, 48–72. Malden, MA:
Wiley-Blackwell.

Campbell, John Edward. 2011. "It Takes an IVillage: Gender, Labor, and
Community in the Age of Television–Internet Convergence." *International
Journal of Communication* 5: 492–510.

Caraway, Brett. 2016. "OUR Walmart: A Case Study of Connective Action."
Information, Communication and Society 19 (7): 907–20. https://doi.org
/10.1080/1369118X.2015.1064464.

Carey, R. Scott. 2013. "Hoosier Whiteness and the Indiana Pacers: Racialized
Strategic Change and the Politics of Organizational Sensemaking." *Sport in
Society* 16 (5): 631–53. https://doi.org/10.1080/17430437.2012.690413.

Chambers, Ross. 1997. "The Unexamined." In *Whiteness: A Critical Reader*,
edited by Mike Hill, 187–203. New York: New York University Press.

Chasin, Alexandra. 2000. *Selling Out: The Gay and Lesbian Movement Goes to*

Market. New York: Palgrave Macmillan.

Child, Ben. 2016. "Twitter Attacks on *Ghostbusters'* Leslie Jones a Symptom of Fan Entitlement." *Guardian,* July 19, 2016. https://www.theguardian.com/.

Chin, Bertha. 2014. "Sherlockology and Galactica.tv: Fan Sites as Gifts or Exploited Labor?" *Transformative Works and Cultures,* no. 15. https://doi.org/10.3983/twc.2014.0513.

Chin, Bertha, Bethan Jones, Myles McNutt, and Luke Pebler. 2014. "*Veronica Mars* Kickstarter and Crowd Funding." *Transformative Works and Cultures,* no. 15. https://doi.org/10.3983/twc.2014.0519.

Christian, Aymar Jean. 2011. "Fandom as Industrial Response: Producing Identity in an Independent Web Series." *Transformative Works and Cultures,* no. 8. https://doi.org/10.3983/twc.v8io.250.

Chun, Wendy Hui Kyong. 2011. "Crisis, Crisis, Crisis, or Sovereignty and Networks." *Theory, Culture and Society* 28 (6): 91–112. https://doi.org/10.1177/0263276411418490.

Cohen, Cathy J. 1997. "Punks, Bulldaggers, and Welfare Queens: The Radical Potential of Queer Politics?" *GLQ* 3 (4): 437–65.

Cohen, Nicole S. 2012. "Cultural Work as a Site of Struggle: Freelancers and Exploitation." *TripleC* 10 (2): 141–55.

Cohen, Sandy. 2006. "Fans Get First Look at *Spider-Man 3*." *Associated Press Online,* July 24, 2006.

Cohen, Sandy. 2007a. "Comic-Con Convention Celebrates Comics, Costumes, Film, Fantasy." *Associated Press Worldstream,* July 27, 2007.

Cohen, Sandy. 2007b. "Judd Apatow and Seth Rogen Talk about *Superbad* and the Years-Long Road It Took to Theaters." *Associated Press,* August 2, 2007.

Cohen, Sandy. 2008a. "Comics, Film and Figurine Fans Flock to Comic-Con." *Associated Press,* July 23, 2008.

Cohen, Sandy. 2008b. "'Twilight' Fans Camp out for a Peek (and a Scream)." *Associated Press Online,* July 25, 2008.

Cohen, Sandy. 2009. "'Twilight' Sequel Draws Fangirls by the Thousands." *Associated Press Online,* July 23, 2009.

Cohen, Stanley. 1972. *Folk Devils and Moral Panics.* New York: Routledge.

Cole, Kai. 2017. "Joss Whedon Is a 'Hypocrite Preaching Feminist Ideals,' Ex-Wife Kai Cole Says (Guest Blog)." The Wrap, August 20, 2017. https://www.thewrap.com/.

Collins, Patricia Hill. 1990. *Black Feminist Thought: Knowledge, Consciousness, and the Politics of Empowerment.* New York: Routledge.

Collins, Steve. 2010. "Digital Fair Prosumption and the Fair Use Defence."

Journal of Consumer Culture 10 (1): 37–55. https://doi.org /10.1177/1469540509354014.

Combahee River Collective. 1981. "A Black Feminist Statement." In *This Bridge Called My Back: Writings by Radical Women of Color,* edited by Cherríe Moraga and Gloria Anzaldúa, 210–18. Watertown, MA: Persephone Press.

Comeau, Troy O. 2007. "Fantasy Football Participation and Media Usage." PhD diss., University of Missouri, Columbia.

Connell, R. W. 2005. *Masculinities.* 2nd ed. Berkeley: University of California Press.

Consalvo, Mia. 2003. "Cyber-Slaying Media Fans: Code, Digital Poaching, and Corporate Control of the Internet." *Journal of Communication Inquiry* 27 (1): 67–86.

Coombe, Rosemary J. 1998. *The Cultural Life of Intellectual Properties: Authorship, Appropriation, and the Law.* Durham, NC: Duke University Press.

Coppa, Francesca. 2008. "Women, *Star Trek,* and the Early Development of Fannish Vidding." *Transformative Works and Cultures,* no. 1. https:// doi.org/10.3983/twc.2008.044.

Coppa, Francesca. 2009. "A Fannish Taxonomy of Hotness." *Cinema Journal* 48 (4): 107–13. https://doi.org/10.1353/cj.0.0136.

Cowling, Mark, and Paul Reynolds. 2004. Introduction to *Making Sense of Sexual Consent,* 1–14. Farnham, UK: Ashgate.

Cox, Adam. 2012. "Live Broadcasting, Gate Revenue, and Football Club Performance: Some Evidence." *International Journal of the Economics of Business* 19 (1): 75–98. https://doi.org/10.1080/13571516.2012.643668.

Crawford, Garry. 2004. *Consuming Sport: Fans, Sport and Culture.* New York: Routledge.

Crenshaw, Kimberle. 1991. "Mapping the Margins: Intersectionality, Identity Politics, and Violence against Women of Color." *Stanford Law Review* 43 (6): 1241–99.

Daniels, Jessie. 2013. "Race and Racism in Internet Studies: A Review and Critique." *New Media and Society* 15 (5): 695–719. https://doi.org/ 10.1177/1461444812462849.

Davis, Chelyen. 1999. "Football Widows Mourn Loss of Husbands—An AP West Virginia Member Exchange." *Associated Press State and Local Wire,* January 6, 1999.

Davis, Lauren. 2013. "Paul Dini: Superhero Cartoon Execs Don't Want Largely Female Audiences." Io9, December 15, 2013. http://io9.gizmodo.com/.

Davis, Nickolas W., and Margaret Carlisle Duncan. 2006. "Sports Knowledge Is Power: Reinforcing Masculine Privilege through Fantasy Sport League Participation." *Journal of Sport and Social Issues* 30 (3): 244–64.

Dawes, Simon. 2014. "Broadcasting and the Public Sphere: Problematising Citizens, Consumers and Neoliberalism." *Media, Culture and Society* 36 (5): 702–19. https://doi.org/10.1177/0163443714536842.

De Kosnik, Abigail. 2009. "Should Fan Fiction Be Free?" *Cinema Journal* 48 (4): 118–24. https://doi.org/10.1353/cj.0.0144.

De Kosnik, Abigail. 2012. "Fandom as Free Labor." In *Digital Labor: The Internet as Playground and Factory*, edited by Trebor Scholz, 98–111. New York: Routledge.

De Kosnik, Abigail. 2013. "Interrogating 'Free' Fan Labor." In *Spreadable Media: Creating Value and Meaning in a Networked Culture*, edited by Henry Jenkins, Sam Ford, and Joshua Green. New York: New York University Press. http://spreadablemedia.org/essays/kosnik/#.UbEevZzqOZQ.

D'Emilio, John. 1993. "Capitalism and Gay Identity." In *The Lesbian and Gay Studies Reader*, edited by Henry Abelove, Michèle Aina Barale, and David M. Halperin, 467–78. New York: Routledge.

Derecho, Abigail. 2006. "Archontic Literature: A Definition, a History, and Several Theories of Fan Fiction." In *Fan Fiction and Fan Communities in the Age of the Internet: New Essays*, edited by Karen Hellekson and Kristina Busse, 61–78. Jefferson, NC: McFarland.

Derhy Kurtz, Benjamin W. L. 2014. "Introduction: Transmedia Practices: A Television Branding Revolution." *Networking Knowledge* 7 (1): 1–6.

Deuze, Mark. 2007. *Media Work*. Cambridge: Polity.

Driscoll, Catherine, and Melissa Gregg. 2011. "Convergence Culture and the Legacy of Feminist Cultural Studies." *Cultural Studies* 25 (4–5): 566–84. https://doi.org/10.1080/09502386.2011.600549.

Duffy, Brooke. 2015. "Amateur, Autonomous, and Collaborative: Myths of Aspiring Female Cultural Producers in Web 2.0." *Critical Studies in Media Communication* 32 (1): 48–64. https://doi.org/10.1080/15295036.2014.997832.

Duggan, Lisa. 2004. *The Twilight of Equality? Neoliberalism, Cultural Politics, and the Attack on Democracy*. Boston, MA: Beacon Press.

Dwyer, Brendan. 2009. "Fantasy Sport Consumer Behavior: An Analysis of Participant Attitudes and Behavioral Intentions." PhD diss., University of Northern Colorado.

Dyer, Richard. 1997. *White*. London: Routledge.

Dyer-Witheford, Nick. 2010. "Digital Labour, Species-Becoming and the

Global Worker." *Ephemera: Theory and Politics in Organization* 10 (3/4): 484–503.

Dyer-Witheford, Nick. 2011. "In the Ruined Laboratory of Futuristic Accumulation." In *Cognitive Capitalism, Education and Digital Labor,* edited by Michael A. Peters and Ergin Bulut, 275–86. New York: Peter Lang.

Dyer-Witheford, Nick, and Greig de Peuter. 2009. "Empire@Play: Virtual Games and Global Capitalism." *Ctheory.* http://www.ctheory.net/.

Edelman, Lee. 2004. *No Future: Queer Theory and the Death Drive.* Durham, NC: Duke University Press.

Edmond, Maura. 2015. "All Platforms Considered: Contemporary Radio and Transmedia Engagement." *New Media and Society* 17 (9): 1566–82. https://doi.org/10.1177/1461444814530245.

Edwards, Lee, Bethany Klein, David Lee, Giles Moss, and Fiona Philip. 2015. "'Isn't It Just a Way to Protect Walt Disney's Rights?' Media User Perspectives on Copyright." *New Media and Society* 17 (5): 691–707. https://doi.org/10.1177/1461444813511402.

Edwards, Leigh H. 2012. "Transmedia Storytelling, Corporate Synergy, and Audience Expression." *Global Media Journal* 12 (20): 1–12.

Eicher-Catt, Deborah. 2003. "The Logic of the Sacred in Bateson and Peirce." *American Journal of Semiotics* 19 (1–4): 95–126.

Elderkin, Beth. 2016. "Steven Universe Artist Quits Twitter over Fan Harassment." Io9, August 13, 2016. http://io9.gizmodo.com/.

Elias, Paul. 2008. "Jury Orders NFL Union to Pay $28.1M to Retirees." *Associated Press State and Local Wire,* November 11, 2008.

England, Paula, and Nancy Folbre. 1999. "The Cost of Caring." *Annals of the American Academy of Political and Social Science* 561 (1): 39–51.

Esposito, Roberto. 2009. *Communitas: The Origin and Destiny of Community.* Palo Alto, CA: Stanford University Press.

Ewick, Patricia, and Susan S. Silbey. 1991. "Conformity, Contestation, and Resistance: An Account of Legal Consciousness." *New England Law Review* 26: 731–49.

Ewick, Patricia, and Susan S. Silbey. 1999. "Common Knowledge and Ideological Critique: The Significance of Knowing that the 'Haves' Come out Ahead." *Law and Society Review* 33 (4): 1025–41. https://doi.org/10.2307/3115157.

Faraci, Devin. 2012. "*Mass Effect 3* Protests Prove Annie Wilkes Is the Patron Saint of Fandom." Birth Movies Death (blog), March 14, 2012. http://birthmoviesdeath.com/.

Faraci, Devin. 2016. "Fandom Is Broken." Birth Movies Death (blog), May 30, 2016. http://birthmoviesdeath.com/.

Fast, Karin, Henrik Örnebring, and Michael Karlsson. 2016. "Metaphors of Free Labor: A Typology of Unpaid Work in the Media Sector." *Media, Culture and Society* 38 (7): 963–78. https://doi.org /10.1177/0163443716635861.

Favale, Marcella. 2014. "Death and Resurrection of Copyright between Law and Technology." *Information and Communications Technology Law* 23 (2): 117–35. https://doi.org/10.1080/13600834.2014.925631.

Federici, Sylvia. 2011. "On Affective Labor." In *Cognitive Capitalism, Education and Digital Labor,* edited by Michael A. Peters and Ergin Bulut, 57–73. New York: Peter Lang.

Feld, Steven. 1988. "Notes on World Beat." *Public Culture* 1 (1): 31–37. https:// doi.org/10.1215/08992363-1-1-31.

Ferguson, Roderick A. 2003. *Aberrations in Black: Toward a Queer of Color Critique.* Minneapolis: University of Minnesota Press.

Fetterman, David M. 1998. *Ethnography: Step by Step.* Thousand Oaks, CA: Sage.

Fiesler, Casey. 2007. "Everything I Need to Know I Learned from Fandom: How Existing Social Norms Can Help Shape the next Generation of User-Generated Content." *Vanderbilt Journal of Entertainment and Technology Law* 10: 729–62.

Fisher, Eran. 2012. "How Less Alienation Creates More Exploitation? Audience Labour on Social Network Sites." *TripleC* 10 (2): 171–83. https:// doi.org/10.31269/triplec.v10i2.392.

Fiske, John. 1992. "The Cultural Economy of Fandom." In *The Adoring Audience: Fan Culture and Popular Media,* edited by Lisa A. Lewis, 30–49. London: Routledge.

Foley, Megan. 2014. "'Prove You're Human': Fetishizing Material Embodiment and Immaterial Labor in Information Networks." *Critical Studies in Media Communication* 31 (5): 365–79. https://doi.org/10.1080 /15295036.2014.939682.

Forsyth, Craig J., and Carol Y. Thompson. 2007. "Helpmates of the Rodeo: Fans, Wives, and Groupies." *Journal of Sport and Social Issues* 31 (4): 394–416.

Foster, Mary. 2002. "Super Bowl Shows Patriotic Colors." *Associated Press Online,* February 3, 2002.

Foucault, Michel. 1972. *The Archaeology of Knowledge and the Discourse on Language.* New York: Pantheon.

Foucault, Michel. 1980. "What Is an Author?" In *Language, Counter-memory, Practice: Selected Essays and Interviews*, edited by Donald F. Bouchard, 113–38. Ithaca, NY: Cornell University Press.

Foucault, Michel. 1990. *The History of Sexuality, Volume 1: An Introduction*. New York: Vintage.

Foucault, Michel. 1995. *Discipline and Punish: The Birth of the Prison*. New York: Vintage.

Foucault, Michel. 2003. *"Society Must Be Defended": Lectures at the Collège de France, 1975–1976*. New York: Picador.

Foucault, Michel. 2008. *The Birth of Biopolitics: Lectures at the Collège de France, 1978–1979*. New York: Picador.

Frank, Thomas. 2000. *One Market under God: Extreme Capitalism, Market Populism, and the End of Economic Democracy*. New York: Doubleday.

Frankenberg, Ruth. 1993. *White Women, Race Matters: The Social Construction of Whiteness*. Minneapolis: University of Minnesota Press.

Fredriksson, Martin. 2014. "Copyright Culture and Pirate Politics." *Cultural Studies* 28 (5–6): 1022–47. https://doi.org/10.1080/09502386.2014.886483.

Freud, Sigmund. (1905) 1995. "Three Essays on the Theory of Sexuality." In *The Freud Reader*, edited by Peter Gay, 239–92. New York: Norton.

Fuchs, Christian. 2010. "Class, Knowledge and New Media." *Media, Culture and Society* 32 (1): 141–50.

Fuchs, Christian. 2012a. "Google's 'New' Terms of Use and Privacy Policy: Old Exploitation and User Commodification in a New Ideological Skin." Christian Fuchs (blog), March 1, 2012. http://fuchs.uti.at/789/.

Fuchs, Christian. 2012b. "The Political Economy of Privacy on Facebook." *Television and New Media* 13 (2): 139–59. https://doi.org/10.1177/1527476411415699.

"Fundraiser." n.d. LGBT Fans Deserve Better. https://lgbtfansdeservebetter.com/fundraiser/.

Gaines, Jane. 1986. "White Privilege and Looking Relations: Race and Gender in Feminist Film Theory." *Cultural Critique*, (4): 59–79. https://doi.org/10.2307/1354334.

Gerlitz, Carolin, and Anne Helmond. 2013. "The Like Economy: Social Buttons and the Data-Intensive Web." *New Media and Society* 15 (8): 1348–65. https://doi.org/10.1177/1461444812472322.

Germain, David. 2008. "Mulder, Scully Believe in *X-Files* Audience." *Associated Press State and Local Wire*, July 23, 2008.

Gibbons, Tom. 2011. "English National Identity and the National Football

Team: The View of Contemporary English Fans." *Soccer and Society* 12 (6): 865–79. https://doi.org/10.1080/14660970.2011.609685.

Gilbert, Anne. 2015. "What We Talk about When We Talk about Bronies." *Transformative Works and Cultures*, no. 20. https://doi.org/10.3983/twc.2015.0666.

Gillespie, Tarleton. 2007. *Wired Shut: Copyright and the Shape of Digital Culture.* Cambridge, MA: MIT Press.

Giulianotti, Richard. 2005. "Sport Spectators and the Social Consequences of Commodification: Critical Perspectives from Scottish Football." *Journal of Sport and Social Issues* 29 (4): 386–410.

Glasner, Eli. 2016. "Fan Fury, Fan Power: The Changing Relationship between Creators and Consumers." CBC News, July 15, 2016. http://www.cbc.ca/.

Goldberg, Dave. 2000. "Unlikely Teams in Unlikely Bowl." *Associated Press Online,* January 29, 2000.

Gordon, Wendy J. 1992. "A Property Right in Self-Expression: Equality and Individualism in the Natural Law of Intellectual Property." *Yale Law Journal* 102: 1533–609.

Gosling, Victoria K. 2007. "Girls Allowed? Marginalization of Female Sports Fans." In *Fandom: Identities and Communities in a Mediated World,* edited by Jonathan Gray, Cornel Sandvoss, and C. Lee Harrington, 250–60. New York: New York University Press.

Government Accountability Office. 2010. "Intellectual Property: Observations on Efforts to Quantify the Economic Effects of Counterfeit and Pirated Goods." http://www.gao.gov/new.items/d10423.pdf.

Gray, Jonathan. 2010. *Show Sold Separately: Promos, Spoilers, and Other Media Paratexts.* New York: New York University Press.

Gray, Jonathan, Cornel Sandvoss, and C. Lee Harrington. 2007. "Introduction: Why Study Fans?" In *Fandom: Identities and Communities in a Mediated World,* edited by Jonathan Gray, Cornel Sandvoss, and C. Lee Harrington, 1–16. New York: New York University Press.

Gray, Mary L. 2012. "Critical Studies as Big Data: Making the Case for Cultural Approaches to Media and Technology Studies." Public lecture, Champaign, IL, April 10, 2012.

Green, Shoshanna, Cynthia Jenkins, and Henry Jenkins. 1998. "Normal Female Interest in Men Bonking: Selections from the *Terra Nostra Underground* and *Strange Bedfellows.*" In *Theorizing Fandom: Fans, Subculture and Identity,* edited by Cheryl Harris and Alison Alexander, 9–38. Creskill, NJ: Hampton Press.

Gregg, Melissa. 2011. *Work's Intimacy.* Cambridge: Polity.

Greven, David. 2013. "'I Love You, Brom Bones': Beta Male Comedies and American Culture." *Quarterly Review of Film and Video* 30 (5): 405–20. https://doi.org/10.1080/10509208.2011.575669.

Guschwan, Matthew. 2011. "Fans, Romans, Countrymen: Soccer Fandom and Civic Identity in Contemporary Rome." *International Journal of Communication* 5: 1990–2013.

Hadas, Leora. 2009. "The Web Planet: How the Changing Internet Divided *Doctor Who* Fan Fiction Writers." *Transformative Works and Cultures,* no. 3. https://doi.org/10.3983/twc.2009.0129.

Hadas, Leora, and Limor Shifman. 2013. "Keeping the Elite Powerless: Fan–Producer Relations in the 'Nu Who' (and New YOU) Era." *Critical Studies in Media Communication* 30 (4): 275–91. https://doi.org/10.1080/15295036.2012.676193.

Halberstam, Judith. 2005. *In a Queer Time and Place: Transgender Bodies, Subcultural Lives.* New York: New York University Press.

Hall, Stuart. (1980) 2001. "Encoding/Decoding." In *Media and Cultural Studies: KeyWorks,* edited by Meenakshi Gigi Durham and Douglas Kellner, 166–76. Malden, MA: Blackwell.

Halverson, Erica Rosenfeld, and Richard Halverson. 2008. "Fantasy Baseball: The Case for Competitive Fandom." *Games and Culture* 3 (3–4): 286–308.

Hamilton, James F., and Kristen Heflin. 2011. "User Production Reconsidered: From Convergence, to Autonomia and Cultural Materialism." *New Media and Society* 13 (7): 1050–66.

Hanmer, Rosalind. 2003. "Lesbian Subtext Talk: Experiences of the Internet Chat." *International Journal of Sociology and Social Policy* 23 (1–2): 80–106. https://doi.org/10.1108/01443330310790453.

Hardt, Michael. 1999. "Affective Labor." *Boundary 2* 26 (2): 89–100.

Harman, Sarah, and Bethan Jones. 2013. "Fifty Shades of Ghey: Snark Fandom and the Figure of the Anti-fan." *Sexualities* 16 (8): 951–68. https://doi.org/10.1177/1363460713508887.

Hartson, H. Rex. 2003. "Cognitive, Physical, Sensory, and Functional Affordances in Interaction Design." *Behaviour and Information Technology* 22 (5): 315–18.

Hassenger, Jesse. 2016. "*Ghostbusters, Frozen,* and the Strange Entitlement of Fan Culture." *AV Club,* May 25, 2016. http://www.avclub.com/.

Hebdige, Dick. 2000. "Object as Image: The Italian Scooter Cycle." In *The Consumer Society Reader,* edited by Martyn J. Lee, 125–61. Malden, MA: Wiley-Blackwell.

Helens-Hart, Rose. 2014. "Promoting Fan Labor and 'All Things Web': A Case Study of *Tosh.o.*" *Transformative Works and Cultures*, no. 15. http://dx.doi.org/10.3983/twc.2014.0491.

Hellekson, Karen. 2009. "A Fannish Field of Value: Online Fan Gift Culture." *Cinema Journal* 48 (4): 113–18. https://doi.org/10.1353/cj.0.0140.

Hellekson, Karen. 2015. "Making Use Of: The Gift, Commerce, and Fans." *Cinema Journal* 54 (3): 125–31. https://doi.org/10.1353/cj.2015.0017.

Herman, Edward S., and Noam Chomsky. 1988. *Manufacturing Consent: The Political Economy of the Mass Media*. New York: Pantheon.

Hermes, Joke. 2015. "Labour and Passion: Introduction to Themed Section." *European Journal of Cultural Studies* 18 (2): 111–16. https://doi.org/10.1177/1367549414563301.

Hernández-Pérez, Manuel, and José Gabriel Ferreras Rodríguez. 2014. "Serial Narrative, Intertextuality, and the Role of Audiences in the Creation of a Franchise: An Analysis of the Indiana Jones Saga from a Cross-Media Perspective." *Mass Communication and Society* 17 (1): 26–53. https://doi.org/10.1080/15205436.2013.788192.

Hesmondhalgh, David. 2006. "Digital Sampling and Cultural Inequality." *Social and Legal Studies* 15 (1): 53–75. https://doi.org/10.1177/0964663906060973.

Hesmondhalgh, David. 2010. "User-Generated Content, Free Labour, and the Cultural Industries." *Ephemera: Theory and Politics in Organization* 10 (3/4): 267–84.

Hess, Amanda. 2016. "The Rise of the Internet Fan Bully." *New York Times*, August 12, 2016. https://www.nytimes.com/.

Hill, DeShawn. 2016. "Diversity in Hollywood and Why Fans Get It Wrong." Film Inquiry (blog), August 5, 2016. https://www.filminquiry.com/.

Hill, Mike. 1997. "Vipers in Shangri-La: Whiteness, Writing, and Other Ordinary Terrors." In *Whiteness: A Critical Reader*, edited by Mike Hill, 1–18. New York: New York University Press.

Hills, Matt. 2002. *Fan Cultures*. London: Routledge.

Hills, Matt. 2014. "Sherlock's Epistemological Economy and the Value of 'Fan' Knowledge: How Producer-Fans Play the (Great) Game of Fandom." In *Sherlock and Transmedia Fandom: Essays on the BBC Series*, edited by Louisa Ellen Stein and Kristina Busse, 27–40. Jefferson, NC: McFarland.

Hills, Matt. 2015. "*Veronica Mars*, Fandom, and the 'Affective Economics' of Crowdfunding Poachers." *New Media and Society* 17 (2): 183–97. https://doi.org/10.1177/1461444814558909.

Hochschild, Arlie Russell. 1983. *The Managed Heart: Commercialization of Human Feeling.* 2nd ed. Berkeley: University of California Press.

Hochschild, Arlie Russell. 1989. *The Second Shift.* New York: Avon Books.

Hochschild, Arlie Russell. 2003. "Love and Gold." In *Global Woman: Nannies, Maids, and Sex Workers in the New Economy,* edited by Barbara Ehrenreich and Arlie Russell Hochschild, 15–31. London: Macmillan.

Hyde, Lewis. 2010. *Common as Air: Revolution, Art, and Ownership.* New York: Farrar, Straus and Giroux.

International Telecommunication Union. 2017. "ICT Facts and Figures 2017." Geneva: International Telecommunication Union. https://www.itu.int/en /ITU-D/Statistics/Documents/facts/ICTFactsFigures2017.pdf.

James, Stephanie. 2013. "Promotional Alternate Reality Games and Brand Ownership." *Participations* 10 (1): 320–21.

Jenkins, Henry. 1992. *Textual Poachers: Television Fans and Participatory Culture.* New York: Routledge.

Jenkins, Henry. 2006a. *Convergence Culture: Where Old and New Media Collide.* New York: New York University Press.

Jenkins, Henry. 2006b. "'Do You Enjoy Making the Rest of Us Feel Stupid?': Alt.Tv.Twinpeaks, the Trickster Author, and Viewer Mastery." In *Fans, Bloggers, and Gamers: Exploring Participatory Culture,* 115–33. New York: New York University Press.

Jenkins, Henry. 2006c. "Interactive Audiences? The 'Collective Intelligence' of Media Fans." In *Fans, Bloggers, and Gamers: Exploring Participatory Culture,* 134–51. New York: New York University Press.

Jenkins, Henry. 2007. "Afterword: The Future of Fandom." In *Fandom: Identities and Communities in a Mediated World,* edited by Jonathan Gray, Cornel Sandvoss, and C. Lee Harrington, 357–64. New York: New York University Press.

Jenkins, Henry. 2013. "Joss Whedon, the Browncoats, and Dr. Horrible." In *Spreadable Media: Creating Value and Meaning in a Networked Culture,* edited by Henry Jenkins, Sam Ford, and Joshua Green. New York: New York University Press. http://spreadablemedia.org/essays/jenkins1 /#.UbSjq5zqOZQ.

Jenkins, Henry. 2014. "Fandom Studies as I See It." *Journal of Fandom Studies* 2 (2): 89–109. https://doi.org/10.1386/jfs.2.2.89_1.

Jenkins, Henry, and Nico Carpenter. 2013. "Theorizing Participatory Intensities: A Conversation about Participation and Politics." *Convergence* 19 (3): 265–86. https://doi.org/10.1177/1354856513482090.

Jenkins, Henry, Sam Ford, and Joshua Green. 2013. *Spreadable Media: Creating Value and Meaning in a Networked Culture*. New York: New York University Press.

Jensen, Joli. 1992. "Fandom as Pathology: The Consequences of Characterization." In *The Adoring Audience: Fan Culture and Popular Media*, edited by Lisa A. Lewis, 9–29. London: Routledge.

Johnson, Derek. 2007. "Fan-tagonism: Factions, Institutions, and Constitutive Hegemonies of Fandom." In *Fandom: Identities and Communities in a Mediated World*, edited by Jonathan Gray, Cornel Sandvoss, and C. Lee Harrington, 285–300. New York: New York University Press.

Johnson, Derek. 2013. *Media Franchising*. New York: New York University Press.

Johnson, Derek. 2014. "'May the Force Be with Katie': Pink Media Franchising and the Postfeminist Politics of HerUniverse." *Feminist Media Studies* 14 (6): 895–911. https://doi.org/10.1080/14680777.2014.882856.

Johnson-Yale, Camille. 2015. "Frozen in Hollywood: Postwar Film Policy and the New Power-Geometry of Globalizing Production Labor." *Critical Studies in Media Communication* 32 (1): 33–47. https://doi.org/10.1080/15295036.2014.998251.

Jones, Bethan. 2014a. "Fannish Tattooing and Sacred Identity." In "Performance and Performativity in Fandom," edited by Lucy Bennett and Paul J. Booth, special issue, *Transformative Works and Cultures*, no. 18. https://doi.org/10.3983/twc.2015.0626.

Jones, Bethan. 2014b. "Fifty Shades of Exploitation: Fan Labor and *Fifty Shades of Grey*." In "Fandom and/as Labor," edited by Mel Stanfill and Megan Condis, special issue, *Transformative Works and Cultures*, no. 15. https://doi.org/10.3983/twc.2014.0501.

Jones, Bethan. 2014c. "Written on the Body: Experiencing Affect and Identity in My Fannish Tattoos." In "Material Fan Culture," edited by Bob Rehak, special issue, *Transformative Works and Cultures*, no. 16. https://doi.org/10.3983/twc.2014.0527.

Jones, Janet Megan. 2003. "Show Your Real Face: A Fan Study of the UK *Big Brother* Transmissions (2000, 2001, 2002)—Investigating the Boundaries between Notions of Consumers and Producers of Factual Television." *New Media and Society* 5 (3): 400–421. https://doi.org/10.1177/14614448030053006.

Jones, Katharine W. 2008. "Female Fandom: Identity, Sexism and Men's Professional Football in England." *Sociology of Sport Journal* 25: 516–37.

Jones, Orlando. 2016. "Foreword: Orlando the Fangirl." In *Seeing Fans: Representations of Fandom in Media and Popular Culture,* edited by Lucy Bennett and Paul Booth, xii–xv. New York: Bloomsbury Academic.

Jones, Richard G., and Carrie A. Wilson-Brown. 2014. "Beta Male Comedies as an Extension of the Bromance Genre: Homosociality and Homoeroticism in *This Is the End.*" Paper presented at the National Communication Association, November 23, 2014, Chicago, IL.

Jones, Sara Gwenllian. 2000. "Histories, Fictions, and *Xena: Warrior Princess.*" *Television and New Media* 1 (4): 403–18. https://doi.org /10.1177/152747640000100403.

Kant, Immanuel. (1790) 2001. *Critique of the Power of Judgment.* Translated by Paul Guyer and Eric Matthews. Revised ed. Cambridge: Cambridge University Press.

Kelty, Christopher M. 2013. "There Is No Free Software." *Journal of Peer Production,* no. 3. http://peerproduction.net/.

Kennedy, David. 2012. "Football Stadium Relocation and the Commodification of Football: The Case of Everton Supporters and Their Adoption of the Language of Commerce." *Soccer and Society* 13 (3): 341–58. https://doi.org /10.1080/14660970.2012.655504.

Kennedy, Peter, and David Kennedy. 2012. "Football Supporters and the Commercialisation of Football: Comparative Responses across Europe." *Soccer and Society* 13 (3): 327–40. https://doi.org /10.1080/14660970.2012.655503.

Kettrey, Heather Hensman, and Whitney Nicole Laster. 2014. "Staking Territory in the 'World White Web': An Exploration of the Roles of Overt and Color-blind Racism in Maintaining Racial Boundaries on a Popular Web Site." *Social Currents* 1 (3): 257–74. https://doi.org/ 10.1177/2329496514540134.

Khanna, Derek S. 2012. "Three Myths about Copyright Law and Where to Start to Fix It." Republican Study Committee RSC Policy Brief, November 16, 2012. https://www.publicknowledge.org/files /withdrawn_RSC_Copyright_reform_brief.pdf.

Kimmel, Michael. 2008. *Guyland: The Perilous World Where Boys Become Men.* New York: Harper Perennial.

Klugman, Matthew. 2015. "'I Love Him in an Absolutely Gay Way': Heterodox Fragments of the Erotic Desires, Pleasures, and Masculinity of Male Sports Fans." *Men and Masculinities* 18 (2): 193–213. https://doi.org /10.1177/1097184X15584911.

Kohnen, Melanie. 2014. "'The Power of Geek': Fandom as Gendered Commodity at Comic-Con." *Creative Industries Journal* 7 (1): 75–78. https://doi.org/10.1080/17510694.2014.892295.

Koulikov, Mikhail. 2010. "Fighting the Fan Sub War: Conflicts between Media Rights Holders and Unauthorized Creator/Distributor Networks." *Transformative Works and Cultures,* no. 5. https://doi.org/10.3983/twc.2010.0115.

Krzywinska, Tanya. 2009. "Arachne Challenges Minerva: The Spinning out of Long Narrative in *World of Warcraft* and *Buffy the Vampire Slayer.*" In *Third Person: Authoring and Exploring Vast Narratives,* edited by Pat Harrigan and Noah Wardrip-Fruin, 385–98. Cambridge, MA: MIT Press.

Kücklich, Julian. 2005. "Precarious Playbour: Modders and the Digital Games Industry." *Fibreculture Journal,* no. 5. http://fibreculturejournal.org/.

Kuehn, Kathleen, and Thomas F. Corrigan. 2013. "Hope Labor: The Role of Employment Prospects in Online Social Production." *Political Economy of Communication* 1 (1). http://www.polecom.org/.

Kusz, Kyle W. 2001. "'I Want to Be the Minority': The Politics of Youthful White Masculinities in Sport and Popular Culture in 1990s America." *Journal of Sport and Social Issues* 25 (4): 390–416.

Lackner, Eden, Barbara Lynn Lucas, and Robin Anne Reid. 2006. "Cunning Linguists: The Bisexual Erotics of Words/Silence/Flesh." In *Fan Fiction and Fan Communities in the Age of the Internet: New Essays,* edited by Karen Hellekson and Kristina Busse, 189–206. Jefferson, NC: McFarland.

Lakoff, George, and Mark Johnson. 2003. *Metaphors We Live By.* Chicago: University of Chicago Press.

Leaver, Tama. 2013. "Joss Whedon, Dr. Horrible, and the Future of Web Media." *Popular Communication* 11 (2): 160–73. https://doi.org/10.1080/15405702.2013.779510.

Lee, Hye-Kyung. 2011. "Participatory Media Fandom: A Case Study of Anime Fansubbing." *Media, Culture and Society* 33 (8): 1131–47. https://doi.org/10.1177/0163443711418271.

Lee, Micky. 2011. "Google Ads and the Blindspot Debate." *Media, Culture and Society* 33 (3): 433–47. https://doi.org/10.1177/0163443710394902.

Lessig, Lawrence. 1999. *Code: And Other Laws of Cyberspace.* New York: Basic Books.

Lessig, Lawrence. 2004. *Free Culture: How Big Media Uses Technology and the Law to Lock Down Culture and Control Creativity.* New York: Penguin.

Lessig, Lawrence. 2006. *Code: Version 2.0.* New York: Basic Books.

Lewis, Lisa A. 1992a. "'Something More than Love': Fan Stories on Film."

In *The Adoring Audience: Fan Culture and Popular Media,* edited by Lisa A. Lewis, 135–59. London: Routledge.

Lewis, Lisa A., ed. 1992b. *The Adoring Audience: Fan Culture and Popular Media.* London: Routledge.

License Global. 2017. "Disney Earnings Decline Slightly in Non–Star Wars Year." License Global, November 10, 2017. http://www.licensemag.com/.

Lin, Judy. 2000. "Growing Comic Conventions Leaves Some Artists Out." *Associated Press State and Local Wire,* July 21, 2000.

Littlejohn, Janice Rhoshalle. 2008. "A Nutty Campaign Brings *Jericho* Back for Season 2." *Associated Press,* February 4, 2008.

Lloyd, Richard. 2006. *Neo-Bohemia: Art and Commerce in the Postindustrial City.* New York: Routledge.

Lobato, Ramon, Julian Thomas, and Dan Hunter. 2011. "Histories of User-Generated Content: Between Formal and Informal Media Economies." *International Journal of Communication* 5: 899–914.

Lothian, Alexis. 2009. "Living in a Den of Thieves: Fan Video and Digital Challenges to Ownership." *Cinema Journal* 48 (4): 130–36. https://doi.org/10.1353/cj.0.0152.

Lothian, Alexis. 2015. "A Different Kind of Love Song: Vidding Fandom's Undercommons." *Cinema Journal* 54 (3): 138–45. https://doi.org/10.1353/cj.2015.0025.

Lothian, Alexis, Kristina Busse, and Robin Anne Reid. 2007. "'Yearning Void and Infinite Potential': Online Slash Fandom as Queer Female Space." *English Language Notes* 45 (2): 103–11.

Lotz, Amanda D. 2007. *The Television Will Be Revolutionized.* New York: New York University Press.

Mangan, Katherine. 2017. "2 Women Say Stanford Professors Raped Them Years Ago." *Chronicle of Higher Education,* November 11, 2017. https://www.chronicle.com/.

Mansell, Robin, and W. Edward Steinmueller. 2013. "Copyright Infringement Online: The Case of the Digital Economy Act Judicial Review in the United Kingdom." *New Media and Society* 15 (8): 1312–28. https://doi.org/10.1177/1461444812470429.

Martens, Todd. 2016. "Creators, Fans and Death Threats: Talking to Joss Whedon, Neil Gaiman, and More on the Age of Entitlement." *Los Angeles Times,* July 25, 2016. http://www.latimes.com/.

Marwick, Alice E. 2008. "To Catch a Predator? The MySpace Moral Panic." *First Monday* 13 (6). http://www.firstmonday.dk/.

Marx, Karl. 1978a. "Capital, Volume One." In *The Marx–Engels Reader,* edited by Robert C. Tucker, 294–438. New York: Norton.

Marx, Karl. 1978b. "Economic and Philosophic Manuscripts of 1844." In *The Marx–Engels Reader,* edited by Robert C. Tucker, 66–125. New York: Norton.

Mauss, Marcel. 2000. *The Gift: The Form and Reason for Exchange in Archaic Societies.* Translated by W. D. Halls. New York: Norton.

McCourt, Tom, and Patrick Burkart. 2007. "Customer Relationship Management: Automating Fandom in Music Communities." In *Fandom: Identities and Communities in a Mediated World,* edited by Jonathan Gray, Cornel Sandvoss, and C. Lee Harrington, 261–70. New York: New York University Press.

McCracken, Grant. 2013. "'Consumers' or 'Multipliers'?" In *Spreadable Media: Creating Value and Meaning in a Networked Culture,* edited by Henry Jenkins, Sam Ford, and Joshua Green. New York: New York University Press. http://spreadablemedia.org/essays/mccracken/#.UbSqA5zqOZQ.

McGuigan, Lee. 2012. "Consumers: The Commodity Product of Interactive Commercial Television, or Is Dallas Smythe's Thesis More Germane than Ever?" *Journal of Communication Inquiry* 36 (4): 288–304. https://doi.org/10.1177/0196859912459756.

McGuigan, Lee, and Vincent Manzerolle. 2015. "'All the World's a Shopping Cart': Theorizing the Political Economy of Ubiquitous Media and Markets." *New Media and Society* 17 (11): 1830–48. https://doi.org/10.1177/1461444814535191.

McRobbie, Angela. 2011. "Reflections on Feminism, Immaterial Labour and the Post-Fordist Regime." *New Formations* 70 (1): 60–76. https://doi.org/10.3898/NEWF.70.04.2010.

McRobbie, Angela, and Sarah L. Thornton. 1995. "Rethinking 'Moral Panic' for Multi-mediated Social Worlds." *British Journal of Sociology* 46 (4): 559–74. https://doi.org/10.2307/591571.

McRuer, Robert. 2006. *Crip Theory: Cultural Signs of Queerness and Disability.* New York: New York University Press.

Meehan, Eileen R. 2000. "Leisure or Labor? Fan Ethnography and Political Economy." In *Consuming Audiences? Production and Reception in Media Research,* edited by Ingunn Hagen and Janet Wasko, 72–92. Cresskill, NJ: Hampton Press.

Mendelson, Scott. 2013. *"Batfleck, Fifty Shades of Grey* and Fan Entitlement Syndrome." *Forbes,* September 5, 2013. http://www.forbes.com/.

Mewett, Peter, and Kim Toffoletti. 2008. "Rogue Men and Predatory Women:

Female Fans' Perceptions of Australian Footballers' Sexual Conduct."
International Review for the Sociology of Sport 43 (2): 165–80.

Mintert, Svenja-Maria, and Gertrud Pfister. 2015. "The FREE Project and
the Feminization of Football: The Role of Women in the European Fan
Community." *Soccer and Society* 16 (2–3): 405–21. https://doi.org/10.1080/
14660970.2014.961383.

Mittell, Jason. 2013. "Forensic Fandom and the Drillable Text." In *Spreadable
Media: Creating Value and Meaning in a Networked Culture,* edited by Henry
Jenkins, Sam Ford, and Joshua Green. New York: New York University
Press. http://spreadablemedia.org/essays/mittell/#.UbSrxJzqOZQ.

Moraga, Cherríe, and Gloria Anzaldúa, eds. 1983. *This Bridge Called My Back:
Writings by Radical Women of Color.* Latham, NY: Kitchen Table Press.

Moretti, Franco. 2005. *Graphs, Maps, Trees: Abstract Models for a Literary
History.* London: Verso.

Müller, Floris, L. van Zoonen, and L. de Roode. 2007. "Accidental Racists:
Experiences and Contradictions of Racism in Local Amsterdam Soccer Fan
Culture." *Soccer and Society* 8 (2/3): 335–50.

Mulvey, Laura. 1988. "Visual Pleasure and Narrative Cinema." In *Feminism
and Film Theory,* edited by Constance Penley, 57–68. New York: Routledge.

Murray, Simone. 2004. "'Celebrating the Story the Way It Is': Cultural Studies,
Corporate Media and the Contested Utility of Fandom." *Continuum* 18 (1):
7–25. https://doi.org/10.1080/1030431032000180978.

Nagel, Joane. 2003. *Race, Ethnicity, and Sexuality: Intimate Intersections,
Forbidden Frontiers.* New York: Oxford University Press.

Nakashima, Ryan. 2009. "Disney Sees Superhero Dollars in Marvel
Unknowns." *Associated Press,* December 28, 2009.

Newitz, Annalee, and Matt Wray. 1997a. Introduction to *White Trash: Race and
Class in America,* edited by Annalee Newitz and Matt Wray, 1–12. New York:
Routledge.

Newitz, Annalee, and Matt Wray. 1997b. "What Is 'White Trash'? Stereotypes
and Economic Conditions of Poor Whites in the United States." In
Whiteness: A Critical Reader, edited by Mike Hill, 168–84. New York: New
York University Press.

Newman, Joshua I. 2007. "Army of Whiteness? Colonel Reb and the Sporting
South's Cultural and Corporate Symbolic." *Journal of Sport and Social Issues*
31 (4): 315–39.

Nielsen, Christian Axboe. 2013. "Stronger than the State? Football
Hooliganism, Political Extremism and the Gay Pride Parades in Serbia."

Sport in Society 16 (8): 1038–53. https://doi.org/10.1080 /17430437.2013.801221.

Nielsen Company. 2017. "The Nielsen Total Audience Report." http:// www.nielsen.com/content/dam/corporate/us/en/reports-downloads /2017-reports/total-audience-report-q2-2017.pdf.

Noble, Safiya Umoja, and Sarah T. Roberts. 2016. "Through Google-Colored Glass(es): Design, Emotion, Class, and Wearables as Commodity and Control." Media Studies Publications Paper 13. https://ir.lib.uwo.ca/cgi /viewcontent.cgi?referer=&httpsredir=1&article=1013&context=commpub.

Noppe, Nele. 2011. "Why We Should Talk about Commodifying Fan Work." In "Textual Echoes," edited by Cyber Echoes, special issue, *Transformative Works and Cultures*, no. 8. https://doi.org/10.3983/twc.2011.0369.

Noppe, Nele. 2015. "Mechanisms of Control in Online Fanwork Sales: A Comparison of Kindle Worlds and Dlsite.com." *Participations* 12 (2): 218–37. https://doi.org/10.3983/twc.2011.0369.

NPR. 2010. "Patton Oswalt and Robert Siegel: Serious Funny Men." *Fresh Air with Terry Gross*. NPR, January 8, 2010. https://www.npr.org/.

Nussbaum, Martha C. 1998. "'Whether from Reason or Prejudice': Taking Money for Bodily Services." *Journal of Legal Studies* 27 (Suppl. 2): 693–723. https://doi.org/10.1086/468040.

Oates, Thomas P. 2012. "Representing the Audience: The Gendered Politics of Sport Media." *Feminist Media Studies* 12 (4): 603–7. https://doi.org /10.1080/14680777.2012.723929.

obsession_inc. 2009. "Affirmational Fandom vs. Transformational Fandom." Dreamwidth, June 1, 2009. https://obsession-inc.dreamwidth.org/82589.html.

Olson, Kathleen K. 2012. "Injunctions and the Public Interest in Fair Use Cases after eBay." *Communication Law and Policy* 17 (3): 235–64. https:// doi.org/10.1080/10811680.2012.687951.

Ouellette, Laurie, and James Hay. 2008. *Better Living through Reality TV: Television and Post-welfare Citizenship*. Malden, MA: Blackwell.

Ouellette, Laurie, and Julie Wilson. 2011. "Women's Work: Affective Labour and Convergence Culture." *Cultural Studies* 25 (4–5): 548–65. https:// doi.org/10.1080/09502386.2011.600546.

Pande, Rukmini. 2016. "Squee from the Margins: Racial/Cultural/Ethnic Identity in Global Media Fandom." In *Seeing Fans: Representations of Fandom in Media and Popular Culture*, edited by Lucy Bennett and Paul Booth, 209–20. New York: Bloomsbury Academic.

Pascoe, C. J. 2007. *Dude, You're a Fag: Masculinity and Sexuality in High School.*

Berkeley: University of California Press.

Pearson, Roberta. 2010. "Fandom in the Digital Era." *Popular Communication* 8 (1): 84–95. https://doi.org/10.1080/15405700903502346.

Peaslee, Robert Moses, Jessica El-Khoury, and Ashley Liles. 2014. "The Media Festival Volunteer: Connecting Online and On-Ground Fan Labor." In "Fandom and/as Labor," edited by Mel Stanfill and Megan Condis, special issue, *Transformative Works and Cultures*, no. 15. http://dx.doi.org/10.3983/twc.2014.0502.

Penley, Constance. 1997. *NASA/Trek: Popular Science and Sex in America.* New York: Verso.

Penley, Constance. 2012. "Interview with Constance Penley." *European Journal of Cultural Studies* 15 (3): 360–79. https://doi.org/10.1177/1367549412440522.

Petersen, Jennifer. 2015. "Is Code Speech? Law and the Expressivity of Machine Language." *New Media and Society* 17 (3): 415–31. https://doi.org/10.1177/1461444813504276.

Poderi, Giacomo, and David J. Hakken. 2014. "Modding a Free and Open Source Software Video Game: 'Play Testing Is Hard Work.'" In "Fandom and/as Labor," edited by Mel Stanfill and Megan Condis, special issue, *Transformative Works and Cultures*, no. 15. https://doi.org/10.3983/twc.2014.0493.

Pope, Stacey. 2013. "'The Love of My Life': The Meaning and Importance of Sport for Female Fans." *Journal of Sport and Social Issues* 37 (2): 176–95. https://doi.org/10.1177/0193723512455919.

Pope, Stacey. 2014. "'There Are Some Daft People Out There!' Exploring Female Sport and Media Fandoms." *Sport in Society* 17 (2): 254–69. https://doi.org/10.1080/17430437.2013.828708.

Pope, Stacey, and John Williams. 2010. "'White Shoes to a Football Match!': Female Experiences of Football's Golden Age in England." *Transformative Works and Cultures*, no. 6. https://doi.org/10.3983/twc.2011.0230.

Postigo, Hector. 2003. "From *Pong* to *Planet Quake*: Post-industrial Transitions from Leisure to Work." *Information, Communication and Society* 6 (4): 593–607. https://doi.org/10.1080/1369118032000163277.

Postigo, Hector. 2009. "America Online Volunteers: Lessons from an Early Co-production Community." *International Journal of Cultural Studies* 12 (5): 451–69. https://doi.org/10.1177/1367877909337858.

Postigo, Hector. 2012. "Cultural Production and the Digital Rights Movement." *Information, Communication and Society* 15 (8): 1165–85.

https://doi.org/10.1080/1369118X.2011.568509.

Postigo, Hector. 2016. "The Socio-technical Architecture of Digital Labor: Converting Play into YouTube Money." *New Media and Society* 18 (2): 332–49. https://doi.org/10.1177/1461444814541527.

Potts, Jason, John Hartley, John Banks, Jean Burgess, Rachel Cobcroft, Stuart Cunningham, and Lucy Montgomery. 2008. "Consumer Co☐creation and Situated Creativity." *Industry and Innovation* 15 (5): 459–74. https://doi.org /10.1080/13662710802373783.

Puar, Jasbir K., and Amit S. Rai. 2002. "Monster, Terrorist, Fag: The War on Terrorism and the Production of Docile Patriots." *Social Text* 20 (3): 117–48.

Rafferty, Karen. 2011. "Class-Based Emotions and the Allure of Fashion Consumption." *Journal of Consumer Culture* 11 (2): 239–60. https://doi.org /10.1177/1469540511403398.

Rahman, Momin. 2011. "The Burdens of the Flesh: Star Power and the Queer Dialectic in Sports Celebrity." *Celebrity Studies* 2 (2): 150–63. https:// doi.org/10.1080/19392397.2011.574850.

Reinhard, CarrieLynn D. 2011. "Gameplay Marketing Strategies as Audience Co-optation: The Story of the Dark Knight, the Cloverfield Monster, and Their Brethren." *International Journal of Communication* 5: 51–77.

Rennels, Tasha R. 2015. "*Here Comes Honey Boo Boo:* A Cautionary Tale Starring White Working-Class People." *Communication and Critical /Cultural Studies* 12 (3): 271–88. https://doi.org/10.1080 /14791420.2015.1053957.

Rich, Adrienne. 1980. "Compulsory Heterosexuality and Lesbian Existence." *Signs* 5 (4): 631–60.

Rindels, Michelle. 2009. "Disney Expo Seeks to Monetize Mouse-Mania." *Associated Press,* September 9, 2009.

Ritzer, George, and Nathan Jurgenson. 2010. "Production, Consumption, Prosumption: The Nature of Capitalism in the Age of the Digital 'Prosumer.'" *Journal of Consumer Culture* 10 (1): 13–36. https://doi.org /10.1177/1469540509354673.

Rob, R., and J. Waldfogel. 2006. "Piracy on the High C's: Music Downloading, Sales Displacement, and Social Welfare in a Sample of College Students." *Journal of Law and Economics* 49: 29–62.

Rodino-Colocino, Michelle. 2012. "Geek Jeremiads: Speaking the Crisis of Job Loss by Opposing Offshored and H-1B Labor." *Communication and Critical/ Cultural Studies* 9 (1): 22–46. https://doi.org/10.1080 /14791420.2011.645490.

Roediger, David R. 1991. *The Wages of Whiteness: Race and the Making of the American Working Class*. London: Verso.

Rommel, Carl. 2011. "Playing with Difference: Football as a Performative Space for Division among Suryoye Migrants in Sweden." *Soccer and Society* 12 (6): 850–64. https://doi.org/10.1080/14660970.2011.609684.

Rose, Carol M. 1998. "The Several Futures of Property: Of Cyberspace and Folk Tales, Emission Trades and Ecosystems." *Minnesota Law Review* 83: 129–82.

Ross, Andrew. 2000. "The Mental Labor Problem." *Social Text* 18 (2): 1–31.

Ross, Andrew. 2012. "In Search of the Lost Paycheck." In *Digital Labor: The Internet as Playground and Factory*, edited by Trebor Scholz, 13–32. New York: Routledge.

Ross, Sharon Marie. 2009. *Beyond the Box: Television and the Internet*. New York: Wiley.

Roth, Dany. 2016. "Why Jason Rothenberg's Apology Fell Flat with *The 100*'s Fans and the Real Lessons to Learn." SyFy Wire, March 27, 2016. http://www.syfy.com/.

Roth, Jenny, and Monica Flegel. 2014. "It's Like Rape: Metaphorical Family Transgressions, Copyright Ownership and Fandom." *Continuum* 28 (6): 901–13. https://doi.org/10.1080/10304312.2014.964175.

Rowe, Douglas J. 2007. "The Film Geek Shall Inherit the Earth." *Associated Press Online*, April 9, 2007.

Rubin, Gayle S. 1975. "The Traffic in Women: Notes on the 'Political Economy' of Sex." In *Toward an Anthropology of Women*, edited by Rayna R. Reiter, 13th printing edition, 157–210. New York: Monthly Review Press.

Rubin, Gayle S. 1993. "Thinking Sex: Notes for a Radical Theory of the Politics of Sexuality." In *The Lesbian and Gay Studies Reader*, edited by Henry Abelove, Michèle Aina Barale, and David M. Halperin, 3–44. New York: Routledge.

Rubin, Gayle S. 2011. "Misguided, Dangerous, and Wrong: An Analysis of Antipornography Politics." In *Deviations: A Gayle Rubin Reader*. Durham, NC: Duke University Press.

Ruddock, Andy. 2005. "Let's Kick Racism Out of Football—And the Lefties Too! Responses to Lee Bowyer on a West Ham Web Site." *Journal of Sport and Social Issues* 29 (4): 369–85.

Russo, Julie Levin. 2009. "User-Penetrated Content: Fan Video in the Age of Convergence." *Cinema Journal* 48 (4): 125–30. https://doi.org/10.1353/cj.0.0147.

Russo, Julie Levin. 2010. "Indiscrete Media: Television/Digital Convergence and Economies of Online Lesbian Fan Communities." PhD diss., Brown University. http://j-l-r.org/diss.

Ryan, Marie-Laure. 2015. "Transmedia Storytelling: Industry Buzzword or New Narrative Experience?" *StoryWorlds* 7 (2): 1–19.

Ryan, Maureen. 2016a. "What TV Can Learn from *The 100* Mess." *Variety* (blog), March 14, 2016. http://variety.com/.

Ryan, Maureen. 2016b. "*The 100* Showrunner Apologizes for Controversial Character Death." *Variety* (blog), March 24, 2016. http://variety.com/.

Ryan, Maureen. 2016c. "'Anyone Can Die?' TV's Recent Death Toll Says Otherwise." *Variety* (blog), April 13, 2016. http://variety.com/.

Sandlin, Jennifer A., and Julie G. Maudlin. 2012. "Consuming Pedagogies: Controlling Images of Women as Consumers in Popular Culture." *Journal of Consumer Culture* 12 (2): 175–94. https://doi.org /10.1177/1469540512446877.

Sandvoss, Cornel. 2003. *A Game of Two Halves: Football, Television, and Globalisation*. London: Routledge.

Sandvoss, Cornel. 2005. *Fans: The Mirror of Consumption*. Malden, MA: Polity.

Sassatelli, Roberta. 2007. *Consumer Culture: History, Theory and Politics*. Los Angeles, CA: Sage.

Sassen, Saskia. 2012. "Interactions of the Technical and the Social: Digital Formations of the Poweful and the Powerless." *Information, Communication and Society* 15 (4): 455–78. https://doi.org/10.1080 /1369118X.2012.667912.

Savage, Christina. 2014. "Chuck versus the Ratings: Savvy Fans and 'Save Our Show' Campaigns." In "Fandom and/as Labor," edited by Mel Stanfill and Megan Condis, special issue, *Transformative Works and Cultures*, no. 15. https://doi.org/10.3983/twc.2014.0497.

Savran, David. 1998. *Taking It Like a Man: White Masculinity, Masochism, and Contemporary American Culture*. Princeton, NJ: Princeton University Press.

Schaeffer, Felicity Amaya. 2012. *Love and Empire: Cybermarriage and Citizenship across the Americas*. New York: New York University Press.

Schimmel, Kimberly S., C. Lee Harrington, and Denise D. Bielby. 2007. "Keep Your Fans to Yourself: The Disjuncture between Sport Studies' and Pop Culture Studies' Perspectives on Fandom." *Sport in Society* 10 (4): 580–600.

Schmidt, Lisa. 2010. "Monstrous Melodrama: Expanding the Scope of Melodramatic Identification to Interpret Negative Fan Responses to

Supernatural." *Transformative Works and Cultures*, no. 4. https://doi.org/
10.3983/twc.2010.0152.

Scholz, Trebor. 2012. "Introduction: Why Does Digital Labor Matter Now?"
In *Digital Labor: The Internet as Playground and Factory*, edited by Trebor
Scholz, 1–9. New York: Routledge.

Schumacher, Thomas G. 1995. "'This Is a Sampling Sport': Digital Sampling,
Rap Music and the Law in Cultural Production." *Media, Culture and Society*
17 (2): 253–73. https://doi.org/10.1177/016344395017002006.

Scodari, Christine. 2012. "'Nyota Uhura Is Not a White Girl': Gender,
Intersectionality, and *Star Trek* 2009's Alternate Romantic Universes."
Feminist Media Studies 12 (3): 335–51. https://doi.org/10.1080
/14680777.2011.615605.

Scolari, Carlos A. 2013. "Lost in the Borderlines between User-Generated
Content and the Cultural Industry." *Participations* 10 (1): 414–17.

Scott, Jason. 2016. "Fandom Culture in 2016: The Good, the Bad and the
Ugly." Popdust, August 12, 2016. http://www.popdust.com/.

Scott, Suzanne. 2007. "Authorized Resistance: Is Fan Production Frakked?" In
Cylons in America: Critical Studies in Battlestar Galactica, edited by Tiffany
Potter and C. W. Marshall, 210–23. New York: Continuum.

Scott, Suzanne. 2009. "Repackaging Fan Culture: The Regifting Economy
of Ancillary Content Models." *Transformative Works and Cultures*, no. 3.
https://doi.org/10.3983/twc.2009.0150.

Scott, Suzanne. 2011. "Revenge of the Fanboy: Convergence Culture and the
Politics of Incorporation." PhD diss., University of Southern California,
Los Angeles. http://digitallibrary.usc.edu/assetserver/controller/item
/etd-Scott-4277.pdf.

Scott, Suzanne. 2013. "Fangirls in Refrigerators: The Politics of (In)visibility in
Comic Book Culture." In "Appropriating, Interpreting, and Transforming
Comic Books," edited by Matthew J. Costello, special issue, *Transformative
Works and Cultures*, no. 13. https://doi.org/10.3983/twc.2013.0460.

Scott, Suzanne. 2015. "The Moral Economy of Crowdfunding and the
Transformative Capacity of Fan-Ancing." *New Media and Society* 17 (2):
167–82. https://doi.org/10.1177/1461444814558908.

Seeger, Anthony. 1992. "Ethnomusicology and Music Law." *Ethnomusicology*
36 (3): 345–59. https://doi.org/10.2307/851868.

Shirky, Clay. 2008. *Here Comes Everybody: The Power of Organizing without
Organizations*. New York: Penguin Press.

Silbey, Susan S. 2005. "After Legal Consciousness." *Annual Review of Law and*

Social Science 1 (1): 323–68. https://doi.org/10.1146
/annurev.lawsocsci.1.041604.115938.

Sillanpaa, Ted. 2014. "History Shows Giants' Sabean Does Bold Deadline
Deals." *Press Democrat,* July 30, 2014.

Smythe, Dallas W. 1977. "Communications: Blindspot of Western Marxism."
Canadian Journal of Political and Social Theory 1 (3): 1–27.

Sperb, Jason. 2010. "Reassuring Convergence: Online Fandom, Race, and
Disney's Notorious *Song of the South.*" *Cinema Journal* 49 (4): 25–45.
https://doi.org/10.1353/cj.2010.0016.

Spigel, Lynn. 1992. *Make Room for TV: Television and the Family Ideal in
Postwar America.* Chicago: University of Chicago Press.

Spivak, Gayatri Chakavorty. 1988. "Can the Subaltern Speak?" In *Marxism
and the Interpretation of Culture,* edited by Lawrence Grossberg and Cary
Nelson, 271–313. Urbana: University of Illinois Press.

Stacy, Mitch. 2009. "Super Bowl Destination: What to See around Tampa."
Associated Press, January 12, 2009.

Stanfill, Mel. 2013. "'They're Losers, but I Know Better': Intra-fandom
Stereotyping and the Normalization of the Fan Subject." *Critical Studies in
Media Communication* 20 (2): 117–34. https://doi.org/10.1080
/15295036.2012.755053.

Stanfill, Mel. 2015. "The Interface as Discourse: The Production of Norms
through Web Design." *New Media and Society* 17 (7): 1059–74. https://
doi.org/10.1177/1461444814520873.

Stein, Louisa Ellen. 2008. "'Emotions-Only' versus 'Special People': Genre in
Fan Discourse." *Transformative Works and Cultures,* no. 1. https://
doi.org/10.3983/twc.2008.043.

Stein, Louisa, moderator. 2014. "Spreadable Media: Creating Value and
Meaning in a Networked Culture" [roundtable]. Paul Booth, Kristina Busse,
Melissa Click, Sam Ford, Henry Jenkins, Xiaochang Li, and Sharon Ross,
respondents. *Transformative Works and Cultures,* no. 17. https://
doi.org/10.3983/twc.2014.0633.

Stockton, Kathryn Bond. 2009. *The Queer Child, or Growing Sideways in the
Twentieth Century.* Durham, NC: Duke University Press.

Stork, Matthias. 2014. "The Cultural Economics of Performance Space:
Negotiating Fan, Labor, and Marketing Practice in *Glee*'s Transmedia
Geography." In "Fandom and/as Labor," edited by Mel Stanfill and Megan
Condis, special issue, *Transformative Works and Cultures,* no. 15. https://
doi.org/10.3983/twc.2014.0490.

Story, Paula. 1998. "Pigskin Gets Wired as Super Bowl Goes High Tech." *Associated Press*, January 24, 1998.

Sullivan, Barbara. 2004. "Prostitution Consent: Beyond the Liberal Dichotomy of 'Free or Forced.'" In *Making Sense of Sexual Consent*, edited by Mark Cowling and Paul Reynolds, 127–39. Farnham, UK: Ashgate.

Sullivan, David B. 2006. "Broadcast Television and the Game of Packaging Sports." In *Handbook of Sports and Media*, edited by Arthur A. Raney and Jennings Bryant, 131–46. Mahwah, NJ: Lawrence Erlbaum.

Švelch, Jaroslav. 2013. "The Delicate Art of Criticizing a Saviour 'Silent Gratitude' and the Limits of Participation in the Evaluation of Fan Translation." *Convergence* 19 (3): 303–10. https://doi.org /10.1177/1354856513486531.

Tan, Leon. 2013. "Intellectual Property Law and the Globalization of Indigenous Cultural Expressions: Māori Tattoo and the *Whitmill versus Warner Bros.* Case." *Theory, Culture and Society* 30 (3): 61–81. https:// doi.org/10.1177/0263276412474328.

Tanaka, Toko. 2004. "The Positioning and Practices of the 'Feminized Fan' in Japanese Soccer Culture through the Experience of the FIFA World Cup Korea/Japan 2002." Translated by Hiroki Ogasawara. *Inter-Asia Cultural Studies* 5 (1): 52–62.

Tang, Terry. 2008. "Phoenix Eager to Show Off Super Bowl Host Role." *Associated Press*, January 14, 2008.

Terranova, Tiziana. 2000. "Free Labor: Producing Culture for the Digital Economy." *Social Text* 18 (2): 33–58. https://doi.org/10.1215 /01642472-18-2_63-33.

Terranova, Tiziana. 2012. "Free Labor." In *Digital Labor: The Internet as Playground and Factory*, edited by Trebor Scholz, 33–57. New York: Routledge.

Tosenberger, Catherine. 2008. "'The Epic Love Story of Sam and Dean': *Supernatural*, Queer Readings, and the Romance of Incestuous Fan Fiction." *Transformative Works and Cultures*, no. 1. https://doi.org/10.3983 /twc.2008.030.

Toula, Christopher M., and Gregory C. Lisby. 2014. "Towards an Affirmative Public Domain." *Cultural Studies* 28 (5–6): 997–1021. https://doi.org /10.1080/09502386.2014.886490.

Turk, Tisha. 2014. "Fan Work: Labor, Worth, and Participation in Fandom's Gift Economy." In "Fandom and/as Labor," edited by Mel Stanfill and Megan Condis, special issue, *Transformative Works and Cultures*, no. 15.

https://doi.org/10.3983/twc.2014.0518.

Turk, Tisha, and Joshua Johnson. 2012. "Toward an Ecology of Vidding." In "Fan/Remix Video," edited by Francesca Coppa and Julie Levin Russo, special issue, *Transformative Works and Cultures*, no. 9. https://doi.org/10.3983/twc.2012.0326.

Tushnet, Rebecca. 2004. "Copy This Essay: How Fair Use Doctrine Harms Free Speech and How Copying Serves It." *The Yale Law Journal* 114 (3): 535–90. https://doi.org/10.2307/4135692.

Tushnet, Rebecca. 2007a. "Payment in Credit: Copyright Law and Subcultural Creativity." *Law and Contemporary Problems* 70 (2): 135–74. https://doi.org/10.2307/27592184.

Tushnet, Rebecca. 2007b. "User-Generated Discontent: Transformation in Practice." *Columbia Journal of Law and the Arts* 31: 101–20.

Tushnet, Rebecca. 2009. "Economies of Desire: Fair Use and Marketplace Assumptions." *William and Mary Law Review* 51 (3): 513–46.

Tushnet, Rebecca. 2014. "All of This Has Happened Before and All of This Will Happen Again: Innovation in Copyright Licensing." *Berkeley Technology Law Journal* 29 (3): 1447–88.

TWC Editor. 2009. "Pattern Recognition: A Dialogue on Racism in Fan Communities." *Transformative Works and Cultures*, no. 3. https://doi.org/10.3983/twc.2009.0172.

Vaidhyanathan, Siva. 2003. *Copyrights and Copywrongs: The Rise of Intellectual Property and How It Threatens Creativity.* New York: New York University Press.

Van Dijck, Jose, and David Nieborg. 2009. "Wikinomics and Its Discontents: A Critical Analysis of Web 2.0 Business Manifestos." *New Media and Society* 11 (5): 855–74.

Veblen, Thorstein. (1899) 2000. "Conspicuous Consumption." In *The Consumer Society Reader,* edited by Martyn J. Lee, 31–47. Malden, MA: Wiley-Blackwell.

Vered, Karen Orr, and Sal Humphreys. 2014. "Postfeminist Inflections in Television Studies." *Continuum* 28 (2): 155–63. https://doi.org/10.1080/10304312.2014.888037.

Walliss, John. 2010. "Fan Filmmaking and Copyright in a Global World: *Warhammer 40,000* Fan Films and the Case of *Damnatus.*" *Transformative Works and Cultures*, no. 5. https://doi.org/10.3983/twc.2010.0178.

Wanzo, Rebecca. 2015. "African American Acafandom and Other Strangers: New Genealogies of Fan Studies." *Transformative Works and Cultures,* no.

20. https://doi.org/10.3983/twc.2015.0699.

Warner, Kristen J. 2015a. "ABC's *Scandal* and Black Women's Fandom." In *Cupcakes, Pinterest, and Ladyporn: Feminized Popular Culture in the Early Twenty-First Century*, edited by Elana Levine, 32–50. Urbana: University of Illinois Press.

Warner, Kristen J. 2015b. *The Cultural Politics of Colorblind TV Casting*. New York: Routledge.

Warner, Kristen J. 2015c. "If Loving Olitz Is Wrong, I Don't Wanna Be Right." *Black Scholar* 45 (1): 16–20. https://doi.org/10.1080/00064246.2014.997599.

Warner, Michael. 1999. "Normal and Normaller: Beyond Gay Marriage." *GLQ* 5 (2): 119–71.

Warner, Michael. 2002. "Publics and Counterpublics." *Public Culture* 14 (1): 49–90.

Waysdorf, Abby. 2015a. "The Creation of Football Slash Fan Fiction." In "European Fans and European Fan Objects: Localization and Translation," edited by Anne Kustritz, special issue, *Transformative Works and Cultures*, no. 19. https://doi.org/10.3983/twc.2015.0588.

Waysdorf, Abby. 2015b. "My Football Fandoms, Performance, and Place." In "Performance and Performativity in Fandom," edited by Lucy Bennett and Paul J. Booth, special issue, *Transformative Works and Cultures*, no. 18. https://doi.org/10.3983/twc.2015.0636.

Weber, Brenda R. 2009. *Makeover TV: Selfhood, Citizenship, and Celebrity*. Durham, NC: Duke University Press.

WeDeservedBetter.com. n.d. "Your Friendly Neighborhood Lurker." Lexawasdeadalready. http://wedeservedbetter.com/post/141388433803/your-friendly-neighborhood-lurker.

Wedgwood, Nikki. 2008. "For the Love of Football: Australian Rules Football and Heterosexual Desire." *Journal of Sport and Social Issues* 32 (3): 311–17.

White, Michele. 2006. *The Body and the Screen: Theories of Internet Spectatorship*. Cambridge, MA: MIT Press.

Wiegman, Robyn. 1999. "Whiteness Studies and the Paradox of Particularity." *Boundary 2* 26 (3): 115–50.

Willis, Ika. 2006. "Keeping Promises to Queer Children: Making Space (for Mary Sue) at Hogwarts." In *Fan Fiction and Fan Communities in the Age of the Internet: New Essays*, edited by Karen Hellekson and Kristina Busse, 153–70. Jefferson, NC: McFarland.

Willis, Margaret M., and Juliet B. Schor. 2012. "Does Changing a Light

Bulb Lead to Changing the World? Political Action and the Conscious Consumer." *Annals of the American Academy of Political and Social Science* 644 (1): 160–90. https://doi.org/10.1177/0002716212454831.

Wilson, Wayne. 2007. "All Together Now, Click: MLS Soccer Fans in Cyberspace." *Soccer and Society* 8 (2/3): 381–98.

Wittel, Andreas. 2012. "Digital Marx: Toward a Political Economy of Distributed Media." *TripleC* 10 (2): 313–33.

Woodmansee, Martha. 1984. "The Genius and the Copyright: Economic and Legal Conditions of the Emergence of the 'Author.'" *Eighteenth-Century Studies* 17 (4): 425–48. https://doi.org/10.2307/2738129.

Yodovich, Neta. 2016. "'A Little Costumed Girl at a Sci-Fi Convention': Boundary Work as a Main Destigmatization Strategy among Women Fans." *Women's Studies in Communication* 39 (3): 289–307. https://doi.org/10.1080/07491409.2016.1193781.

Young, Helen. 2014. "Race in Online Fantasy Fandom: Whiteness on Westeros.org." *Continuum* 28 (5): 737–47. https://doi.org/10.1080/10304312.2014.941331.

Zelizer, Viviana A. 2000. "The Purchase of Intimacy." *Law and Social Inquiry* 25 (3): 817–48.

Zhang, Lin, and Anthony Y. H. Fung. 2014. "Working as Playing? Consumer Labor, Guild and the Secondary Industry of Online Gaming in China." *New Media and Society* 16 (1): 38–54. https://doi.org/10.1177/1461444813477077.

Zubernis, Lynn, and Katherine Larsen. 2012. *Fandom at the Crossroads: Celebration, Shame and Fan/Producer Relationships.* Newcastle upon Tyne, UK: Cambridge Scholars.

Bloom, Harold, 188
Bolin, Göran, 169
Bonilla-Silva, Eduardo, 25
Bonini, Tiziano, 136, 151
Bourdieu, Pierre, 78
boyd, danah, 16, 140
Boyle, James, 108, 175
Brabham, Daren C., 150, 160, 179
Brady, Bobby, 194
Brennan Center for Justice, 115
Bridges, Elizabeth, 1
broadcasting, 111, 209n3
Brock, André, 26
bromance, 64
Brooker, Will, 115, 120
Brown, Brian, 131
Bruns, Axel, 161
Buffy the Vampire Slayer, 50, 58, 63, 135–36
Busse, Kristina, 35, 38, 147, 151; on gender inequality, 38, 41; on gender representations, 34, 36, 42, 195
Butler, Judith, 54, 64, 74
buzz, 144–45

Campbell, Bruce, 66, 154, 192–93
Campbell, Colin, 83
Campbell, John Edward, 153
Campfire, 12, 32, 43, 48, 135, 140–41, 162; and fan engagement, 94–95, 147–48, 149; marketing strategies of, 96, 111, 145
capitalism, 82, 128, 176; and labor, 159, 167, 174; value system of, 165–66, 169
The Captains, 29
Caraway, Brett, 157

cease-and-desist letters, 115, 120, 146–47, 205–6n10
Chambers, Ross, 24, 54
Chapman, Mark David, 22
Chasin, Alexandra, 83
children, 194; and age-based normativity, 44–46; fans compared to, 56–58; legal scare tactics against, 115–17
Children's Online Privacy Protection Act (COPPA), 44–45, 207n10
Chin, Bertha, 132
Chuck, 58, 65, 103, 146; Save Our Show campaign for, 103, 136, 141–42
Cinema Journal, 132
close reading, 15
coercive positivity, 155
cognitive affordance, 14
Cohen, Cathy, 53
Cohen, Nicole S., 131, 159
Cohen, Sandy, 88, 148, 154
Cohen, Stanley, 184–85, 186–87
color blindness, 25, 28, 30, 31
Comeau, Troy O., 98
Comic-Con, 33, 57, 88, 144; backlash at, 39–40, 70; New York, 44; San Diego, 14, 32–33, 39–40, 89
comics: and gender, 32–33, 38; *Simpsons* spoofs on, 32–33, 51, 61, 67
coming-out theme, 71
commons: as mode of production, 177–79; public domain as, 108, 126, 129, 174–75, 177; of resistance, 157; turned into private property, 175
consent, 179–80; and labor, 170–74

emotional labor, 151, 155

enclosure of fandom: and consent, 179–80; consequences of, 178–79; and gift economy, 177–78; and labor arrangements, 176–77; as model, 174–80

encoding, 118

Espenson, Jane, 58

ESPN, 13, 45, 86–87, 97, 138, 148; TOS of, 114, 123

Esposito, Roberto, 165

Ewick, Patricia, 106

exchange value, 163, 165, 169

The Express, 28, 192

Facebook: and buzz, 144–45; likes on, 139, 140–41, 155

failed masculinity, 18, 49–53, 183

fair use, 106, 115, 172; and Content ID, 119–20; and labor-benefit framework, 128–29; legal determination of, 113, 209n1; and TOS agreements, 122, 124

false consciousness, 173

family appeal, 45–46

Family Guy, 135

The Fan, 59–60, 66, 100, 191

fan (concept), 3, 4, 5, 6, 7, 16

fan desire: and attendance at sports events, 85, 86, 87; and consumption, 88, 92, 98, 100–103, 183; domestication of, 18, 82, 83–84; and industry desire, 81, 82, 100–101, 180–81; management of, 9–10, 83–84, 100–102, 103, 183; social nature of, 103; stigma around, 81

fan entitlement discourse, 184, 185–86, 189

fan fiction, 71, 98, 105, 115, 177; feminized nature of, 31, 37–38, 162

fan film, 118; masculinized nature of, 35, 37–38, 162

fan hero character, 20, 192, 195–96

fan identity, 25, 151–52

fan labor. *See* labor, fan

fan management, 2–3, 9–10; and biopolitics, 10–11; of desire, 9–10, 83–84, 100–102, 103, 183; as domestication, 11, 42, 78, 101, 103, 115, 151, 156, 179, 183–84, 197, 206n11

fan portrayals: as bullies and monsters, 187–89; of failed masculinity, 18, 49–53, 183; as failures, 59–60; of fanboy, 33–34, 48, 195; of fangirl and women fans, 32, 34, 38, 39, 41–42, 206n4; and homosociality, 64–66; as immature, 56–60; and performativity, 54–55; as virgin and creep, 61–64

fan studies, 22–23, 30–31, 70, 80, 81, 132–33

fan violence, 188, 189

Fanalysis, 66, 69, 154

fanboy, 33–34, 48, 195

Fanboys, 10, 50, 51, 154; sexuality depiction in, 61–62, 65–67

fandom's future, 19–20; dark, 184–89; light, 190–97

fangirl, 34, 38, 39. *See also* women fans

fan-industry relationship: audience commodity built into, 134–35, 137;

backlash in, 21, 34, 39–40, 41, 54, 70, 164, 179, 184–89, 206n1; and benefits from fan labor, 131–32, 133, 142, 145, 150–51, 156–58, 169–70; and fan resistance, 1–2, 156–57, 165–66, 173, 177; and fan surveillance, 139–42, 156; future of, 19–20, 183–97; imbalance in, 173; and industry legal action, 106, 114–17; lack of transparency in, 173, 197; nonalignment of desires and interests in, 82, 100–101, 180–81; and Terms of Service, 12–13, 44–45, 112, 114–15, 120–25, 148, 171, 172–73

FanLib, 176, 178–79, 210n7

fans of color, 29–30, 55, 162

fantasy sports, 97–98, 142, 209n3

Faraci, Devin, 188, 189

Fast, Karin, 150, 153

Favale, Marcella, 113, 115

feminism, 172; women of color, 53

Fever Pitch, 62, 66, 68, 69, 73–74, 99; stuck-in-childhood narrative of, 57–58

Fey, Tina, 41

Fiesler, Casey, 105

Fifty Shades of Grey, 164

Fisher, Eran, 167

Fiske, John, 80

Foley, Megan, 132

For Love of the Game, 57

Ford, Sam, 82, 88, 134, 145, 151, 190

The 40-Year-Old Virgin, 57, 61, 68, 73, 208n9

Foucault, Michel, 6, 10–11, 13, 81, 114

Frank, Thomas, 9

Frankenberg, Ruth, 7, 27

free lunch production and logic, 142–44, 156

Freud, Sigmund, 82

Friday Night Lights: film, 28; TV show, 28, 45–46

Fuchs, Christian, 128, 131

functional affordance, 14

Fung, Anthony Y. H., 180

Fury, David, 50

Gaiman, Neil, 187

Gaines, Jane, 35

Galaxy Quest, 100

Game 6, 59, 153

game modding, 35, 37–38, 150, 162, 167, 210nn2–3

Gamergate, 21, 34, 189, 206n1

gender: and normativity, 30–42; performativity of, 54–55; and sexuality, 64. *See also* masculinity; women

General Agreement on Tariffs and Trade (1994), 127

Gerlitz, Carolin, 139, 140, 155

Germain, David, 135

Getty Images, 118–19

Ghostbusters all-female remake, 34, 186

gift economy, 170, 176, 210n4; as concept, 163–66; and industry enclosure, 177–78; and labor exploitation, 179

Gilbert, Anne, 33

Gillespie, Tarleton, 108, 118, 125–26

Giulianotti, Richard, 80

Glee, 180

Goldman, Katie, 41

Gosling, Victoria K., 31–32, 40

legal strategy, 115, 117, 171; on fan
consumption, 7, 88, 91, 99; on fan
participation and labor, 131, 147;
on fans as poachers, 172, 174; on
male-female differences, 37, 38
Jensen, Joli, 69
Jericho, 191, 192
Johnson, Derek, 35–36, 41, 97
Johnson, Mark, 188
Johnson-Yale, Camille, 159
Jones, Bethan, 132, 164
Jones, Katharine W., 31
Jones, Orlando, 39
Jurgenson, Nathan, 161

Kant, Immanuel, 78
Karlsson, Michael, 150, 153
Kennedy, David, 151, 180
Kettrey, Heather Hensman, 26
Kick-Ass, 142
Kickstarter, 135, 141, 150, 151–52, 180
Kimmel, Michael, 52–53, 58, 59
Knowles, Harry, 69, 146
Kontner, Jim, 50
Kring, Tim, 68
Kripke, Eric, 37
Krzywinska, Tanya, 96–97, 99
Kuehn, Kathleen, 162
Kurtz, Benjamin W. L. Derhy, 95
Kusz, Kyle, 25

labor: alienated and nonalienated,
167–69; under capitalism, 174;
and exchange value, 163, 165, 169;
and intellectual property, 128–29;
and leisure, 158, 160–61, 166–67,
175; Marxist view of, 131–32, 156,
161; pleasurable, 166–67, 168–70,

173–74; precarious, 159–60;
turning workers into, 176; and
use value, 83, 163, 165, 169
labor, fan, 19, 130–57, 183; benefits
to industry of, 131–32, 133, 142,
145, 150–51, 156–57, 158, 169–70;
as calling card, 161–62; character
of, 166–70; and consent, 170–74;
content labor, 148–51; exploitation
of, 131–32, 156–57, 161, 166, 168,
169, 179, 181; and fan use value,
163; as free lunch, 142–44; and
gift economy, 163–66, 179, 210n4;
as legal gray area, 171–72; lovebor,
151–56, 165–66, 168; need for
new approach to, 156–57, 173–74,
181; as normative, 130, 143, 148,
153, 156, 166; and professional-
amateur slippage, 160–61;
promotional labor, 144–48; as
sharecropping arrangement, 176–
77; and technological advances,
130–31, 133; in time of precarity,
159–63; work of being watched,
139–42
Lakoff, George, 188
Laster, Whitney Nicole, 26
law and legal action, 18, 104–29;
and authorship, 109–10; and
copyright law, 107–14; and
creativity, 107–8, 109–10, 112–13,
126, 127–29, 209n2; and defense
of public interest, 127–29; and
fair use determination, 113,
209n1; and fan labor, 171–72; and
labor-benefit framework, 128–29;
popular beliefs about, 104–6; and
scare tactics, 114–17; technological

self-control, 55, 56, 60–61, 62, 63, 73, 75–76; as socially constructed, 24–25; and white male backlash, 21, 34, 39–40

The Winning Season, 88

women: and consumption, 78, 80; employment of, 162; and fan fiction, 31, 37–38, 162; marginalization of, 37–42; portrayed as emotional, 39; and teen television, 36; and Title IX, 40; white male backlash against, 21, 39–40

women fans, 32, 206n4; as fangirl, 34, 38, 39; as media characters, 41–42

Woodmansee, Martha, 109

work of being watched, 139–42, 156, 176

world building, 92–93

Writers Guild of America (WGA), 160

Xena: Warrior Princess, 191

X-Files, 135

YouTube, 68, 117, 128, 132; Content ID system of, 119–20

Zhang, Lin, 180